KARL MARX
AND FRIEDRICH ENGELS

GARLAND REFERENCE LIBRARY
OF SOCIAL SCIENCE
(VOL. 23)

KARL MARX AND FRIEDRICH ENGELS
An Analytical Bibliography

Cecil L. Eubanks

GARLAND PUBLISHING, INC. • NEW YORK & LONDON
1977

© 1977 by Cecil L. Eubanks
All rights reserved

Library of Congress Cataloging in Publication Data
Eubanks, Cecil L
  Karl Marx and Friedrich Engels.

  (Garland reference library of social science ; v. 23)
  1. Marx, Karl, 1818-1883--Bibliography. 2. Engels,
Friedrich, 1820-1895--Bibliography. I. Title.
Z8551.67.E94 [HX39.5]   016.3354   75-24779
ISBN 0-8240-9957-5

PRINTED IN THE UNITED STATES OF AMERICA

For Flora

CONTENTS

Introduction	ix
The Writings of Marx and Engels	
Karl Marx—Individual Works	1
Karl Marx—Collected Works	10
Friedrich Engels—Individual Works	13
Friedrich Engels—Collected Works	18
Karl Marx and Friedrich Engels—Individual Works	19
Karl Marx and Friedrich Engels—Collected Works	22
Books on Marx and Engels	26
Articles on Marx and Engels	78
Doctoral Dissertations on Marx and Engels	154

INTRODUCTION

A specter is haunting the world -- the corpus of Marx-Engels scholarship. So enormous is its scope and so varied is its content that it would indeed take 'a holy alliance' to evaluate it effectively. What is more, there is no indication that the literature by and on Marx and Engels will cease growing. With the recent translations of the <u>Grundrisse</u> and the emergence into English of the entire body of writings by Marx and Engels we are likely to see in the next decade an even more intense interest in Marxian thought. The bibliographer, scholar and student can only raise their collective hands and cry with Lenin, "what is to be done?"

The answer must simply be, to begin or rather to continue. This bibliography and the evaluative comments herein are meant to be just that, a beginning, a putting together of a comprehensive bibliography of the works of Marx and Engels and their interpreters, along with some indication of how those works may be judged and utilized. Before embarking upon the task of discussing those works in detail it is necessary to make a few remarks about the general character of the bibliography that follows this essay.

As mentioned above, this work is intended to be a comprehensive bibliography of those writings by and about Marx and Engels either written or translated into English, including books, monographs, articles, chapters from books and doctoral dissertations. In the secondary literature the criteria for inclusion was whether or not a particular work contributed to the understanding of the thought of Marx and Engels. While this standard was applied with liberality it should be noted at the outset that neither the history of Marxist movements nor that ponderous body of literature called Marxism-Leninism was considered to be the subject matter of concern here. This does not mean that there are no selections from Marxist-Leninist literature included in the bibliography. There are representative samplings throughout. It means simply that Marx and Engels, not Lenin, not Mao and not the history of various communist revolutions were the primary focus of attention.

This separation of Marx and Engels from the variety of movements that they spawned, including Marxist-Leninist thought is both a useful and necessary one. If the literature on Marx and Engels is vast and close to being unmanageable, the body of works on Marxist-Leninist thought is nearly impenetrable. More important, because of the unavailability of many of the writings of Marx and Engels until very recently, it becomes necessary to insist that our understanding of them begin simply with them. That means a concerted effort must be undertaken to know what it is they were intending prior to any examination of the results of those intentions in the modern world. Such a distinction between Marxian (i.e., concerned with Marx and Engels), as opposed to Marxist (i.e., concerned with adherence to the thought of Marx and Engels), is not an easy one to make in a completely consistent fashion. Many works on Marx and Engels were written by Marxists, and they have been included here. The distinction is nonetheless useful in spite of its clumsiness. It gives us the impetus at least toward collecting and perhaps reading that body of thought which is necessary to an understanding of its creators. Only then can we proceed, perhaps in another bibliogrpahy, to a consideration of the effects of that thought in the world. These issues of selection, of exclusion and inclusion, will perhaps become clearer as we proceed to a more systematic examination of the contents of the bibliography.

The Writings of Marx and Engels

The complete collected works of Marx and Engels do not exist in any language. The first full scale attempt at putting together a complete edition in original languages was begun in Russia in 1927. Largely due to the efforts of D. Riazanov, (who was a victim of the Stalinist purges), and later V. Adoratsky, this never to be completed project was of enormous significance; because it introduced to the world previously unknown writings of Marx and Engels. Especially important was the publication of Volume III of the Historisch-Kritische Gesamtsausgabe (referred to as MEGA), which included The Economic and Philosophic Manuscripts of 1844. This led to an important change in Marxian scholarship centering attention on the early Marx and ultimately raising the question of the compatibility of that early Marx with the later writer of Capital. A second effort at collecting the works of Marx and Engels was launched in 1950 by the Institute of Marxism-Leninism of the Central Committee of the Socialist Unity Party of Germany. It is simply referred to as Werke (MEW). Finally, there is currently a joint project underway in Moscow and Berlin directed by their respective Institutes of Marxism-Leninism to publish a complete collection of the works of Marx and Engels in original languages. This edition, which will easily comprise one hundred volumes, will contain all of the works, plus drafts, unpublished manuscripts, preparatory materials, notes and all available correspondence. In effect this will be a completed version of MEGA.

Alas, these publishing efforts of the last 50 years have had a minimal effect on the English speaking world. The English reader of Marx and Engels has had to rely upon individually translated editions, on a variety of specialized collections of the writings of Marx and Engels and on the two volume selected works anthology first published in Moscow in 1935, (MESW). In 1975, however, International Publishers Company and Lawrence & Wishart Limited began the publication of a 50 volume English collection of the works of Marx and Engels, (Collected Works). This collection will contain all works published in the lifetime of Marx and Engels, a large selection of unpublished manuscripts and all known correspondence. To date six volumes of this project have been completed and published. But, while the complete English edition of the collected works does not exist and while the Marxian specialist eagerly awaits the completion of the above mentioned projects, it can be said that in the anthologies and translations of individual works we do have a very representative sampling of the writings. What follows is a seriatim listing of the more important of those writings of Marx and Engels as well as a descriptive analysis of each.*

"The Difference Between the Democritean and Epicurean Philosophies of Nature"

This is Marx's doctoral dissertation which was accepted by the faculty of the University of Jena on April 15, 1841. In the dissertation Marx examines the physics of Democritus and Epicurus, criticizing the former's deterministic empiricism and lauding the latter's notion of a free self, conscious of itself and capable of effecting change in the world. Even more important are the notes to the dissertation in which Marx grapples with the notion of philosophy as praxis. Philosophy after Hegel, he contends, must measure the world in terms of its criticism of the world. Philosophy must become worldly. Since the notion of a nexus between theory and practice is a central one in the thought of Marx this early discussion is of great interest.

---

*For a similar and more complete analysis of all the important writings of marx the reader may wish to consult a work to which I am heavily indebted, D. McLellan, The Thought of Karl Marx. See also J. Lachs, Marxist Philosophy: A Bibliographic Guide and J. M. Bochenski et al., Guide to Marxist Philosophy: An Introductory Bibliography. as well as Robert C. Tucker's notes in The Marx-Engels Reader.

The dissertation and the notes, or portions of each, can be found in <u>Karl Marx - Frederick Engels: Collected Works</u> Volume 1; D. McLellan, <u>The Early Texts</u>; D. Livergood, <u>Marx's Philosophy of Action</u>; and L. Easton and K. Guddat, <u>Writings of the Young Marx on Philosophy and Society</u>.

"Proceedings of the Rhenish Parliament on Thefts of Wood" and "The Poverty of the Moselle Wine Growers."

These are articles written in 1842 for the <u>Rheinische Zeitung</u>, a newspaper which Marx edited. Though something of an embarassment to Marx in later years they represent an early attempt at examining the relevance of economics to certain social and political matters. His analysis of the laws on wood thefts led him to conclude that they were in reality a reflection of the desires and interests of the ruling class. His documented description of the poverty that existed in the Moselle wine district stressed the importance of objectively determined economic conditions. In both pieces Marx not only began to explore the relationships that existed between economics and politics but also began to relate political change to certain liberal democratic reforms, especially universal suffrage and a free press.

These articles or portions thereof are found in the <u>Collected Works</u> Volume 1; McLellan, <u>The Early Texts</u>; and Easton and Guddat, <u>Writings of the Young Marx on Philosophy and Society</u>.

Critique of Hegel's Philosophy of Right

An incomplete and unpublished work written in 1843, the critique attacks Hegel's major political treatise. Relying heavily upon Feuerbach, Marx criticizes Hegel's views on the state, bureaucracy, voting and democracy itself. The realities of the state are subjected to a careful examination and are found to be not at all like Hegel's ideal form. The essay contains further development of Marx's own views on democracy, revealing that at this time he was much taken with the idea of a humanistic democracy, with universal suffrage. The true democracy may even involve the disappearance of Hegel's revered state.

This work can be found in the Collected Works Volume 3; Easton and Guddat, Writings of the Young Marx on Philosophy and Society; and as a separate publication edited by J. O'Malley.

On the Jewish Question

One of the more important of Marx's early writings, this piece was a two part article written in 1843 and published in 1844 in the Deutsch-Französische Jahrbücher which Marx was co-editing with Arnold Ruge. It is a polemical review of Bruno Bauer's Judaism and Christianity. Once again the state is subjected to criticism, as is the classical liberal view of human rights. Social emancipation of the Jews, indeed of all humans, will come only when the gap between the atomistic existence of the individual in civil society and the abstract existence of the citizen in the state is overcome. Then and only then will the communal being fully emerge. In the second part of the essay Marx borders on antisemitism by calling for an end to "huckstering" - later to be more properly named "Capitalism." It is evident in this work that Marx has moved beyond the sphere of politics and now considers full emancipation as necessary in the everyday life of work. Thus, he introduces the theory of alienated labor for the first time.

The standard translation of this work is T. B. Bottomore's in Early Writings edited by Bottomore. It can also be found in several anthologies: Easton and Guddat, Writings of the Young Marx on Philosophy and Society; McLellan, The Early Texts; and R. C. Tucker, The Marx-Engels Reader. It is also in Volume 3 of the Collected Works and has been published separately.

Contribution to the Critique of Hegel's Philosophy of Right: Introduction

This is one of Marx's most important essays. It was written as an introduction to the unpublished Critique of Hegel's Philosophy of Right and published separately in the Deutsch-Französische Jahrbücher in 1844. The theme of a nexus between philosophy and the world is taken up again and pushed to a radical conclusion. German emancipation, human self-realization (here the two are equated), can come in "the formation of a class with radical chains," the proletariat. The notion of a universal class, a class in chains which would become the redeeming force of history makes its first appearance in this essay.

The "Introduction:" is found in Bottomore, Early Writings; Easton and Guddat, Writings of the Young Marx on Philosophy and Society; McLellan, The Early Texts; Tucker, The Marx-Engels Reader; and Volume 3 of the Collected Works.

Economic and Philosophic Manuscripts of 1844

The Paris Manuscripts as these essays are often called represent the apex of the writings of the early Marx. Unpublished until 1932 they had a great impact on Marxian scholarship, because in them the relationship between German philosophy and the writings of the mature Marx are clarified and the theory of alienated labor is fully explored for the first time. Marx felt that in these essays he had united the materialism of Feuerbach with the idealism of Hegel by rooting alienation in the real world of "flesh and blood." In so doing he begins to develop the materialist view of history by contending that human degradation had reached its final stage in the relationship between worker and production in capitalist society. The solution to the problem of alienation would be found in communism, particularly in the abolition of private property.

This work is published separately in an edition translated by M. Milligan and edited by D. Struik. It can also be found in the following anthologies: Bottomore,

Early Writings; Easton and Guddat, Writings of the Young Marx on Philosophy and Society; and Tucker, The Marx-Engels Reader. The Bottomore translation made its first American appearance in Erich Fromm's Marx and the Nature of Man. The manuscripts can also be found in Volume 3 of the Collected Works.

The Condition of the Working Class in England

Engels first major work is this study of political economy in an urban society, published in 1845. He gathered much of his material for it during a two year sojourn in Manchester, England. Engels examines in some detail the life of the proletariat - the industrial workers, miners, farmers, and immigrants - and sees a horrible misery that will yield ultimately to inner necessity. The concentration of capital and continuing commercial crises will reduce all to the status of proletariat and drive them toward revolutionary action. Working independent of Marx, Engels had arrived at similar conclusions, indeed here Engels was the teacher on matters of political economy. This study is evidence of his grasp of the nature of capitalism and the role of the proletariat in history.

This work can be found in part in Tucker, The Marx-Engels Reader and in Volume 4 of the Collected Works. It is also published separately.

The Holy Family

The Holy Family published in 1845 is the first

collaborative work of Marx and Engels, although Marx wrote all but about 16 pages of it. The work is long, difficult and very polemical, much of it an attack on Bruno Bauer and the young Hegelians. It is also a paean to Feuerbach, (Marx later referred to this as a "cult of Feuerbach"), in that Marx and Engels develop a humanistic materialist view of history in it. Ideas, they contend, require men before they become a force in history. Once again the proletariat is depicted as playing a necessary historic role in that redemptive history.

Excerpts from The Holy Family can be found in Easton and Guddat, Writings of the Young Marx on Philosophy and Society and Tucker, The Marx-Engels Reader. It is also published separately and can be found in Volume 4 of the Collected Works.

Theses on Feuerbach

These very short jottings of Marx were written in 1845 and found by Engels after Marx's death. He published them in 1888 as an appendix to his Ludwig Feuerbach and the End of Classical German Philosophy. The cult of Feuerbach had evidently gone far enough. Here Marx discusses the weaknesses of all materialisms including Feuerbach's. They lack the active element of Hegel's philosophy which is itself too abstract. Marx instead outlines his synthesis of the two - the unity of theory and practice. The final thesis is the best known aphoristic comment in all of the Marxian literature. "The philosophers have only interpreted the world in various ways; the point is to change it."

The Theses can be found in most anthologies of Marx and Engels, including Easton and Guddat, <u>Writings of the Young Marx on Philosophy and Society</u>; Tucker, <u>The Marx-Engels Reader</u>; and T. Bottomore and M. Rubel, <u>Selected Writings in Sociology and Social Philosophy</u>. They can also be located in the 1888 edition of Engels' <u>Ludwig Feuerbach and the End of Classical German Philosophy</u> and in many editions of <u>The German Ideology</u> (as an appendix). They are also in Volume 5 of the <u>Collected Works</u>.

The German Ideology

This second collaboration between Marx and Engels was written in 1845-46 but never published in their lifetime. Part of the difficulty in getting it published was its length, near 700 pages, and its nature. It is a long satirical polemic on Max Stirner and Bruno Bauer. Marx later said he and Engels had abandoned the work to the "gnawing mice." It had served one important purpose, that of self-clarification. Part I of the work is a very important section on Feuerbach wherein Marx, who most probably wrote this section, gives us a mature discussion of the theory of historical materialism while elaborating on the <u>Theses on Feuerbach</u>. It contains an examination of the historical methodology Marx used and a brief application of that methodology to existing bourgeois society, along with some predictions for the future communist state. The division of labor will be abolished, society will be stateless and we shall be free to "hunt in the morning, fish in the afternoon, breed cattle in the evening and criticize after dinner." The conclusions of Part I on historical materialism are its most important contents. Human consciousness is linked to economic development, to life. Discussed as it is in political and economic terms, this serves as an important restatement of the more idealistic theory of history found in the Paris Manuscripts.

Because this work was never published, indeed is in some ways incomplete, and because of its many marginal notes, it offers great latitude to an editor. It is therefore often published separately in a variety of ways, usually with Part I intact and selections from Parts II and III, (along with an appendix containing the Theses on Feuerbach). Part One is also included in Easton and Guddat, Writings of the Young Marx on Philosophy and Society; and Tucker, The Marx-Engels Reader. The entire work can be found in Volume 5 of the Collected Works.

The Poverty of Philosophy

This work which was first published in 1847 is an answer to Proudhon's Philosophy of Poverty. It is the first of Marx's thorough examinations of economics and contains a discussion of surplus value, the birth of capitalism, land, rent, the division of labor and the rise of trade unions. In all of this Marx sees social relations, i.e., the class structure of society as a reflection of the productive process and attacks Proudhon for believing that mere changes in the nature of money and the commodity exchange system would bring relief to the worker. Proudhon had failed to see the "real" inner contradictions of society and the transforming qualities of those contradictions. Revolution would come as a result of the rising consciousness of the proletariat.

Marx viewed this essay as one of his most important. He recommended that those who wished to understand Capital should read the Manifesto and Poverty of Philosophy. Since The German Ideology was not published in his lifetime, this was the first public account of historical materialism.

The Poverty of Philosophy is published separately and excerpted in many anthologies including Tucker, The Marx-Engels Reader, and Easton and Guddat, Writings of the Young Marx on Philosophy and Society. It is also found in Volume 6 of the Collected Works.

The Communist Manifesto

The shortest, most concise and clearest of the writings of Marx and Engels is the Manifesto, published in 1848. It is a commissioned work, Marx and Engels having been asked by the Communist League to write a manifesto for that organization. Engels prepared a draft, "The Principles of Communism" which was a series of twenty-five questions and answers. Marx is acknowledged as having given the pamphlet

Inaugural Address and Rules of the Working Men's
International Association (1864) Selected Works
Volume 1.

Secret Diplomatic History of the Eighteenth Century
Published separately.

Friedrich Engels

"Outline of a Critique of Political Economy" Volume
3 Collected Works.

The Peasant War in Germany and Germany: Revolution and
Counter Revolution Published separately.

"Speech at the Graveside of Marx" (1883) Volume 2
Selected Works.

Karl Marx and Friedrich Engels

Journalism: Especially Articles from the New York Daily
Tribune. The American Journalism of Marx and Engels
edited by H. M. Christman.

Articles for the New American Encyclopedia. Articles
in the New American Cyclopaedia edited by H. Draper.

Selected Correspondence, 1846-1895. Translated by
Dona Torr.

In the section of the bibliography entitled "Writings of Marx and Engels" a variety of separate editions of the major individually published works are listed. In addition there are many collected writings mentioned. These require some evaluational comment. The early writings of Marx are available in four good selections: D. McLellan, Early Writings; T. B. Bottomore, Early Writings; L. Colletti, Early Writings; and L. Easton and K. Guddat, Writings of the Young Marx on Philosophy and Society. Specialized collections are becoming increasingly popular and the more important ones include: The Eastern Question, On Colonialism, Karl Marx on Colonialism and Modernization, Letters to Dr.

Kugelmann, Marx on China and Marx on Economics. The Karl
Marx Library edited by Saul Padover is in the process of
publishing an entire library of specialized works including:
On America and the Civil War, On Freedom of Press and
Censorship, On Revolution and On the First International.
More general collections are the Pelican Library Political
Writings and D. McLellan's Karl Marx Reader which promises
to be the best selection available. To date the single most
popular and attractive short collection of the writings of
Marx is T. Bottomore and M. Rubel, Selected Writings in
Sociology and Social Philosophy.

The works of Engels also have been collected on a
specialized basis. The more important collections are:
Engels on Capital, Engels as Military Critic, The Housing
Question and Articles from the Labour Standard.

Finally, the writings of Marx and Engels combined
include the already mentioned Selected Works and Collected
Works as well as Robert Tucker's fine Marx-Engels Reader
and L. Feuer's Basic Writings on Politics and Philosophy.
Specialized collections of both writers that are noteworthy
are: The American Journalism of Marx and Engels, Articles
from the Neue Rheinische Zeitung, 1848-49, Ireland and the
Irish Question, Marx and Engels on Literature and Arts and
Marx and Engels on Malthus.

This completes the descriptive summary of the writings
of Marx and Engels. What remains is the awesome burden of
attempting to make some sense out of the vast secondary

literature. That task must begin with attention being given to the men themselves, to their biographers and to the intellectual and personal relationship they shared.

The Biographers of Marx and Engels

The biographers of Marx and Engels and their readers face several serious problems. First, whether or not the biographer's intent is to present an intellectual history, some familiarity with the ideas of Marx and/or Engels is essential to an understanding of their personal and political life. More often than not the skills necessary for investigating those ideas are not combined with the talents of the historian of persons and events. The tendency in the literature is toward personal biographies with some few political ones and a leaving of intellectual matters to those who have the daring to wade through the literature produced by Marx and Engels. This is not an unreasonable division of labor, although it would be useful if more of the biographers exhibited at least a nodding acquaintance with the philosophical views of their subject.

A second difficulty in the biographical literature is the fact that Marx and Engels are the prime intellectual movers of that twentieth century phenomenon known as Marxism. Hence, an objective analysis of their lives and achievements is very unlikely. There are a good many biographies that are excessively sympathetic, bordering on the hagiographical, while others tend toward an exorcism rite, treating Marx or

Engels as demons of the modern world.

Finally, it is not unreasonable to expect that some serious attention would be given to Marx and Engels combined. Their relationship after 1845 was so close, both in terms of intellectual development and personal acquaintance, that it is difficult to understand why the literature has not one adequate account of their lives together. Indeed Engels has few biographies at all, either singly or in combination with those of Marx.

It should not be surprising that given the above difficulties the number of biographies worth serious attention is not high. Among that group, however, are some successes, a few of high merit.

The biographical studies of Marx far outnumber those of Engels. Among the sympathetic reviews of Marx's life there are four interesting, readable and reasonably adequate accounts: Heinrich Gemkow, et al., <u>Karl Marx: A Biography</u>; Arnold Kettle, <u>Karl Marx</u>; Karl Korsch, <u>Karl Marx</u>, and John Lewis, <u>The Life and Teaching of Karl Marx</u>. The documentation is especially good in the Gemkow work, and while there is divided opinion on the utility of Korsch, it is interesting to read the account of an ex-communist. John Lewis' biography is probably the best of the four mentioned, very reasonable and highly favorable. The first biography of Marx written in English was John Spargo's <u>Karl Marx: His Life and Work</u>. A socialist and sympathetic biographer, Spargo spent thirteen years collecting material for this work. Two other important sympathetic biographies are Wilhelm Liebknecht, <u>Karl Marx: Biographical Memoirs</u> and David Riazanov, <u>Karl Marx: Man, Thinker and Revolutionist</u>. Liebknecht was a personal friend of Marx's and thus gives something of an insiders view, while Riazanov, the initial editor of the Marx-Engels Collected Works presents a very informed set of lectures on Karl Marx and his thought. Finally, from the standpoint of reading an example of pure sentimental idolatry, the student of Marx may wish to consult Evgeniia Stepanova, <u>Karl Marx: Short Biography</u>.

In the category of critical biographies there are three worth consulting: Leopold Schwartszchild, <u>The Red Prussian: The Life and Legend of Karl Marx</u>; Otto Rühle, <u>Karl Marx: His Life and Work</u> and E. H. Carr, <u>Karl Marx: A Study in Fanaticism</u>. Schwartzschild's is the weakest of the three and Ruhle's is a dubious psycho-historical work that presents Marx as something of a neurotic. (A more legitimate and interesting attempt at studying Marx from the psycho-historical viewpoint is J. E. Siegel, "Marx's Early Development: Vocation, Rebellion and Realism.") Carr's biography, however, deserves careful attention. It is a highly controversial work that attempts to place Marx in the context of his social milieu, often characterizing him as a sinister and fanatical man; but it remains the best written and reasoned of the critical studies on the life of Marx.

Popular and speciality biographies on Marx are great in number but not high in quality. There are some interesting and informative works in this grouping, however. In the 1930's Edmund Wilson wrote a long series of biographical articles for the New Republic. Some are insightful and all are readable. Robert Payne's Marx is probably the "standard" popular study. Well written, somewhat hostile and very graphic and thorough in its detailed account of the personal life of Marx this work suffers from inadequate understanding of the philosophy of Marx. In the specialty realm Boris Nicolaievsky and Otto Maenchen-Helfen have written a good political life of Marx, Karl Marx: Man and Fighter, and Werner Blumenberg has constructed an intriguing work, complete with photographs, entitled Karl Marx: An Illustrated Biography. A final speciality item that is extremely interesting is a collection of Reminiscences of Marx put together by the Institute of Marxism-Leninism in Moscow.

The "journeyman" histories of Marx, which is to say those that are sound on life and ideas but by no means complete, have two among their number of special merit, one very old and one relatively new. Max Beer's The Life and Teachings of Karl Marx is an adequate work that is somewhat out of date. Joel Carmichael's Karl Marx: The Passionate Logician is a more recent and shorter introduction to the life and thought of Marx.

Many Marxian scholars maintain that the "definitive" biography of Marx has yet to be written. Whatever the merits of that argument there are several very fine examples of the biographers art on Marx which ought to be read. Isaih Berlin's Karl Marx: His Life and Environment was first published in 1939, so it is rather dated. Nonetheless it remains one of the finest short biographies and is especially strong in integrating the intellectual development of Marx's thought with his life. Michael Evans, in Karl Marx, has more recently written a life of Marx which will stand along side Berlin as another good example of the biography which presents a life and teachings in a highly sophisticated manner. Another recent work, published in 1975, which is difficult to describe but rich in content is Maximilien Rubel and Margaret Manale, Marx without Myth: A Chronological Study of His Life and Work. Presenting little if any narrative, Rubel and Manale have compiled a vast amount of information on Marx and placed it in the framework of a yearly chronology of the life and activities. A good reference work, it would be even more useful if it were better indexed. For years the "authoritative" biography of Marx has been Franz Mehring's Karl Marx: The Story of His Life. It remains so for many. Mehring's is an affectionate biography of sound scholarship but despite its appeal is now out of date because of its unavoidable weaknesses in covering the early Marx. It has been supplanted by the most complete biography of Marx written, David McLellan's Karl Marx: His Life and Thought. One of the foremost living scholars on Marx, McLellan's study is a highly balanced one; and it contains an extremely competent integration of the personal and

Engels first met Marx in the Fall of 1844 after having corresponded over an essay that Engels had published in the Deutsch-Französische Jahrbücher. Marx was very impressed with the essay entitled "Outlines of a Critique of Political Economy." He was equally taken by another work on which Engels was working at the time, <u>The Condition of the Working Class in England</u>. In this early phase of their relationship it was Engels who acted as teacher and Marx the pupil, although Marx would quickly assume the lead in investigating the realm of political economy.

The relationship begun in this initial correspondence and meeting was a close and lifelong one. Engels supported Marx for a good bit of that time, although not entirely and not in luxury. He apparently willingly but not so happily lived in Manchester, England for twenty years running the family business so that he could support Marx and the socialist cause. At times he did so at considerable personal sacrifice. This financial support continued after Marx's death when Engels, who was close to Marx's daughters as well, maintained his support of the family and bequeathed a portion of his estate to them.

Engels was more than benefactor to Marx. He was his closest friend and intellectual ally. During twenty years of correspondence they wrote one another constantly and Marx managed to visit Manchester frequently. The collaboration between the two men has a certain intellectual specialization to it. Marx, after the initial lead provided by Engels and

Moses Hess, wrote primarily on social and economic philosophy. Engels became more interested in natural science and military history. This division of labor would become more apparent and more important in the final years of Engels' life when he would devote himself to the philosophy of science. Marx was easily the more profound of the two but his writing was turgid, difficult to understand and not always accessible. Yet Engels was possessed of his own share of brilliance and wit. If he was not as philosophically sophisticated as Marx or as well educated, he could and did show himself to be a creative mind and skillful analyzer of practical conditions, as well as a better writer.

The most interesting and perhaps most controversial period of their relationship is the late years when Marx is drawn closer to positivism (although not as close as Engels) and assists Engels in the writing of Anti-Dühring. After the death of Marx, Engels continued his role as benefactor of the family and literary executor of Marx's writings; and he began to publish his own works - Ludwig Feuerbach and the End of Classical German Philosophy and The Origin of the Family, Private Property and the State. These works had as much impact on the development of Marxism as any of the writings of Marx.

It is easy to see that the relationship between Marx and Engels presents an intriguing area of study not only in terms of the intellectual differences between the two men and subsequent interpretations of each but also because of

the personal character of their lives together. If that
relationship is ever to be fully apprehended there are a
number of sources to which we must turn.

Most obviously a proper grasp of Marx and Engels is
had only by consulting their writings. A summary of those
available in English has already been given. Beyond that
the richest source is the vast correspondence between the
two men and between Marx and his family. Unfortunately
there are two problems with the correspondence, (the
Briefwechsel). First, all the letters have not been translated into English, although there is a good selection of
the correspondence, and the Collected Works in English will
eventually contain the complete edition. If the first
problem can be corrected the second cannot. The letters
have been sifted and those which might have caused Engels
an embarrassment were destroyed. What is left is warm and
cordial with little indication of any friction between the
two men and not much information on how Marx felt about
Engels and his writings. Despite the disappointing character of the letters, they contain some valuable materials;
and at least two scholars have examined them on their own
terms. Oscar J. Hammen (See "Alienation Communism and
Revolution in the Marx-Engels 'Briefwechsel'.") and Norman
Levine. Mr. Levine has devoted a good bit of attention to
Marx and Engels. (See his "Anthropology in the Thought of
Marx and Engels; Marxism and Engelism: Two Differing Views
of History," and The Tragic Deception: Marx contra Engels.)

The Tragic Deception ends with a psychological analysis of the relationship between Marx and Engels where the symbiotic quality of their association is emphasized. Marx is seen as being emotionally dependent upon Engels. He is free to show his affection without feeling threatened; while Engels, the essentially other-directed personality, needs Marx to establish his own identity. Marx needed a disciple. Engels was quite willing to be one. Levine's psychological analysis of this relationship is supported by Berlin's biography of Marx.

The secondary literature on Marx and Engels is not entirely devoted to the correspondence. There are a number of scholars who have examined the writings as well as the correspondence and made careful distinctions between Marx and Engels, as well as profound assessments of their relationship.

Norman Levine's Tragic Deception is not simply a psycho-history, indeed it is primarily an attempt to distinguish between the philosophical differences between Marx and Engels. Oscar J. Hammen's The Red '48ers: Karl Marx and Friedrich Engels is a fine account of the political activities of Marx and Engels during the 1848 revolutions. Gerorge Lichtheim, an always careful and brilliant intellectual historian, discusses the variations of the theory of Marx and Engels in his Marxism An Historical and Critical Study; as does A. James Gregor in A Survey of Marxism. Sidney Hook analyzes Engels' philosophical

writings in Reason, Social Myths, and Democracy. Ernst
Mandel, The Formation of the Economic Thought of Karl Marx
and A. Walicki, The Controversy over Capitalism both consider discrepancies in the economic theory of Marx and
Engels, the latter discussing differences over the readiness
of Russia to be a revolutionary nation. L. Krader argues
that distinctions between Marx and Engels are traceable to
disagreements over theory and practice. (See The Works of
Marx and Engels in Ethnology Compared.) Finally Zbigniew
Jordan in The Evolution of Dialectical Materialism examines
the philosophical variations of the two men over the fundamental issue of materialism.

The relationship of Engels to Marx, it can be seen,
is a crucial one. Engels was the first revisionist and the
subsequent progenitor of what the world believed was Marxism.
But his was only a beginning. Other interpreters and
revisionists of Marx have arisen by the hundreds. It is
necessary in the final section of this introduction to say
something sensible and useful about the secondary literature
on Marx and Engels that these interpreters have created.

The Interpreters of Marx and Engels

Karl Marx is in the tradition of the grand theorists,
i.e., he is among those who attempt an all encompassing view
of the world and cannot be categorized by the conventional
labels of acedemicians. In one sense this is entirely appro-
priate given Marx's view of the dehumanizing effects of

fragmented labor. It means, however, that Marx is many things to many people, that his thought is examined for a variety of reasons, and that the secondary literature on him (and on Engels) is staggering. There is Marx the economist, the sociologist, the revolutionary, the historian, the philosopher writing on a variety of concepts such as alienation, praxis, nature, man, epistemology, money, commodities, value, politics and the state. The bibliography of secondary works that follows this introduction is an endeavor to collect the writings of those who see in Marx and Engels one or more of those concepts. It is divided into three sections: Books on Marx and Engels; Articles on Marx and Engels, (including major review articles); and Doctoral Dissertations on Marx and Engels. The bibliography is intended to be a comprehensive gathering of the literature into one convenient source. It is also intended to be a "browsing bibliography". The researcher, the student and the casual observer can, if they "read" it, find something of interest or speciality they will wish to peruse. It is assumed, for example, that the reader interested in literary criticism and Marxian thought will discover Peter Demetz' <u>Marx, Engels and the Poets: Origins of Marxist Literary Criticism</u> or perhaps be further intrigued by William Johnston's article on Karl Marx's own poetry, "Karl Marx's Verse of 1836-1837 as a Foreshadowing of His Early Philosophy." The complete evaluation of this literature is an impossible and presumptuous task. What can and will be development of Marxism-Leninism is not the major concern of this bibliography, the above mentioned works are necessary inclusions because they represent initial attempts to actualize Marx and Engels. They are legitimate attempts at interpreting Marx and Engels. The same cannot be said of subsequent developments in the Marxist-Leninist ideology, such as Stalinism or Maoism. Their lack of resemblance to Marx and Engels, and their ideological character warrant their omission.

Some good general studies of the development of Marxism which has been so crudely described above are George Lichtheim, Marxism: A Historical and Critical Study and A. James Gregor, A Survey of Marxism. A short introduction to the same subject can be had in Sidney Hook's Marx and the Marxists: The Ambiguous Legacy. Lewis Coser's "Marxist Thought in the First Quarter of the 20th Century" illustrates the dependency of these various early theories of Marxism on the social location and backgrounds of their authors and their intended audiences. The classic history of the development of the thought of Marx and Engels through Lenin into twentieth century Russia is Dialectical Materialism by Gustav Wetter.

Revisionism did not cease, of course, with the establishment of totalitarian Marxism. If anything it flourished under the burden of attempting to understand what had been done to Marx. Revisionist writings continue to be produced, primarily in Eastern Europe, or by Marxists in noncommunist dominated countries. Leopold Labedz' Revisionism: Essays in the History of Marxist Ideas is a good introduction to the continuation of that trend. Wolfgang Leonhard's Three Faces of Marxism: The Political Concepts of Soviet Ideology, Maoism and Humanist Marxism is also a very useful exploration of the varieties of Marxism existent today. Five original revisionist works present a more intriguing view of the originality of Marxist interpreters: Leszek Kolakowski's The Alienation of Reason and Toward a Marxist Humanism: Essays on the Left Today and Gajo Petrovic's Marx in the Mid-Twentieth Century and Milovan Djilas' The New Class are among the best contemporary examples while Antonio Labriola's Essays on the Materialist Conception of History and Georg Lukacs' History and Class Consciousness are older illustrations of this type of thought. Although Lukacs later became an apologist, his work is the most remarkable of all mentioned. The revisionist, or neo-Marxists as they have been called, frequently object to the positivistic determinism of Soviet Marxism. They argue for a more human, Hegelian Marx. Lukacs did this before having knowledge of The Economic and Philosophic Manuscripts of 1844.

The division of thought among the Marxists between orthodoxy and revisionism roughly corresponds to the major emphases that exist in the Marxian literature on the early and later Marx, or the study of Marx before 1848 and after. Considering Marx in terms of these two great periods of his life has been both an academic and an ideological enterprise.

Often the lines between the university and the party have been obscured. However, the schema of an early and late Marx is useful in orienting our attention toward works that were written in one of the two periods. Whether they fit into the academic-ideological debate over which is more important, the late or early Marx, many interpreters can be located in either of these two "camps" simply because of the writings of Marx they are emphasizing in their analyses, or because of the conceptual framework they are using in their approach to Marx. Those who are in the early Marx category choose to center attention on pre-1848 writings particularly The Economic and Philosophic Manuscripts. The concepts of alienation and the influence of Hegel are central in their approach to Marx. The late Marx enthusiasts, or simply those who concentrate on the period after 1848 regard the Manifesto and Capital as the two most significant works in the Marxian literature. They are interested in and write about surplus value, historical materialism, the critique of capitalism or revolutionary politics. It is useful, then, to consider a major portion of the writings of Marx in light of this twofold categorization.

For many years the two most important studies of the early Marx were H. P. Adams' Karl Marx in His Early Writings, the first of its kind in English, and Sidney Hook's From Hegel to Marx. Both works are dated now, but Hook's is still a valuable source for understanding the young Hegelians and their relationship to Marx. David McLellan's work, Marx before the Marxists has supplanted Hook, and L. Dupre's The Philosophical Foundations of Marxism is a better general introduction to the early Marx than Adams. A relatively new work which also analyzes the development of the early Marx up to the Paris Manuscripts and which vividly illustrates the search for a revolutionary catalyst in the historical process is Dick Howard's The Development of the Marxian Dialectic. A more highly specialized study is J. Maguire, Marx's Paris Writings. Not to be neglected in the examinations of Marx's early writings are Auguste Cornu, The Origins of Marxist Thought; N. Rotenstreich, Basic Problems of Marx's Philosophy and J. Hyppolite, Studies on Marx and Hegel. Cornu traces Marx's intellectual development in the early years. Rotenstreich centers his attention on the Theses on Feuerbach while Hyppolite's set of essays focusses concern on the Critique of Hegel's Philosophy of Right as well as Capital. Hyppolite's analysis is difficult but highly rewarding. The work in this category of the early Marx that is most highly "charged" with the attempt to "prove" Marx was a humanist is Erich Fromm's Marx's Concept of Man. Fromm introduced the controversy over the early versus the late Marx into the United States. In addition to including Bottomore's translation of the Paris Manuscripts in his book Fromm included a provocative introduction which rejected Capital and argued that Marx was essentially an existentialist humanist. A more profound elaboration of the same theme is Ernst Bloch's On Karl Marx. An eschatologist, and theologian of hope, Bloch analyses the early writings, especially the Theses on Feuerbach and places Marx in his own idealist framework. H. Koren's Marx and the Authentic Man is a shorter version of the same humanistic theme.

The older Marx is defended against these "charges" of humanism most ably by L. Althusser in For Marx and to a lesser extent in Reading Capital. In one sense the debate was easily won by the proponents of the older Marx because they could argue that Marx had matured, outgrown his early flirtation with humanism. This is precisely what Althusser does. Marx is seen as having made the break with his youthful self when he left the Rhineland for Paris or in an epistemological sense when he elaborated on the Theses on Feuerbach in The German Ideology. Althusser's argument is that Marx now became the mature social scientist ready to produce Capital. Daniel Bell's The End of Ideology, and Adam Ulam's The Unfinished Revolution essentially make the same argument as Althusser although not as forcefully nor in the context of a structuralist defense of Marx.

Outside the confines of the debate on the early versus the late Marx but nonetheless concerned primarily with writings and developments after 1848 are a number of works of high quality. On the development of historical materialism, especially in the post-1848 writings it is essential that the students of Marx and Engels consult Lichtheim's Marxism as well as the oldest and perhaps ablest work on the subject Karl Marx's Interpretation of History by M. M.

that a new generation of scholars will continue to pursue Marx in light of the more complete literature.

This does not by any criteria exhaust the possible commentary on the interpreters of Marx. It does provide a general guide for using the bibliography. Two final comments are necessary: one bibliographic, the other an admonition. Where, the general reader may intelligently ask, can one go in this literature to gain a simple and accurate introduction to the ideas of Marx? H. J. Koren's <u>Marx and the Authentic Man</u> is a valuable first contact with the thought of Marx. It is a beginner's treatise with some biographical information and some intellectual history. Koren also contrasts the "Authentic Man" of Marx with the inauthenticity of the applications of Marx in the U.S.S.R. David McLellan's biography is also a fine combination of materials on life and thought, carefully presented and easily understood. John Plamenatz has, in all probability given the authoritative general introduction to the writings of Marx in Volume 2 of <u>Man and Society</u>.

Finally, this cautionary note. Outside the realm of intense political debates on ideology or academic disputes over the young Marx versus the old, far removed from the historiography of what has happened to Marx and Engels and their writings there is a clear indication at least in the essays of Marx that he was an utopian thinker, not an ideological one. The writings are dynamic, ever changing and evolving in character. Capturing the final Marx, then, will be tantamount to seizing nothing. It will, in the ultimate sense, only render more truth to Marx's statement to his son-in-law Paul Lafargue: ". . . what is certain is that I am no Marxist."

Acknowledgments

There are many persons to whom I am indebted for assistance in the preparation of this work: the staff of the Louisiana State University Library, for their able and willing assistance on bibliographic matters; Mrs. Myrtle Bolner, for her daily consultative advice on bibliographic style; Mrs. Lucille Tynes, typist extraordinaire; the students of my Marx-Engels seminar, for providing much of the initial impetus for this work; Dr. Irwin A. Berg, Dean of the College of Arts and Sciences, for financial assistance in the preparation of the manuscript; and Ms. Candace Pickering for her unselfish and devoted attention to the demands of my work at the expense of hers. Finally, a neglected family must be acknowledged for their forbearance: my wife, Judith and children, Rebecca, Christopher and Jessica. I thank all of those named for their contributions to whatever merit this work may have. The deficiencies in it are wholly my own.

Baton Rouge, La.
May, 1977

THE WRITINGS OF MARX AND ENGELS

Karl Marx - Individual Works

Capital

Capital. Translated by Samuel Moore, and Edward Aveling. Edited by Dona Torr. New York: International Publishing Co., 1939.

Capital. Edited by F. Engels. Translated from the 3rd German edition by S. Moore and E. Aveling. Revised with additional translation from the 4th German edition by Marie Sachey and Herbert Lamm. Chicago, Encyclopaedia Britannica, 1955. (Also includes The Manifesto of the Communist Party, by K. Marx and F. Engels. Translated by S. Moore and edited by F. Engels.)

Capital. Translated from the 4th German edition by Eden and Cedar Paul. Introduction by G. D. H. Cole. New York: E. P. Dutton; London: Lawrence & Wishart, 1957.

Capital. 3 vol. Moscow: Progress Publishers, 1965-66.

Capital. Translated by S. W. Ryazanskaya. New York: International Publishers Co., 1971.

Capital: A Critical Analysis of Capitalist Production. Translated from the 3rd German edition by S. Moore and E. Aveling. Edited by F. Engels. London: S. Sonnenschein & Co., 1909; London: Wm. Glaisher, 1920.

Capital: A Critical Analysis of Capitalist Production. Translated from the 3rd German edition by S. Moore and E. Aveling. Edited by F. Engels. A photographic reprint of the stereotyped edition of 1889 with a supplement including changes made by Engels in the 4th German edition, Engels' preface to the 4th German edition with notes, Marx's preface to the French edition and notes on the English edition. Edited and translated by Dona Torr. London: George Allen & Unwin, 1966; New York: International Publishers Co., 1948.

Capital: A Critical Analysis of Capitalist Production. 3 vol. Translated from the 3rd German edition by S. Moore and E. Aveling. Edited by F. Engels. Moscow: Foreign Languages Publishing House, 1962.

1

Capital: A Critical Analysis of Capitalist Production.
Translated by S. Moore and E. Aveling. London:
Lawrence & Wishart, 1974.

Capital: A Critique of Political Economy. 3 vol.
Edited by Julian Borchardt. Translated by Stephen
Trask. Chicago: Charles H. Kerr, 1906-09.

Capital: A Critique of Political Economy. 3 vol.
Chicago: Charles H. Kerr & Co., 1925-26.

Capital: A Critique of Political Economy. 3 vol.
Translated from the 3rd German edition by S. Moore
and E. Aveling. Edited by F. Engels. Chicago:
Charles H. Kerr & Co., 1932-33.

Capital: A Critique of Political Economy. New York:
Modern Library, 1936.

Capital: A Critique of Political Economy. 3 vol.
Edited by F. Engels. London: Lawrence & Wishart,
1959; New York: International Publishers Co., 1967.

Capital: A Critique of Political Economy, The Process
of Capitalist Production. London: George Allen &
Unwin, 1928.

Capital: A Critique of Political Economy, The Process
of Capitalist Production. Translated from the 4th
German edition by Eden and Cedar Paul. New York:
International Publishers Co., 1929.

Capital: A Critique of Political Economy, The Process
of Capitalist Production. Translated from the 3rd
German edition by Samuel Moore and Edward Aveling.
Edited by F. Engels and amplified according to the
4th German edition by Ernest Untermann. New York:
Modern Library, 1936.

Capital: A Critique of Political Economy, The Process
of Capitalist Production. 2 vol. Translated from
the 4th German edition by Eden and Cedar Paul.
Introduction by G. D. H. Cole. New York: E. P.
Dutton & Co., 1946; London: J. M. Dent & Sons, 1951.

Capital: Abridged. Introduction by John Strachey.
New York: Thomas Nelson & Sons, 1937.

Das Kapital: A Critique of Political Economy. Edited
by F. Engels. Condensed for modern readers by Serge
L. Levitsky. Chicago: Henry Regnery Co., 1959.

The People's Marx. Abridged popular edition of the three volumes of Capital. Edited by Julian Borchardt. Translated by Stephen L. Trask. London: International Bookshops, 1921.

The Civil War in France
(Also referred to as The Paris Commune when published along with two addresses on the Franco-Prussian War given by Marx to the General Council of the International.)

The Civil War in France: An Address of the General Council of the International Workingmen's Association. London: E. Truelove, 1871.

The Civil War in France Preceded by the Two Manifestoes of the General Council of the International on the Franco-Prussian War. Historical introduction by R. W. Postgate. London: Labour Publishing Co., 1921.

The Civil War in France. Introduction by F. Engels. Enlarged edition including two Manifestoes on the Franco-Prussian War and other writings of Marx and Engels on the Paris Commune. Chicago: Charles H. Kerr & Co., 1934.

The Civil War in France. Introduction by F. Engels. London: Lawrence & Wishart, 1941; New York: International Publishers Co., 1962; Moscow: Foreign Languages Publishing House, 1963.

The Civil War in France. New York: International Publishers Co., 1968; Moscow: Progress Publishers, 1972.

The Civil War in France: The Paris Commune. New York: International Publishers Co., 1968.

The Paris Commune. Introduction by F. Engels. Edited with notes by Lucien Sanial. New York: New York Labor News, 1960.

The Paris Commune, 1871. New edition. Edited and introduced by Christopher Hitchens. London: Sidgwick & Jackson, 1971.

The Class Struggles in France, 1848-1850

The Class Struggles in France, 1848-1850. Edited by C. P. Dutt. Introduction by F. Engels. New York: International Publishers Co.; London: Martin Lawrence, 1935.

The Class Struggles in France, 1848-1850. Introduction by F. Engels. Moscow: Foreign Languages Publishing House; Progress Publishers, 1960.

The Class Struggles in France, 1848-1850. Translated by Henry Kuhn. Introduced by F. Engels. New York: New York Labor News Co., 1967.

The Class Struggles in France, 1848-1850. London: Lawrence & Wishart, 1942; Moscow: Foreign Languages Publishing House, 1960; New York: International Publishers Co., 1964; Moscow: Progress Publishers, 1972.

A Contribution to the Critique of Political Economy

A Contribution to the Critique of Political Economy. Translated by N. I. Stone from the 2nd German edition. Appendix containing Marx's introduction. New York: International Library Publishing Co., 1904; Chicago: Charles H. Kerr & Co., 1918.

A Contribution to the Critique of Political Economy. Translated by S. W. Ryazanskaya. Edited by Maurice Dobb. Introduction by Maurice Dobb. New York: International Publishers Co., 1970; Moscow: Progress Publishers, 1970; London: Lawrence & Wishart, 1971.

Critique of Hegel's Philosophy of Right. Translated by Annette John and Joseph O'Malley. Edited with an introduction and notes by Joseph O'Malley. New York: Cambridge University Press, 1971.

Critique of the Gotha Programme

Critique of the Gotha Programme. New York: International Publishers Co., 1938; Moscow: Foreign Languages Publishing House, 1947; Moscow: Progress Publishers, 1971.

Critique of the Gotha Programme. Includes "Contribution to the Critique of the Social-Democratic Draft Programme of 1891" by F. Engels. Moscow: Foreign Languages Publishing House, 1959.

Critique of the Gotha Programme. Edited by C. P. Dutt. Appendices by Marx, Engels and Lenin. Moscow: Co-operative Publishing Society of Foreign Workers in the U.S.S.R., 1933; New York: International Publishers Co., 1938; London: Lawrence & Wishart, 1943.

The Gotha Program, and Did Marx Err? by Daniel De Leon.
New York: New York Labor News Co., 1935.

"The Difference between the Democritian and Epicurean Philosophy of Nature." Doctoral Dissertation. Activity in Marx's Philosophy. Norman D. Livergood. The Hague: Martinis Nijhoffs, 1967; New York: Universal Distributors, 1967.

The Eighteenth Brumaire of Louis Bonaparte

The Eighteenth Brumaire of Louis Bonaparte. Translated by Daniel De Leon. Chicago: Charles H. Kerr & Co., 1919.

The Eighteenth Brumaire of Louis Bonaparte. Translated by Eden and Cedar Paul. London: G. Allen & Unwin; New York: International Publishers Co., 1926.

The Eighteenth Brumaire of Louis Bonaparte. Edited by C. P. Dutt. With explanatory notes. New York: International Publishers Co., 1935.

The Eighteenth Brumaire of Louis Bonaparte. Edited by C. P. Dutt. Includes Marx's preface to the 2nd edition and Engels' preface to the 3rd edition. New York: International Publishers Co., 1935.

The Eighteenth Brumaire of Louis Bonaparte. Translated by Daniel De Leon. Introduction by Eric Hass. Preface by K. Marx, F. Engels and Daniel De Leon. New York: New York Labor News Co., 1951.

The Eighteenth Brumaire of Louis Bonaparte. With explanatory notes. New York: International Publishers Co., 1964.

The Economic and Philosophic Manuscripts of 1844

The Economic and Philosophic Manuscripts of 1844. Translated by T. B. Bottomore. In Marx's Concept of Man by Erich Fromm. New York: Frederick Ungar Publishing Co., 1961.

The Economic and Philosophic Manuscripts of 1844. Translated by Martin Milligan. Edited with an introduction by Dirk J. Struik. New York: International Publishers Co., 1969; London: Lawrence & Wishart, 1970.

Free Trade

> Free Trade: A Speech Delivered before the Democratic Club, Brussels, Belgium, January 9, 1848. With an extract from La Miserie de la Philosophie. Translated by Florence W. Wischnewetsky. Preface by F. Engels. Boston: Lee & Shepard; New York: C. T. Dillingham, 1888.
>
> Free Trade. An Address Delivered before the Democratic Association of Brussels, Belgium, January 9, 1848. Translated by Florence Kelley. Preface by F. Engels. New York: New York Labor News Co., 1921.
>
> Marx on Cheapness. Being some Portions of "The Discourse on Free Trade" Delivered by Marx before the Democratic Association of Brussels, January 9, 1848. Translated by Robert Rives La Monte. Chicago: Charles H. Kerr & Co., 1907.

Grundrisse - Outlines of a Critique of Political Economy

> The Grundrisse. Edited and translated by David McLellan. New York: Harper & Row Publishers, 1971.
>
> Grundrisse: Foundations of the Critique of Political Economy. Translated with a foreword by Martin Nicolaus. London: Allen Lane, New Left Review; New York: Vintage Books, 1973.
>
> "Notes on Machines." Economy and Society. 1(1972): 244-254. (An excerpt from Grundrisse.)
>
> Pre-capitalist Economic Formations. Translated by Jack Cohen. Edited with an introduction by E. J. Hobsbawm. London: Lawrence & Wishart, 1964; New York: International Publishers Co., 1965. (Part of Grundrisse.)
>
> The First English Translation of Marx's "Notes on Machines." Translated by Ben Brewster. Leicester University: Sublation, 1966.

On the Jewish Question

> On the Jewish Question. Cincinnati: H. U. C., J. I. R., 1958.
>
> A World without Jews. Translated and introduced by D. D. Runes. New York: Philosophical Library, 1959.

A World without Jews. Translated with an introduction
and epilogue by Dagobert D. Runes. 4th enlarged
edition. New York: Philosophical Library, 1960; Ann
Arbor, Mich.: University Microfilms, 1971. (First
unexpurgated English publication of papers originally
published in the Deutsch-Französische Jahrbücher
under the title "Zur Judenfrage.")

"Political Indifferentism." Bulletin of the Society for the
Study of Labour History. 20(1970): 19-23. (Believed to
be the first English translation of L'indefferenza in
materia politica, which appeared in Almanacco Republicano
in January, 1873.)

The Poverty of Philosophy

    The Poverty of Philosophy: Being a Translation of the
"Misere de la Philosophie" (A Reply to "La Philosophie
de la Misere" of M. Proudhon). Translated by H.
Quelch. Preface by F. Engels. London: Twentieth
Century Press, 1900; Chicago: Charles H. Kerr & Co.,
1934.

    The Poverty of Philosophy. Introduction by F. Engels.
Edited by C. P. Dutt and V. G. Chattopadhaya. London:
Martin Lawrence, 1936; New York: International Publishers Co., 1963.

    The Poverty of Philosophy. Introduction by F. Engels.
New York: International Publishers Co., 1964.

    The Poverty of Philosophy. Answer to the "Philosophy
of Poverty" by M. Proudhon. London: Lawrence &
Wishart, 1956; Moscow: Progress Publishers, 1966.
(Translated from the French edition of 1847. Corrections made by Engels for the 2nd French edition
and the German edition of 1885-1892.)

    The Poverty of Philosophy. Moscow: Progress Publishers, 1968.

Secret Diplomatic History of the Eighteenth Century
(Accompanied by The Story of the Life of Lord Palmerston.)

    Secret Diplomatic History of the Eighteenth Century.
Edited by Eleanor Marx Aveling. London: S. Sonnenschein & Co., 1899.

The Story of the Life of Lord Palmerston. Edited by
Eleanor Marx Aveling. London: S. Sonnenschein & Co.,
1899.

Secret Diplomatic History of the Eighteenth Century and
The Story of the Life of Lord Palmerston. Edited with
an introduction and notes by Lester Hutchinson.
London: Lawrence & Wishart; New York: International
Publishers Co., 1969.

Theories of Surplus Value
(Volume IV of Capital.)

    Theories of Surplus Value. New York: International
    Publishers Co., 1952.

    Theories of Surplus Value. Translated by Renate
    Simpson. Edited by S. Ryazanskaya. London: Lawrence
    & Wishart, 1969.

    Theories of Surplus Value. (Vol. 4 of Capital). Translated by Emile Burns. Edited by S. Ryazanskaya. New
    York: Universal Distributors Co., 1963; Moscow:
    Progress Publishers, 1969.

    Theories of Surplus Value. (Vol. 4 of Capital.) Translated by Jack Cohen and S. W. Ryazanskaya. Edited by
    S. W. Ryazanskaya and Richard Dixon. Moscow:
    Progress Publishers, 1971.

    Theories of Surplus Value: A Selection from the Volumes
    Published between 1905 and 1910 as "Theorien über den
    Mehrwert." Edited by Karl Kautsky. Translated by G.
    A. Bonner and Emile Burns. London: Lawrence &
    Wishart, 1954; New York: International Publishers Co.,
    1952; New York: Augustus M. Kelly, 1966.

    History of Economic Theories from the Physiocrats to
    Adam Smith. (Volume IV, Part 1 of Capital.) Edited
    by Karl Kautsky. Translated by Terence McCarthy.
    New York: Langland Press, 1952.

Value, Price and Profit
(Sometimes titled Wages, Price and Profit.)

    Value, Price and Profit. New York: Universal Distributors, 1947; Moscow: Foreign Languages Publishing
    House, 1947.

Value, Price and Profit: Addressed to Workingmen.
Edited by Eleanor Marx Aveling. Introduction by
Lucien Sanial. Preface by Daniel De Leon. New
edition. New York: New York Labor News Co., 1933.

Value, Price and Profit: Addressed to Working Men.
Edited by Eleanor Marx Aveling. Preface by Edward
Aveling. Chicago: Charles H. Kerr & Co., 1935;
London: George Allen & Unwin, 1951.

Value, Price and Profit: Addressed to Working Men.
Edited by Eleanor Marx Aveling. Moscow: Co-operative
Publishing Society of Foreign Workers in the U.S.S.R.,
1933; New York: International Publishers Co., 1969.

Wages, Price and Profit. Moscow: Progress Publishers,
1970.

Wage, Labor and Capital

Wage, Labor and Capital. Translated by J. L. Joynes.
Chicago: Charles H. Kerr & Co., 1918.

Wage-Labor and Capital. Preface by F. Engels. Translated by Harriet E. Lothrop. New York: New York
Labor News Co., 1921.

Wage-Labor and Capital. Revised Edition. Chicago:
Charles H. Kerr & Co., 1935.

Wage-Labor and Capital. Introduction by F. Engels.
Revised translation. New York: International Publishers Co., 1937; Chicago: Charles H. Kerr & Co.,
1948.

Wage-Labor and Capital. New York: International
Library Publishing Co., 1900; New York: International
Publishers Co., 1947; Moscow: Progress Publishers,
1970.

Wage-Labour and Capital. Translated by J. L. Joynes.
London: Modern Press, 1885; New York: International
Publishers Co., 1899.

Wage-Labour and Capital. New edition. Translated by
J. L. Joynes. London: Twentieth Century Press, 1912.

Wage, Labour and Capital. London: Modern Books, 1929;
Martin Lawrence, 1932.

Wage Labour and Capital. Introduction by F. Engels. London: Lawrence & Wishart, 1947; Moscow: Foreign Languages Publishing House, 1954; New York: International Publishers Co., 1969.

Karl Marx - Collected Works

Articles on India. 2nd Indian edition. Bombay: People's Publishing House, 1951; Ann Arbor, Mich.: University Microfilms, 1970.

Capital, the Communist Manifesto and other Writings by Karl Marx. Edited with an introduction by Max Eastman. New York: Modern Library, 1932. (Includes an unpublished essay on Marxism by Lenin.)

Early Texts. Translated and edited by David McLellan. New York: Barnes & Noble, 1971; Oxford: Basil Blackwell & Mott, 1971.

Early Writings. London: Universal Distributors, 1963.

Early Writings. Translated and edited by T. B. Bottomore. London: C. A. Watts & Co., 1963.

Early Writings. Translated and edited by T. B. Bottomore. Foreword by Erich Fromm. New York: McGraw Hill Book Co., 1964.

Early Writings. Introduction by Lucio Colletti. Translated by Rodney Livingston & Gregor Benton. New York: Vintage Books; London: New Left Review; Harmondsworth: Penguin, 1975. (Part of the Pelican Marx Library.)

The Eastern Question: A Reprint of Letters Written 1853-1856 Dealing with the Events of the Crimean War. Edited by Eleanor Marx Aveling and Edward Aveling. London: S. Sonnenschein, 1897; New York: Burt Franklin, 1968; Augustus M. Kelley, 1969.

The Essential Marx. Edited by Ernst Fischer in collaboration with Franz Marek. Translated by Anna Bostock. New York: Herder & Herder, 1970. (Published in London under the title Marx in His Own Words.)

Essential Writings of Karl Marx. Selected and with an introduction and notes by David Caute. London: McGibbon & Kee, 1967; New York: The Macmillan Co., 1968; New York: Collier Books, 1970.

The Essentials of Marx. Introduction and notes by Algernon Lee. New York: Vanguard Press, 1926. Revised edition, New York: Rand School Press, 1946.

The Ethnological Notebooks of Karl Marx. Studies of Morgan, Phear, Maine, Lubbock. Transcribed and edited with an introduction by Lawrence Krader. Assen: Van Gorcum, 1972.

The First International & After. Edited with an introduction by David Fernbach. Vol. 3 Political Writings. New York: Random House, 1974.

The Karl Marx Dictionary. Edited by Morris Stockshammer. New York: Philosophical Library; London: Peter Owen, 1965.

Karl Marx: Economy, Class and Social Revolution. Edited with an introductory essay by Z. A. Jordan. New York: Charles Scribner's Sons; London: Michael Joseph, 1971.

Karl Marx: Essential Writings. Edited by Frderic L. Bender. New York: Harper & Row Publishers, 1972.

Karl Marx on Colonialism and Modernization: His Dispatches (sic) and Other Writings on China, India, Mexico, and the Middle East & North Africa. Edited with an introduction by Shlomo Avineri. Garden City, N.Y.: Doubleday & Co., 1969.

Karl Marx Reader. Edited by David McLellan. New York: Oxford University Press, Forthcoming.

Karl Marx: Selected Papers. Introduced by F. Borkenau. Frankfurt-Main, Hamburg: Fischer Bucherei, 1956.

Karl Marx: Selected Works. New York: International Publishers Co., 1937.

Letters on India. Edited by B. P. L. Bedi and Freda Bedi. Model Town, Lahore: Contemporary India Publications, 1937.

Letters to Dr. Kugelmann. New York: International Publishers Co., 1934; London: Lawrence & Wishart, 1941.

The Living Thoughts of Karl Marx. Presented by Leon Trotsky. Foreword by Sidney Hook. Translated with an introductory essay by Charles Malamuth. Greenwich, Conn.: Fawcett Publications, 1963.

Marx in His Own Words. Edited by Ernst Fischer and Franz Marek. London: Allen Lane, 1970.

Marx on China: Articles from the New York Daily Tribune.
Introduction and notes by Dona Torr. London: Lawrence &
Wishart, 1968; New York: Gordon Press, 1975.

Marx on Economics. Edited by Robert Freedmen. Introduction
by Harry Schwartz. New York: Harcourt, Brace & World;
Harmondsworth: Penguin Books, 1961.

Marx versus Russia. Edited with an introduction by J. A.
Doerig. Afterword by Hans Kohn. New York: Frederick
Ungar Publishing Co., 1962.

Notebook on the Paris Commune: Press Excerpts & Notes.
Edited by Hal Draper. Berkeley, Calif.: Independent
Socialist Press, 1971.

On America and the Civil War. Arranged and edited with an
introduction and new translation by Saul K. Padover.
Vol. 2. The Karl Marx Library. New York: McGraw Hill,
1972.

On Colonialism: Articles from the New York Tribune and Other
Writings. New York: International Publishers Co., 1972.

On Freedom of the Press & Censorship. Translated with an
introduction by Saul K. Padover. Vol. 4. The Karl Marx
Library. New York: McGraw Hill, 1974.

On Revolution. Edited by Saul K. Padover. Vol. 1. The
Karl Marx Library. New York: McGraw Hill, 1972.

On Socialist Movement Treasuries. Edited by John Loeb. New
York: Voluntary Press, 1955.

On the First International. Arranged and edited with an
introduction and new translation by Saul K. Padover. Vol.
3. The Karl Marx Library. New York: McGraw Hill, 1973.

Political Writings. Edited with an introduction by David
Fernbach. Vol. 1: The Revolutions of 1848; Vol. 2: Surveys
from Exile; Vol. 3: The First International & After. The
Vintage Marx Library. London: Allen Lane, New Left Review,
1973; New York: Random House, 1974.

Revolution and Counter-Revolution: Or, Germany in 1848.
Edited and collected by Eleanor Marx Aveling. Chicago:
Charles H. Kerr & Co., 1907; London: George Allen & Unwin,
1937. Revised edition. London: George Allen & Unwin,
1971. (It should be noted that these articles were actual-
ly written by Engels. See citation under works of Engels.)

The Revolutions of 1848. Edited by David Fernbach. Vol. 1.
Political Writings. New York: Random House, 1974.

Selected Essays. Translated by H. J. Stenning. New York: International Publishers Co., 1926. Reprint of 1926 edition. Freeport, N.Y.: Books for Libraries, 1968.

Selected Works. Prepared by the Marx-Engels-Lenin Institute under the editorship of V. Adoratsky. English editor, C. P. Dutt. Moscow: Co-operative Publishing Society of Foreign Workers in the U.S.S.R., 1935; New York: International Publishers Co., 1936; London: Lawrence & Wishart, 1943.

Selected Works. 2nd English edition. Edited by I. B. Lasker. Moscow: Foreign Languages Publishing House, 1946; London: Lawrence & Wishart, 1947.

Selected Writings in Sociology and Social Philosophy. Edited with an introduction and notes by T. B. Bottomore & Maximilien Rubel. Texts translated by T. B. Bottomore. London: F. Franklin Watts, 1961; Harmondsworth, Middlesex, England: Penguin Books, 1965.

Selected Writings in Sociology and Social Philosophy. Newly translated by T. B. Bottomore. Edited with an introduction and notes by T. B. Bottomore and Maximilien Rubel. Foreword by Erich Fromm. New York: McGraw Hill, 1964.

Surveys from Exile. Edited by David Fernbach. Vol. 2. Political Writings. London: Allen Lane, New Left Review; New York: Random House, 1973.

Texts on Method. Translated and edited by Terrell Carver. New York: Barnes & Noble; Oxford: Blackwell, 1975.

Wage-Labour and Capital and Value, Price and Profit. New York: International Publishers Co., 1976.

The Wisdom of Karl Marx. New York: Philosophical Library, 1967.

Writings of the Young Marx on Philosophy and Society. Translated and edited by Loyd D. Easton and Kurt H. Guddat. Garden City, N.Y.: Anchor Books, Doubleday & Cp., 1967.

Friedrich Engels - Individual Works

Anti-Dühring: Herr Eugen Dühring's Revolution in Science

    Anti-Dühring: Herr Eugen Dühring's Revolution in Science. London: Lawrence & Wishart, 1959; Moscow Foreign Languages Publishing House, 1962; Moscow: Progress Publishers, 1969.

Herr Eugen Dühring's Revolution in Science (Anti-Dühring). Chicago: Charles H. Kerr & Co., 1935; London: Lawrence & Wishart, 1940.

Herr Eugen Dühring's Revolution in Science (Anti-Dühring). Edited by E. Wattenberg. New York: Universal Distributors, 1947.

Herr Eugen Dühring's Revolution in Science (Anti-Dühring). Translated by Emile Burns. Edited by C. P. Dutt. London: Martin Lawrence, 1935; New York: International Publishers Co., 1966.

Landmarks of Scientific Socialism, "Anti-Dühring." Translated and edited by Austin Lewis. Chicago: Charles H. Kerr & Co., 1907.

The Bakuninists at Work: Review of the Uprising in Spain in the Summer of 1873. Translated by Bryan Bean. Moscow: Progress Publishers, 1971.

The Condition of the Working Class in England in 1844

> The Condition of the Working Class in England in 1844. Appendix written in 1886 and Preface in 1887 by F. Engels. Translated by Florence K. Wischnewetsky. New York: J. W. Lowe Co., 1887.
>
> The Condition of the Working Class in England in 1844. Preface written in 1892 by F. Engels. Translated by Florence K. Wischnewetsky. London: S. Sonnenschein & Co., 1943; George Allen & Unwin, 1952.
>
> The Condition of the Working Class in England in 1844. London: George Allen & Unwin, 1955.
>
> The Condition of the Working Class in England. Translated and edited by W. O. Henderson and W. H. Chaloner. New York: The Macmillan Co., 1958; Oxford: Basil Blackwell & Mott, 1971; Stanford, Calif.: Stanford University Press, 1968.
>
> The Condition of the Working Class in England from Personal Observation and Authentic Sources. Moscow: Progress Publishers, 1973.

Dialectics of Nature

> Dialectics of Nature. Moscow: Foreign Languages Publishing House; New York: Universal Distributors, 1966.

Dialectics of Nature. Translated and edited by Clemens Dutt. Preface and notes by J. B. S. Haldane. London: Lawrence & Wishart, 1941; New York: International Publishers Co., 1962; Moscow: Progress Publishers, 1972.

Germany: Revolution and Counter Revolution

> Germany: Revolution and Counter Revolution. New York: International Publishers; London: Lawrence & Wishart, 1933.
>
> Germany: Revolution and Counter Revolution. Edited by E. Marx. New York: International Publishers; London: Lawrence & Wishart, 1969.

Karl Marx, Speech at the Graveside of Karl Marx. Moscow: Foreign Languages Publishing House, 1955.

Ludwig Feuerbach and the End of Classical German Philosophy

> Ludwig Feuerbach and the End of Classical German Philosophy. Moscow: Foreign Languages Publishing House, 1950; Moscow: Progress Publishers, 1969. (Also contains Marx's Theses on Feuerbach.)
>
> Ludwig Feuerbach and the Outcome of Classical German Philosophy. New York: International Publishers Co., 1941.
>
> Ludwig Feuerbach and the Outcome of Classical German Philosophy. Edited by I. B. Lasker. Moscow: Foreign Languages Publishing House, 1946; London: Lawrence & Wishart, 1947.
>
> Ludwig Feuerbach and the Outcome of Classical German Philosophy. Appendix of other material of Marx and Engels relating to dialectical materialism. Edited by C. P. Dutt. London: Lawrence & Wishart, 1936; New York: International Publishers Co., 1970.
>
> Feuerbach: The Roots of the Socialist Philosophy. Translated with a critical introduction by Austin Lewis. Chicago: Charles H. Kerr & Co., 1916.

The Origin of the Family, Private Property and the State

> The Origin of the Family, Private Property and the State. Translated by Ernest Untermann. Chicago: Charles H. Kerr & Co., 1910.
>
> The Origin of the Family, Private Property and the State. Translated by Alice West and Dona Torr. London: Lawrence & Wishart, 1943.
>
> The Origin of the Family, Private Property and the State. 4th edition. Moscow: Foreign Languages Publishing House, 1959.
>
> The Origin of the Family, Private Property and the State. Introduction by Evelyn Reed. New York: Pathfinder Press, 1972.
>
> The Origin of the Family, Private Property and the State. In the Light of the Researches of Lewis H. Morgan. (Appendix: A newly discovered case of group marriage 1892.) New York: International Publishers Co., 1942; London: Lawrence & Wishart, 1946; Moscow: Foreign Languages Publishing House, 1952.
>
> The Origin of the Family, Private Property and the State. In the Light of the Researches of Lewis H. Morgan. Introduction and notes by Eleanor B. Leacock. Moscow: Progress Publishers, 1968; New York: International Publishers Co., 1972.
>
> The Origin of the Family. Boston: New England Free Press, 1970?

The Part Played by Labor in the Transition from Ape to Man. New York: International Publishers Co., 1950; Moscow: Foreign Languages Publishing House, 1953; Progress Publishers, 1972. (An unfinished essay, broken off in mid-sentence.)

The Peasant War in Germany

> The Peasant War in Germany. Moscow: Foreign Languages Publishing House, 1956.
>
> The Peasant War in Germany. New edition. Introduction by D. Riazanov. Translated by M. J. Olgin. New York: International Publishers Co., 1966.
>
> The Peasant War in Germany. Edited by Vic Schneierson. Moscow: Progress Publishers, 1969.

Peaceful Revolution versus Violence: Can Socialism be
Achieved Peacefully? Translated by Henry Kuhn. Appendix
by Daniel De Leon. New York: New York Labor News Co.,
1966. (Originally published as an introduction to Marx's
Die Klassenkampfe in Frankreich 1848 bis 1850.)

Principles of Communism

    Principles of Communism. Translated by Max Bedacht.
    New York: Daily Worker Publishing Co., 1925. (Engels
    early draft of the Communist Manifesto.)

    Principles of Communism. Translated by Paul M. Sweezy.
    New York: Monthly Review Press, 1963.

The Revolutionary Act: Military Insurrection or Political
and Economic Action? Translated by Henry Kuhn. Appendix
by Daniel De Leon. New York: New York Labor News Co.,
1935.

The Role of Force in History: A Study of Bismark's Policy
of Blood and Iron. Translated by Jack Cohen. Edited by
Ernest Wangermann. New York: International Publishers Co.;
London: Lawrence & Wishart, 1968.

Socialism: Utopian and Scientific

    Socialism: Utopian and Scientific. Translated by
    Edward Aveling. Special introduction by F. Engels.
    Chicago: Charles H. Kerr & Co., 1918; New York:
    International Publishers Co., 1945; London: George
    Allen & Unwin, 1950; Moscow: Progress Publishers,
    1970.

    Socialism: Utopian and Scientific. New York: Pathfinder
    Press, 1972.

    Socialism, Utopian and Scientific: With the Essay on
    "The Mark." Translated by Edward Aveling. New York:
    International Publishers Co., 1968.

    Socialism: From Utopia to Science. Translated by Edward
    Aveling. New York: New York Labor News Co., 1947.

    The Development of Socialism from Utopia to Science.
    Translated by Daniel De Leon. New York: New York
    Labor News Co., 1898.

The Development of Socialism: From Utopia to Science.
New York: New York Labor News Co., 1900.

Historical Materialism. From the author's introduction
to Socialism, Utopian and Scientific. Prefatory note
by L. Sanial. New York: New York Labor News Co.,
1938.

On Historical Materialism. New York: International
Publishers Co., 1940. (Introduction to Socialism:
Utopian and Scientific.)

The Mark: An Essay on the Primitive Form and Collective
Land Ownership in Germany. New York: New York
Labor News Co., 1902.

The Mark. New York: New York Labor News Co., 1928.
(Written as an appendix to Socialism: Utopian and
Scientific.)

Friedrich Engels - Collected Works

Articles from the Labour Standard (1881). Moscow: Progress
Publishers, 1965.

The British Labour Movement: Articles from the Labour
Standard, May 7 to August 6, 1881. New York: International
Publishers Co., 1940; London: Lawrence & Wishart, 1944.

The Correspondence (of) F. Engels and Paul and Laura Lafargue.
Moscow: Foreign Languages Publishing House, 1959.

The Correspondence (between) Frederick Engels (and) Paul and
Laura Lafargue. Translated by Yvonne Kapp. 2 vol. London:
Lawrence & Wishart, 1959-60.

Engels as Military Critic: Articles Reprinted from the Volunteer Journal and the Manchester Guardian of the 1860's.
Introduction by W. H. Chaloner and W. O. Henderson.
Manchester, England: Manchester University Press, 1959;
New York: Barnes & Noble, 1960; Westport, Conn.: Greenwood
Press, 1976.

Engels on Capital: Synopsis, Reviews, Letters and Supplementary Material. 2nd edition. Translated and edited by
Leonard E. Mins. New York: International Publishers Co.,
1974.

The Housing Question. Moscow: Progress Publishers, 1970.
(Reprint of three articles written for the Leipzig
Volksstadt, 1872.)

18

The Housing Question. Edited by C. P. Dutt. New York: International Publishers, 1935; London: Lawrence & Wishart, 1942; Moscow: Foreign Languages Publishing House, 1955.

The Fourteenth of March 1883: Frederick Engels on the Death of Karl Marx. New York: International Publishers Co., 1933.

"Frederick Engels on the Conduct of the Franco-Prussian War. Excerpts from Pall Mall Gazette, 1870-1871." Edited by L. S. Feuer. Science & Society 5(1941): 362-71.

The German Revolutions: The Peasant War in Germany, and Germany: Revolution and Counter-Revolution. Edited, with an introduction by Leonard Krieger. Chicago: University of Chicago Press, 1967.

Karl Marx, 1818-1883: Extracts from Reminiscences of Marx by Wilhelm Liebknecht and Paul Lafargue. Four Letters of Engels on the Death of Marx; Engels Speech at the Graveside of Marx; for the Anniversary of Marx's Death, 14 March, 1883. London: Lawrence & Wishart, 1941.

Notes on the War: Sixty Articles Reprinted from the "Pall Mall Gazette," 1870-1871. Edited by Friedrich Adler. Translated by Marianne Pollak. Vienna: Wiener Volksbuchandlung, 1923.

Selected Writings. Edited with an introduction by W. O. Henderson. Harmondsworth: Penguin, 1967.

Karl Marx and Friedrich Engels - Individual Works

The Communist Manifesto

> The Communist Manifesto. Authorized English Translation. Edited and annotated by F. Engels. Chicago: Charles H. Kerr & Co., 1908. (Also includes No Compromise by Wilhelm Liebknecht.)

> The Communist Manifesto of Karl Marx and Friedrich Engels. Introduction and explanatory notes by D. Ryazanoff. Translation of Manifesto by M. Lawrence. Translation of introduction and notes by Eden and Cedar Paul. London: Martin Lawrence; New York: International Publishers Co., 1930.

> The Communist Manifesto. Authorized English translation. Edited and annotated by Frederick Engels. New York: New York Labor News Co., 1939.

The Communist Manifesto. Preface by F. Engels.
Chicago: Great Books Foundation, 1947.

The Communist Manifesto. Centenary edition. Translated by Samuel Moore. London: Lawrence & Wishart, 1948.

The Communist Manifesto. Preface by F. Engels. Introduction by Milton Mayer. Chicago: Henry Regnery Co., 1949.

The Communist Manifesto. Introduction by Stefan T. Possony. Translated by Samuel Moore. Chicago: Henry Regnery Co., 1958.

The Communist Manifesto. Authorized English translation by Samuel Moore. Edited and annotated by F. Engels. Centennial edition. New York: New York Labor News Co., 1959.

The Communist Manifesto: Socialist Landmark. A new appreciation written for the Labour Party by Harold J. Laski, together with the original text of the authorized English translation. Translation by Samuel Moore. London: George Allen & Unwin, 1961.

The Communist Manifesto. New York: Russell & Russell, 1963.

The Communist Manifesto. Introduction by Francis B. Randall. Translated by Samuel Moore. Edited by Joseph Katz. Afterword by Grigory Glezerman. New York: Washington Square Press, 1965.

The Communist Manifesto. Introduction by A. J. P. Taylor. Translated by Samuel Moore. Harmondsworth: Penguin, 1967.

The Communist Manifesto. Translated by Samuel Moore. Introduction by Stephen J. Tonsor. Chicago: Henry Regnery Co., 1969.

The Communist Manifesto. Introduction by Leon Trotsky. New York: Pathfinder Press, 1971.

The Communist Manifesto. Preface by F. Engels. Introduction by William P. Fall. Belmont, Mass.: American Opinion, 1974.

Manifesto of the Communists. New York: Schoerr & Franz, 1883.

Manifesto of the Communist Party. Authorized English
translation. Edited and annotated by F. Engels.
Chicago: Charles H. Kerr & Co., 1888. (Also includes
The Civil War in France by K. Marx.)

Manifesto of the Communist Party. Authorized English
version. Edited and annotated by F. Engels. Chicago:
Charles H. Kerr & Co., 1911.

Manifesto of the Communist Party. Authorized English
translation. Edited and annotated by F. Engels.
New York: Socialist Literature Co., 1912.

Manifesto of the Communist Party. Translated by Eden
and Cedar Paul. London: Modern Books, New York:
Workers Library Publications, 1929.

Manifesto of the Communist Party. Authorized English
translation. Edited and annotated by F. Engels.
Translated by Samuel Moore. Chicago: Charles H.
Kerr & Co., 1947; New York: International Publishers
Co., 1948.

Manifesto of the Communist Party. Translated by S.
Moore. Edited by F. Engels. Moscow: Foreign
Languages Publishing House, 1957.

Manifesto of the Communist Party. Authorized English
translation. Translated by S. Moore. Edited and
annotated by F. Engels. Moscow: Progress Publishers,
1969.

The Birth of the Communist Manifesto. Includes full
text of the Manifesto, all prefaces by Marx and
Engels, early drafts by Engels and other supplementary material. Edited and annotated with an introduction by Dirk J. Struik. New York: International
Publishers Co., 1971.

The Communist Manifesto by Marx and Engels. Principles
of Communism by Friedrich Engels; A New Translation
by Paul M. Sweezy. The Communist Manifesto after
100 Years by Paul M. Sweezy and Leo Huberman. New
York: Monthly Review Press, 1964; New York: Modern
Reader Paperbacks, 1968.

The German Ideology

The German Ideology. Translated and edited by S.
Ryazanskaya. New York: Universal Distributors, 1964;
London: Lawrence & Wishart, 1965.

The German Ideology. New York: International Publishers Co., 1947; Moscow: Progress Publishers, 1972.

The German Ideology. Parts 1 and 3. New York: International Publishers Co., 1962.

The German Ideology. Parts I and III. Edited with an introduction by R. Pascal. Translated by W. Lough and C. P. Magill. London: Lawrence & Wishart, 1942; New York: International Publishers Co., 1960. (Also includes appended Theses on Feuerbach by Karl Marx.)

The German Ideology. Part One, with Selections from Parts Two and Three, Together with Marx's "Introduction to a Critique of Political Economy." Edited with an introduction by C. J. Arthur. London: Lawrence & Wishart, 1970; New York: International Publishers Co., 1972. (Also includes Marx's Theses on Feuerbach.)

Feuerbach - Opposition of the Materialist and Idealist Outlooks: The First Part of The Germany Ideology. Published in accordance with the text of the original manuscript. London: Lawrence & Wishart, 1973.

The Holy Family: Or, Critique of Critical Critique. Translated by R. Dixon. Moscow: Foreign Languages Publishing House, 1956; London: Lawrence & Wishart, 1957; Ann Arbor, Mich.: University Microfilms, 1973.

Karl Marx and Friedrich Engels - Collected Works

The American Journalism of Marx and Engels. Edited by H. M. Christman. New York: New American Library of World Literature, 1966.

Articles from the "Neue Rheinsche Zeitung." 1848-49. Translated by S. Ryazansky. Edited by Bernard Isaacs. Complied by R. Ivyanskaya and A. Fomenko. Moscow: Progress Publishers, 1972.

Articles in the New American Cyclopaedia. Edited with an historical introduction by Hal Draper. Berkeley, Calif.: Independent Socialist Press, 1969.

Articles on Britain. Moscow: Progress Publishers, 1971.

The Civil War in the United States. New York: International Publishers, 1937.

The Civil War in the United States. Edited by Richard Enmale. New York; International Publishers Co., 1940; London: Lawrence & Wishart, 1938.

The Civil War in the United States. Centennial edition. New York: Citadel Press; International Publishers Co., 1961.

Basic Writings on Politics and Philosophy. Edited by Lewis S. Feuer. Garden City, N.Y.: Anchor, Doubleday & Co., 1959.

The Cologne Communist Trial. Translated with an introduction and notes by Rodney Livingston. London: Lawrence & Wishart; New York: International Publishers Co., 1971.

The Communist Manifesto. With Selections from The Eighteenth Brumaire of Louis Bonaparte and Capital by K. Marx. Edited by Samuel H. Beer. New York: Appleton-Century-Crofts, 1955.

Dynamics of Social Change. Edited by H. Selsam, D. Goldway and H. Martel. New York: International Publishers Co., 1970.

The First Indian War of Independence, 1857-59. New York: Universal Distributors, 1960; Moscow: Progress Publishers, 1968.

Ireland and the Irish Question: A Collection of Writings by Karl Marx and Friedrich Engels. Translated by Angela Clifford, K. Cook and B. Bean. Edited by R. Dixon. New York: International Publishers Co., 1972.

Karl Marx and Friedrich Engels on Reactionary Prussianism. New York: International Publishers Co., 1944.

Karl Marx and Friedrich Engels on Religion. Moscow: Foreign Languages Publishing House, 1957.

Karl Marx, Frederick Engels: Collected Works,
Volume 1 Karl Marx: 1835-43.
Volume 2 Frederick Engels: 1838-42.
Volume 3 Marx and Engels: 1843-44.
Volume 4 Marx and Engels: 1844-45.
Volume 5 Marx and Engels: 1845-47.
Volume 6 Marx and Engels: 1845-48.
London: Lawrence & Wishart; New York: International Publishers Co., 1973-1976.

Karl Marx, Friedrich Engels: The Uncollected Writings of the New York Daily Tribune. Vol. I. New York: Urizen Books, Forthcoming.

Letters to Americans, 1848-1895. New York: International Publishers Co., 1969.

Literature and Art. New York: International Publishers Co., 1947.

Marx and Engels on India. Edited with a preface by Mulk Ray Anand. Allehabad: Socialist Book Club, 1933.

Marx and Engels on Literature and Arts: A Selection of Writings. Edited by Lee Bagandall and Stefan Morawski. Introduction by Stefan Morawski. St. Louis, Mo.: Telos Press, 1973.

Marx and Engels on Malthus: Selections from the Writings of Marx and Engels, Dealing with the Theories of Thomas Robert Malthus. Edited with an introductory essay and notes by Ronald L. Meek. Translated by Dorothea L. Meek and Ronald L. Meek. London: Lawrence & Wishart, 1953; New York: International Publishers Co., 1963.

The Marx-Engels Reader. Edited by Robert C. Tucker. New York: W. W. Norton & Co., 1972.

Marx and Engels on the Population Bomb: Selections from the Writings of Marx and Engels Dealing with the Theories of Thomas Robert Malthus. Edited by Ronald L. Meek. Translated by Dorothea L. Meek and Ronald L. Meek. Foreword by Steve Weissman. 2nd edition. Berkeley, Calif.: Ramparts Press, 1971.

On Colonialism. 4th enlarged edition. Moscow: Progress Publishers, 1968.

On Colonialism: Articles from the New York Tribune and Other Writings. New York: International Publishers Co., 1972.

On Historical Materialism. Edited by T. Borodulina. New York: International Publishers Co., 1975.

On Religion. New York: International Publishers Co., 1955.

On Religion. Introduction by Reinhold Niebuhr. New York: Schocken Books, 1964.

On Society and Social Change: With Selections by F. Engels. Edited with an introduction by Neil J. Smelser. Chicago: University of Chicago Press, 1973.

On the Labor Party: Selections from the Writings of Karl Marx and Friedrich Engels. Toronto: Workers Vanguard Publishing Association, 1962.

On the Paris Commune. Moscow: Progress Publishers, 1971.

Reactionary Provisionism. New York: Oxford University Press, 1948.

The Revolution of 1848-49: Articles from the Neue Rheinische Zeitung. Translated by S. Ryazanskaya. New York: International Publishers Co., 1972.

Revolution in Spain. New York: International Publishers Co., 1939; Westport, Conn.: Greenwood Press, 1975.

The Russian Menace to Europe: A Collection of Articles, Speeches, Letters, and News Dispatches by Karl Marx and Friedrich Engels. Selected and edited by Paul W. Blackstock and Bert F. Hoselitz. Glencoe, Ill.: The Free Press, 1952; London: George Allen & Unwin, 1953.

Society and Revolution. New Delhi, India: Peoples Publishing House, 1971.

Selected Correspondence of Karl Marx and Frederick Engels. Translated by I. Lasker. Edited by S. Ryazanskaya. 2nd revised enlarged edition. Moscow: Progress Publishers, 1965.

Selected Correspondence, 1846-1895. Translated by Dona Torr. New York: International Publishers Co., 1942; London: Lawrence & Wishart, 1956; Westport, Conn.: Greenwood Press, 1975.

Selected Works. 2 vol. London: Lawrence & Wishart; Moscow: Progress Publishers; New York: International Publishers Co., 1968.

Writings on the Paris Commune. Edited by Hal Draper. New York: Monthly Review Press, 1971.

BOOKS ON MARX AND ENGELS

Abbo, John A. "Modern Times: Marx." Political Thought: Men and Ideas. Westminster, Md.: The Newman Press, 1960. Pp. 320-35.

Acton, H. B. The Illusion of the Epoch: Marxism-Leninism as a Philosophical Creed. Boston: Beacon Press, 1957.

_____. What Marx Really Said. New York: Schocken Books, 1967; London: MacDonald & Co., 1967.

Adams, Henry P. Karl Marx in His Earlier Writings. London: George Allen & Unwin, 1940; New York: Russell & Russell, 1965.

Adelman, Irma. "Karl Marx." Theories of Economic Growth and Development. Stanford, Calif.: Stanford University Press, 1961. Pp. 60-93.

Ader, E. B. Communism: Classic and Contemporary. Woodbury, N.Y.: Barron's Educational Series, 1970.

Adoratskii, Vladimir V. Dialectical Materialism: The Theoretical Foundation of Marxism-Leninism. New York: International Publishers Co., 1934.

_____. History of the Communist Manifesto of Marx and Engels. New York: International Publishers Co., 1936.

Afanas'ev, Viktor G. Marxist Philosophy: A Popular Outline. Moscow: Progress Publishers, 1964.

Ahaluwalia, J. S. Marxism and Contemporary Reality. Bombay-New York: Asia Publishing House, 1973.

Aiken, H. D. "Dialectics and Materialism: Karl Marx and Friedrich Engels." Age of Ideology. Edited by H. D. Aiken. Boston: Houghton Mifflin Co., 1957. Pp. 183-201.

Alexander, Albert. Karl Marx, the Father of Modern Socialism. New York: Franklin Watts, 1969.

Almond, Gabriel A., et al. The Appeals of Communism. Princeton, N.J.: Princeton University Press, 1954.

Althusser, Louis. For Marx. Translated by Ben Brewster. London: Allen Lane, 1969; New York: Vintage Books, 1970.

Althusser, Louis, and Balibar, Etienne. Reading Capital. Translated by Ben Brewster. New York: Pantheon Books, 1971.

Apter, D. "Political Studies and the Search for a Framework." African Perspectives. Edited by C. Allen and R. W. Johnson. New York: Cambridge University Press, 1970. Pp. 213-24.

Aptheker, Hebert, ed. Marxism and Alienation; A Symposium. New York: Humanities Press, 1965.

_____. Marxism and Democracy: A Symposium. New York: Humanities Press, 1965.

Arendt, Hannah. The Human Condition. Chicago: University of Chicago Press, 1958.

_____. "Tradition and the Modern Age." Between Past and Future. New York: Viking Press, 1968. Pp. 17-40.

Aron, Raymond. Main Currents in Sociological Thought. Volume I: Montesquieu, Comte, Marx, Tocqueville, the Sociologists and the Revolution of 1848. Translated by Richard Howard and Helen Weaver. New York: Anchor, Doubleday & Co., 1965.

_____. Marxism and the Existentialists. New York: Simon & Schuster, 1970.

_____. The Opium of the Intellectuals. London: Martin Secker & Warburg, 1957.

Arvon, H. Marxist Esthetics. Translated by H. R. Lane. Ithaca, N.Y.: Cornell University Press, 1973.

Ash, William. Marxism and Moral Concepts. New York: Monthly Review Press, 1964.

Aveling, E. B. Student's Marx: Introduction to "Capital." New York: Charles Scribner's Sons, n.d.

Avineri, Shlomo. "Consciousness and History: List der Vernunst in Hegel and Marx." New Studies in Hegel's Philosophy. Edited by Warren E. Steinkraus. New York: Holt, Rinehart & Winston, 1971. Pp. 108-18.

_____. "Introduction." Karl Marx on Colonialism and Modernization. Garden City, N.Y.: Doubleday & Co., Anchor Books, 1969. Pp. 1-28.

_____. The Social and Political Thought of Karl Marx. London: Cambridge University Press, 1968.

Avineri, Shlomo, ed. Marx's Socialism. New York: Lieber-Atherton, 1973.

Axelos, K. Alienation, Praxis, and Techne in the Thought of
Karl Marx. Austin, Texas: University of Texas at Austin
Press, 1976.

Baffrey, Stephen A. The Red Myth: A History of Communism
from Marx to Khrushchev. Stanford, Calif.: Stanford University, 1962.

Balinky, A. Marx's Economics; Origin and Development.
Lexington, Mass.: D. C. Heath & Co., 1970.

Balz, Albert George Adam. The Value Doctrine of Karl Marx.
Morningside Heights, N.Y.: King's Crown Press, 1943.

Banks, Joseph Ambrose. Marxist Sociology in Action: A Sociological Critique of the Marxist Approach to Industrial
Relations. Harrisburg, Pa.: Stackpole Books, 1970;
London: Faber & Faber, 1970.

Barbei, W. J. A History of Economic Thought. New York:
Frederick A. Praeger, 1968.

Baron, Paul A. Marxism and Psychoanalysis. New York:
Monthly Review Press, 1960.

Barzun, J. M. Darwin, Marx, and Wagner. Revised Edition.
New York: Doubleday & Co., 1958.

Basu, N. Political Philosophy after Hegel and Marx.
Calcutta: Asia Publishing House, 1956.

Baxandall, L. Marxism and Aesthetics: A Selective Annotated
Bibliography. New York: Humanities Press, 1969.

Beach, W. G. "Karl Marx and the Socio-economic Theory of
Social Change." Growth of Social Thought. New York:
Charles Scribner's Sons, 1939. Pp. 153-66.

Becker, Carl L. "Marxian Philosophy of History." Everyman
His Own Historian. New York: F. S. Crofts & Co., 1935.
Pp. 113-31.

Beer, Max. A Guide to the Study of Marx. London: Labor
Research Department, 1932.

_____. "Karl Marx." General History of Socialism and
Social Struggles. Vol. 2. New York: Russell & Russell,
1957. Pp. 56-87.

_____. The Life and Teachings of Karl Marx. Translated
by T. C. Partington and H. J. Sterling. Revised edition.
2 v. Boston: Small, Maynard & Co., 1924.

Bell, Daniel. "The Debate on Alienation." Revisionism. Edited by Leopold Labedz. New York: Frederick A. Praeger, 1962. Pp. 195-211.

_____. "In Search of Marxist Humanism: The Debate on Alienation." Political Thought Since World War II. Edited by Wladyslaw J. Stankiewicz. New York: Free Press of Glencoe, 1964. Pp. 143-58.

_____. Marxian Socialism in the United States. Princeton, N.J.: Princeton University Press, 1967.

_____. "Two Roads from Marx: The Themes of Alienation and Exploitation and Workers Control in Socialist Thought." The End of Ideology. New Revised Edition. New York: Collier Books, 1962.

Bender, Frederic L. "Introduction: The Betrayal of Marx." The Betrayal of Marx. Edited by Frederic L. Bender. New York: Harper & Row, Publishers, 1975. Pp. 1-52.

Bendix, Reinhard, and Lipset, Seymour M. "Karl Marx's Theory of Social Classes." Class, Status and Power: A Reader in Social Stratification. Edited by Reinhard Bendix and S. M. Lipset. Berkeley, Calif.: California Hall, 1954. Pp. 26-35.

Berger, P. L., ed. Marxism and Sociology: Views from Eastern Europe. New York: Appleton-Century-Crofts, 1969.

Berki, Robert N. "The Marxian Concept of Bourgeois Ideology: Some Aspects and Perspectives." Knowledge and Belief in Politics: The Problem of Ideology. Edited by Robert Benewick, R. N. Berki, and B. C. Parekh. New York: St. Martins Press, 1973. Pp. 88-114.

_____. "Perspectives in the Marxian Critique of Hegel's Political Philosophy." Hegel's Political Philosophy. Edited by Zbigniew A. Pelczynski. London: Cambridge University Press, 1971. Pp. 149-219.

_____. Socialism. New York: St. Martins Press, 1975.

Berlin, Isaiah. Historical Inevitability. New York: Oxford University Press, 1955.

_____. Karl Marx: His Life and Environment. Reprint of 1939 edition. 3rd edition. New York: Oxford University Press, 1963.

Bernal, J. D. Marx and Science. London: Lawrence & Wishart, 1952.

Bernstein, Edward. Evolutionary Socialism. New York: Schocken Books, 1961.

_____. Ferdinand LaSalle as a Social Reformer. Grosse Point, Mich.: Scholarly Press, 1970.

Bernstein, Richard. Praxis and Action: Contemporary Philosophies of Human Activity. Philadelphia: University of Pennsylvania Press, 1971.

Bernstein, Samuel. Beginnings of Marxian Socialism in France. New York: Elliot Publishing Co., 1933.

_____. "From Social Utopia to Social Science." Essays in Political and Intellectual History. New York: Paine-Whitman Publishers, 1955. Pp. 113-20.

Bernstein, Samuel, ed. A Centenary of Marxism. New York: Science & Society, 1948.

Berolzheimer, F. The World's Legal Philosophies. Reprint of 1912 ed. Translated by Rachel S. Jastrow. New York: Augustus M. Kelley, 1968.

Bevan, Ruth A. Marx and Burke: A Revisionist View. La Salle, Ill.: Open Court Publishing Co., 1973.

Birdseye, C. F. American Democracy v. Prussian Marxism. Chicago: Fleming H. Revelle & Co., 1920.

Blake, W. J. An American Looks at Karl Marx. New York: Cordon Co., 1939.

Bloch, Ernst. On Karl Marx. New York: Herder and Herder, 1971.

Bloom, S. F. "Man of His Century: A Reconsideration of the Historical Significance of Karl Marx." The Making of Modern Europe. Vol. 2. Edited by Herman Ausubel. New York: The Dryden Press, 1951. Pp. 765-82.

_____. The World of Nations: A Study of the National Implications in the Work of Karl Marx. New York: Columbia University Press, 1941.

Blumenberg, Werner. Karl Marx; An Illustrated Biography. Translated by Douglas Scott. London: New Left Books, 1972. Also published as Portrait of Marx. New York: Herder and Herder, 1972.

_____. Portrait of Marx: An Illustrated Biography. Translated by Douglas Scott. New York: Herder and Herder, 1972.

Bober, M. Karl Marx's Interpretation of History. New York: W. W. Norton & Co., 1965.

Bochenski, J. M., ed. Guide to Marxist Philosophy: An Introductory Bibliography. Chicago: Swallow Press, 1972.

Bochenski, J. M., and Niemeyer, G. eds. Handbook on Communism. New York: Frederick A. Praeger, 1962.

Bogardus, Emory S. "Marx and Socialistic Thought." Development of Social Thought. New York: Longmans, Green & Co., 1940. Pp. 246-60.

Bose, Arun and Kirori, Mal. Marxian and Post-Marxian Political Economy: An Introduction. New York: Penguin Books, Inc., 1975.

Bottomore, Thomas Burton. Marxist Sociology. New York: Holmes & Meier, 1975.

Bottomore, Thomas Burton, ed. Karl Marx. Englewood Cliffs, N.J.: Prentice-Hall, 1973.

Boudin, Louis B. The Theoretical System of Karl Marx in Light of Recent Criticism. Reprint of 1907 edition. New York: Monthly Review Press, 1968.

Boulding, Kenneth E. A Primer on Social Dynamics: History as Dialectics and Development. New York: The Free Press, 1970.

Bouquet, Alan C. Karl Marx and His Doctrines. London: Society for Promoting Christian Knowledge, 1950.

Bouscaren, Anthony T. Communism: Theory and Practice. New York: Paulist Press, 1960.

Bowle, John. "Marx and Engels, I." Politics and Opinions in the Nineteenth Century. New York: Oxford University Press, 1954. Pp. 298-324.

_____. "Marx and Engels, II." Politics and Opinions in the Nineteenth Century. New York: Oxford University Press, 1954. Pp. 325-47.

Brameld, Theodore B. A Philosophic Approach to Communism. Chicago: University of Chicago Press, 1933.

Brecht, Arnold. Political Theory: The Foundations of Twentieth-Century Thought. Princeton, N.J.: Princeton University Press, 1959.

Bromfield, Louis. "Thomas Jefferson vs. Karl Marx." Few Brass Tacks. New York: Harper & Brothers, 1946. Pp. 191-222.

Browder, Earl R. Keynes, Foster and Marx. Yonkers, N.Y.: Earl Browder, 1950.

_____. Marx and America: A Study of the Doctrine of Impoverishment. Westport, Conn.: Greenwood Press, 1974.

Brown, Bruce. Marx, Freud, and the Critique of Everyday Life: Toward a Permanent Cultural Revolution. New York: Monthly Review Press, 1973.

Brown, W. M. Teachings of Marx for Girls and Boys. Galion, Ohio: Bradford-Brown Educational Co., n.d.

Brus, Wlodzimierz. The Economics and Politics of Socialism: Collected Essays. London: Routledge & Kegan Paul, 1973.

Buber, Martin. Paths in Utopia. Translated by R. F. C. Hull. New York: The Macmillan Co., 1950.

Bukharin, Nikolai. Historical Materialism: A System of Sociology. New York: International Publishers Co., 1925.

Burke, K. A Grammar of Motives. Berkeley, Calif.: University of California Press, 1969.

Burns, Edward McNall. Ideas in Conflict: The Political Theories of the Contemporary World. New York: W. W. Norton & Co., 1960.

Burns, Emile. An Introduction to Marxism. New and revised edition. (Also published as What is Marxism?) New York: International Publishers Co., 1966.

_____. What is Marxism? New York: International Publishers Co., 1957.

Butterfield, Herbert. "Marxist History." History and Human Relations. New York: British Book Centre, 1951. Pp. 66-100.

Calvert, P. A Study of Revolution. New York: Oxford University Press, 1970.

Cameron, J. M. Scrutiny of Marxism. New York: The Macmillan Co., 1949; London: SCM Press, 1948.

Cameron, K. N. Marx and Engels Today: A Modern Dialogue on Philosophy and History. Hicksville, N.Y.: Exposition Press, 1976.

Carleton, G. Friedrich Engels' The Shadow Prophet. London: Pall Mall Press, 1965.

Carmichael, Joel. Karl Marx, The Passionate Logician. New York: Charles Scribner's Sons, 1970; London: Rapp and Whiting, 1968.

Carr, E. H. "The Communist Manifesto." Studies in Revolution. New York: The Macmillan Co., 1950. Pp. 15-37.

_____. "A Historical Turning Point: Marx, Lenin, Stalin." Revolutionary Russia. Edited by Richard Pipes. Garden City, N.Y.: Doubleday Anchor Books, 1969. Pp. 282-94.

_____. "Ideological Impact." Soviet Impact on the Western World. New York: The Macmillan Co., Pp. 84-102.

_____. Karl Marx: A Study in Fanaticism. London: J. M. Dent & Sons, 1934.

Carroll, L. R. The Pixylated Prophet: The Man Who Captured the Minds of a Generation. Billings, Mont.: The Guardian, 1948.

Catlin, George Edward Gordon. "Marx and His Predecessors." Story of the Political Philosophers. New York: McGraw-Hill Book Co., 1939. Pp. 543-601.

Chadwick, Owen. "Karl Marx." The Secularization of the European Mind in the Nineteenth Century. New York: Cambridge University Press, 1976. Pp. 48-87.

Chamberlin, W. H. "Ten Mistakes of Marx; Excerpt from 'Evolution of a Conservative'." Anthology of Conservative Writing in the United States, 1932-1960. Edited by A. G. Heinsohn. Chicago: Henry Regnery Co., 1962. Pp. 32-41.

Chambre, Henri. From Karl Marx to Mao Tse Tung: A Systematic Survey of Marxism-Leninism. New York: P. J. Kenedy & Sons, 1963.

Chang, S. H. M. The Marxian Theory of the State. New York: Russell & Russell, 1965.

Childs, David. Marx and the Marxists; An Outline of Practice and Theory. London: Benn; New York: Barnes & Noble, 1973.

Clarke, J. S. Marxism and History. London: National Council of Labor Colleges Publishing Society, 1929.

Clarye, Alasdair. "Marx." Work and Play: Ideas and Experience of Work and Leisure. New York: Harper & Row Publishers, 1975. Pp. 45-62.

Coates, J. B. Leaders of Modern Thought. New York: Longmans, Green & Co., 1947.

Coates, Z. K. The Life and Teachings of Friedrich Engels. New York: Universal Distributors, 1946.

Cohen, R. S. "On the Marxist Philosophy of Education." Modern Philosophies and Education. National Society for the Study of Education. Edited by Nelson B. Henry. Chicago: University of Chicago Press, 1955. Pp. 175-214.

Coker, Francis William. "Karl Marx." Recent Political Thought. New York: D. Appleton-Century Co., 1934. Pp. 35-65.

Cole, George Douglas Howard. A History of Socialist Thought. Vol. 1-5. London: Macmillan & Co., 1953.

_____. The Meaning of Marxism. London: Victor Gollancz, 1948.

_____. What Marx Really Meant. New York: Alfred A. Knopf, 1934; London: Victor Gollancz, 1934.

Colegrove, K. W. Democracy versus Communism. Princeton, N. J.: D. Van Nostrand Co., 1957.

Colletti, Lucio. Marxism and Hegel. Translated by Lawrence Garner. Atlantic Highlands, N.J.: Humanities Press, 1973.

_____. "Marxism as a Sociology." From Rousseau to Lenin: Studies in Ideology and Sociology. Translated by John Merrington and Judith White. New York: Monthly Review Press, 1972. Pp. 3-44.

_____. "Marxism: Science or Revolution?" From Rousseau to Lenin: Studies in Ideology and Sociology. Translated by John Merrington and Judith White. New York: Monthly Review Press, 1972. Pp. 229-36.

Collins, Henry, and Abramsky, Chimen. Karl Marx and the British Labour Movement: Years of the First International. London: Macmillan & Co.; New York: St. Martin's Press, 1965.

Commons, J. R. "Karl Marx and Samuel Gompers." Understanding the American Past. Edited by Edward N. Saveth. Boston: Little, Brown & Co., 1954. Pp. 376-83.

Connolly, William E. Political Science and Ideology. New York: Atherton Press, 1967.

Conway, A. W. Veritas; A Synopsis of Marxian Communism. Baltimore, Md.: J. H. Furst, 1940.

Conze, Edward. An Introduction to Dialectical Materialism. London: N.C.L.C. Publishing Co., 1936.

Coolidge, Olivia E. Makers of the Red Revolution. Boston: Houghton Mifflin Co.; Toronto: Thomas Allen, 1963.

Cooper, David, ed. Congress on the Dialectics of Liberation. London, 1967; New York: Collier Books, 1969.

Cooper, Rebecca. The Logical Influence of Hegel on Marx. Seattle, Wash.: University of Washington Press, 1925.

Cork, J. "John Dewey and Karl Marx." John Dewey: Philosopher of Science and Freedom. Edited by Sidney Hook. New York: Dial Press, 1950. Pp. 331-50.

Cornford, Francis M. "The Marxist View of Ancient Philosophy." Unwritten Philosophy, and Other Essays. London: Cambridge University Press, 1950. Pp. 117-37.

Cornforth, Maurice C. Communism and Human Values. New York: International Publishers, 1972.

_____. Dialectical Materialism: An Introductory Course. 3 vol. 3rd Revised Edition. London: Lawrence & Wishart, 1961-62.

_____. Historical Materialism. New York: International Publishers, 1954.

_____. Marxism and Linguistic Philosophy. New York: International Publishers, 1966.

Cornu, Auguste. "Hegel, Marx, and Engels." Philosophy for the Future. Edited by Roy W. Sellers, Vivian J. McGill, and Marvin Farber. New York: The Macmillan Co., 1949. Pp. 41-60.

_____. The Origins of Marxian Thought. Springfield, Ill.: C. C. Thomas, 1957.

Coser, Lewis A. Masters of Sociological Thought: Ideas in Historical and Social Context. New York: Harcourt Brace Jovanovich, 1971.

Coser, Lewis A., and Howe, Irving. "Images of Socialism." The Radical Papers. Edited by Irving Howe. New York: Doubleday & Co., 1966. Pp. 13-32.

Cot, P. "Karl Marx." Torch of Freedom. Edited by E. Ludwig and H. B. Kranz. New York: Rinehart & Co., 1943. Pp. 257-79.

Cowley, Malcolm. "Footnotes to a Life of Marx." Think Back on Us. Edited by Henry David Piper. Carbondale, Ill.: Southern Illinois University Press, 1967. Pp. 104-9.

Cox, R. H., ed. Ideology, Politics and Political Theory. Belmont, Calif.: Wadsworth Publishing Co., 1970.

Croce, Benedetto. Essays on Marx and Russia. Translated by A. A. De Gennato. New York: Frederick Ungar Publishing Co., 1966.

_____. Historical Materialism and the Economics of Karl Marx. Translated by C. M. Meredith. New York: Russell & Russell, 1966.

Cuddihy, J. M. The Ordeal of Civility. New York: Basic Books, 1974.

Curtis, M., ed. Marxism. New York: Atherton Press, 1970.

Czobel, A., and Kahn, C. Karl Marx as Labor Defender, 1348-1871. New York: International Labor Defence, 1933.

Dahrendorf, Ralf. Class and Class Conflict in Industrial Society. Stanford, Calif.: Stanford University Press, 1959.

Daniels, R. V. "Marxian Theories of Historical Dynamics." Sociology and History: Theory and Research. Edited by Werner J. Cahnman and Alvin Boskoff. New York: The Free Press of Glencoe, 1964. Pp. 62-85.

_____. The Nature of Communism. New York: Random House, 1962.

Dannenberg, Karl. Karl Marx; The Man and His Work. New York: The Radical Review Publishing Association, 1918.

Davis, Horace Bancroft. Nationalism and Socialism: Marxist and Labor Theories of Nationalism to 1917. New York: Monthly Review Press, 1967.

De George, R. T. The New Marxism; Soviet and East European Marxism Since 1956. New York: Pegasus, 1968.

De Leon, Daniel. The Gotha Program and Did Marx Err? New York: New York Labor News Co., 1922.

_____. James Madison and Karl Marx. New York: New York Labor News Co., 1920.

_____. Karl Marx. New York: Socialist Labor Party, 1924.

_____. Marx on Mallock. New York: New York Labor News Co., 1908.

Delfgaauw, B. M. I. The Young Marx. Glen Rock, N.J.: The Newman Press, 1962.

Demetz, Peter. Marx, Engels and the Poets: Origins of Marxist Literary Criticism. Revised and enlarged by the author. Translated by Jeffrey L. Sammons. Chicago: University of Chicago Press, 1967.

Desai, Meghnad. Marxian Economic Theory. New Edition. London: Gray-Mills Publishers, 1974.

Deutscher, Issac. Heretics and Renegades; and Other Essays. London: Hamish Hamilton, 1955.

_____. "Marx and Russia." Russia in Transition. New York: Coward-McCann, 1957. Pp. 158-67.

Deverall, R. L. G. The Communist Gospel of Peace According to Marx, Mao-Tse-Tung, Lenin, and Stalin. Tokyo: Publisher Unknown, 1952.

Diamond, S. "Anthropology in Question." Reinventing Anthropology. Edited by Dell H. Hymes. New York: Pantheon Books, 1973. Pp. 401-29.

Diggs, B. J. The State, Justice, and the Common Good: An Introduction to Social and Political Philosophy. Glenview, Ill.: Scott, Foresman & Co., 1974.

Djilas, Milovan. The New Class: An Analysis of the Communist System. New York: Frederick A. Praeger, 1957.

_____. The Unperfect Society: Beyond the New Class. Translated by Dorian Cooke. New York: Harcourt, Brace & World, 1969.

Dobb, Maurice H. "Lecture on Marx." On Economic Theory and Socialism. New York: International Publishers Co., 1955. Pp. 178-204.

_____. Marx as an Economist. London: Lawrence & Wishart; New York: International Publishers Co., 1945.

_____. Political Economy and Capitalism. New York: International Publishers Co., 1939.

Dodd, M. H. "Some Historical Reflections on Planning and the Market." Essays in Honour of E. H. Carr. Edited by C. Abramsky. Hamden, Conn.: The Shoe String Press, Archon Books, 1974. Pp. 324-38.

Doherty, John J. The Concept of Man in Communist Philosophy. Washington, D.C.: Catholic University of America Press, 1955.

Downs, Robert B. "High Priest of the Proletariat." Molders of the Modern Mind. New York: Barnes & Noble, 1961. Pp. 256-9.

_____. "Prophet of the Proletariat." Books that Changed the World. Chicago: American Library Association, 1956. Pp. 85-97.

Downton, J. V., and Hart, D. K., eds. Perspectives on Political Philosophy. 2 vol. New York: Holt, Rinehart & Winston, 1971.

Drachkovitch, Milorod M., ed. Marxist Ideology in the Contemporary World, Its Appeals and Paradoxes. New York: Frederick A. Praeger, 1966.

Draper, Hal. Karl Marx's Theory of Revolution. Part One: The State and Bureaucracy. 2 vol. New York: Monthly Review Press, Forthcoming.

Drennen, D. A. Karl Marx's Communist Manifesto. Woodbury, N.Y.: Barrow's Educational Service, 1972.

Dridzo, S. A. Marx and the Trade Unions. New York: International Publishers Co., 1935.

Drucker, Henry M. The Political Uses of Ideology. New York: Barnes & Noble, 1975.

Dunayevskaya, Raya. Marxism and Freedom from 1776 until Today. Preface by Herbert Marcuse. New York: Twayne Publishers, 1964.

_____. Philosophy and Revolution: From Hegel to Sartre, and from Marx to Mao. New York: Delacorte Press, 1973.

Duncan, Graeme Campbell. Marx and Mill: Two Views of Social Conflict and Social Harmony. Cambridge, England: Cambridge University Press, 1973.

Duncker, Hermann. Introduction to Marxism. New York: Universal Distributors, 1962.

Dunning, William Archibald. A History of Political Thinkers, from Rousseau to Spencer. New York: The Macmillan Co., 1926.

Dupre, Louis K. The Philosophical Foundations of Marxism. New York: Harcourt, Brace & World, 1966.

Eastman, Max. "Higher Criticism of the Marxian Bible." Art and the Life of Action. New York: Alfred A. Knopf, 1934. Pp. 121-33.

_____. Marx, Lenin and the Science of Revolution. Westport, Conn.: Hyperion Press, 1973.

_____. Marxism: Is it Science? New York: W. W. Norton & Co., 1940.

Eaton, John. Marx against Keynes. London: Lawrence & Wishart, 1951.

_____. Political Economy: A Marxist Textbook. New York: International Publishers Co., 1949.

Ebenstein, W. Communism in Theory and Practice. New York: Holt, Rinehart & Winston, 1964.

_____. Today's isms: Communism, Fascism, Capitalism, Socialism. 7th ed. Englewood Cliffs, N.J.: Prentice Hall, 1973.

Edwards, Stewart, ed. The Communards of Paris, 1871. Ithaca, N.Y.: Cornell University Press, 1973.

Egbert, Donald Drew. Socialism and American Art in the Light of European Utopianism, Marxism and Anarchism. Princeton, N.J.: Princeton University Press, 1969.

_____. Social Radicalism and the Arts. New York: Alfred A. Knopf, 1970.

Ellis, Harry B. Ideas and Ideologies: Communism, Socialism, and Capitalism. Cleveland, Ohio: World Publishing Co., 1968.

Ellis, Richard W. Bernard Shaw and Karl Marx: A Symposium, 1884-1889. New York: Random House, 1930.

Ellwood, Charles Abrams. "Economic Social Philosophers." The Story of Social Philosophy. New York: Prentice-Hall, 1938. Pp. 324-43.

Emmett, W. H. The Marxian Economic Handbook. New York: International Publishing Co., 1925; London: G. Allen & Unwin, 1936.

Evans, Michael. Karl Marx. Bloomington, Ind.: Indiana University Press, 1975.

Faurot, J. H. The Philosopher and the State. San Francisco: Chandler Publishing Co., 1971.

Federn, Karl. The Materialist Conception of History. London: Macmillan & Co., 1939; Westport, Conn: Greenwood Press, 1971.

Fedoseyev, P. N. et al. Karl Marx: A Biography. Translated by Yuri Sdobnikov. Moscow: Progress Publishers, 1973.

Feinstein, Charles Hilliard, ed. Socialism, Capitalism and Economic Growth: Essays Presented to Maurice Dobb. Cambridge, England: Cambridge University Press, 1967.

Ferguson, John M. "Karl Marx and Post-Marxian Socialism.' Landmarks of Economic Thought. New York: Longmans, Green & Co., 1950. Pp. 213-31.

Fetscher, Irving. Marx and Marxism. New York: Herder & Herder, 1971.

Feuer, Lewis S. Marx and the Intellectuals: A Collection of Post-Ideological Essays. Garden City, N.Y.: Doubleday & Co., 1969.

_____. "What is Alienation? The Career of a Concept." Sociology on Trial. Edited by Maurice Stein and Arthur Vidich. Englewood Cliffs, N.J.: Prentice-Hall, 1963. Pp. 127-47.

Fichter, Joseph Henry. "Marx, Man, and Machinery." Roots of Change. New York: D. Appleton-Century Co., 1939. Pp. 181-200.

Fisher, Ernst, and Marek, Franz. Marx in His Own Words. Translated by Anna Bostock. London: Allen Lane, 1970.

Fisher, Harold Henry. The Communist Revolution: An Outline of Strategy and Tactics. Stanford, Calif.: Stanford University Press, 1955.

Flakser, D. Marxism, Ideology and Myths. New York: Philosophical Library, 1971.

Fleischer, Helmut. Marxism and History. Translated by E. Mosbacher. New York: Harper & Row Publishers, 1974.

Fleischmann, E. "The Role of the Individual in Pre-revolutionary Society: Stirner, Marx, and Hegel." Hegel's Political Philosophy. Edited by Zbigniew A. Pelczynski. London: Cambridge University Press, 1971. Pp. 220-9.

Florence, Ronald. Marx's Daughters: Eleanor Marx, Rosa Luxemburg, Angelica Balabanoff. New York: Dial Press, 1975.

Foner, Phillip Sheldon, ed. When Karl Marx Died: Comments in 1883. New York: International Publishers Co., 1973.

Forman, J. D. Communism: From Marx's Manifesto to 20th Century Reality. New York: New Viewpoints, 1973.

Foster, William Z. History of the Three Internationals: The World Socialist and Communist Movements from 1848 to the Present. New York: International Publishers, 1955.

Fox, Ralph Winston. Marx, Engels, and Lenin on Ireland. New York: International Publishers, 1940.

Frank, Waldo David. "With Marx, Spinoza." The American Jungle. New York: Farrar & Rinehart, 1937. Pp. 240-53.

Frankel, C. "Social Criticism and Programs of Reform: Early Marxism." Chapters in Western Civilization. 2 vol. Edited by the Contemporary Civilization Staff of Columbia College. New York: Columbia University Press, 1948. Pp. 116-21.

Freedman, Robert, ed. Marxist Social Thought. New York: Harcourt, Brace & World, 1968.

Freehof, S. B. Marx, Freud, and Einstein. New York: International Publishers Co., 1935.

Friedrich, Carl J. "Marx, Marxism, and the Totalitarian Challenge." An Introduction to Political Theory. New York: Harper & Row, 1967. Pp. 43-58.

Friedrichs, Robert W. A Sociology of Sociology. New York: The Free Press, 1970.

Fromm, Erich. Beyond the Chains of Illusion. New York: Simon & Schuster, 1967.

_____. Marx's Concept of Man. With a Translation from Marx's Economic and Philosophical Manuscripts. New York: Frederick Ungar Publishing Co., 1966.

_____. "Problems of Interpreting Marx." The New Sociology: Essays in Social Science and Social Theory in Honor of C. Wright Mills. Edited by Irving L. Horowitz. New York: Oxford University Press, 1964. Pp. 188-95.

Fromm, Erich, ed. Socialist Humanism. Garden City, N.Y.: Doubleday & Co., 1966.

Fry, L. C. Catechism of Karl Marx's "Capital." St. Louis, Mo.: Economic Publishing Co., 1905.

Fuerst, N. "The Age of Wagner?" The Victorian Age of German Literature. University Park, Pa.: Pennsylvania State University Press, 1966. Pp. 177-205.

Fulton, Robert Brank. Original Marxism -- Estranged Offspring. Boston: Christopher Publishing House, 1960.

Gallacher, William. Marxism and the Working Class. London: Lawrence & Wishart, 1943.

Gandhi, Madan G. Gandhi and Marx: Study in Ideological Polarities. Chandigarh: Vikas Bharti, 1969.

Garaudy, Roger. Karl Marx: The Evolution of His Thought. New York: International Publishers Co., 1967.

_____. Marxism in the 20th Century. New York: Charles Scribner's Sons, 1970.

Gay, Peter J. The Dilemma of Democratic Socialism: Edward Bernstein's Challenge to Marx. New York: Collier Books, 1962.

Gemkow, Heinrich, et al. Karl Marx: A Biography. Columbia, Mo.: South Asia Books, 1975.

Gersch, A. On the Theory of Exchange Value. Würzburg: A. Gersch, 1969.

Gesell, Silvio. Karl Marx in Error: His Capital Theory Clearly and Undeniably Refuted as Unscientific. Huntington Park, Calif.: Free Economy Association, 1952.

Giddens, Anthony. Capitalism and Modern Social Theory: An Analysis of the Writings of Marx, Durkheim and Max Weber. Cambridge, England: Cambridge University Press, 1971.

_____. The Class Structure of the Advanced Societies. New York: Barnes & Noble, 1973.

Gide, Charles. "Marxism." History of Economic Doctrines. By Charles Gide and Charles Rist. Boston: D. C. Heath & Co., 1948. Pp. 452-84.

Gillman, Joseph M. The Falling Rate of Profit: Marx's Law and Its Significance to Twentieth Century Capitalism. London: D. Dobson, 1957; New York: Cameron Associates, 1958.

Gilson, Etienne Henry. "The Breakdown of Modern Philosophy." The Unity of Philosophical Experience. New York: Charles Scribner's Sons, 1937. Pp. 271-95.

Girardi, Giulio. Marxism and Christianity. New York: The Macmillan Co., 1968.

Godelier, M. Rationality and Irrationality in Economics. Translated by Brian Pearce. New York: Monthly Review Press, 1972.

Golding, C. "Karl Marx, Visionary." Great Names in History 356 B.C. -- A.D. 1910. Philadelphia: J. B. Lippencott Co., 1936. Pp. 284-89.

Golob, Eugene O. "From Hegel and Ricardo to Marx and Engels." The "Isms." New York: Harper & Brothers, 1954. Pp. 193-228.

_____. The "Isms": A History and Evaluation. New York: Harper & Brothers, 1954.

Gottheil, F. M. Marx's Economic Predictions. Evanston, Ill.: Northwestern University Press, 1966.

Gouldner, Alvin W. The Coming Crisis of Western Sociology. New York: Basic Books, 1970.

Grant, George P. "Marxism." Philosophy in the Mass Age. New York: Hill & Wang, 1960. Pp. 66-79.

Gray, Alexander. The Socialist Tradition: Moses to Lenin. New York: Longmans, Green & Co., 1946.

Gray, J. L. "Karl Marx and Social Philosophy." The Social and Political Ideas of Some Representative Thinkers of the Victorian Age. Edited by F. J. C. Hearnshaw. London: George G. Harrap & Co., 1933. Pp. 116-49.

Gregor, A. James. A Survey of Marxism: Problems in Philosophy and the Theory of History. New York: Random House, 1965.

Grem, June. Karl Marx, Capitalist. Oak Park, Ill.: Enterprise Publications, 1972.

Grossman, H. "The Evolutionist Revolt Against Classical Economics." Essays in Economic Thought: Aristotle to Marshall. Edited by Joseph J. Spengler and William R. Allen. Chicago: Rand McNally & Co., 1960. Pp. 500-24.

Guest, David A. Lectures on Marxist Philosophy. New York: International Publishers Co., 1963.

Gupta, K. C. A Critical Examination of Marxist Philosophy. Calcutta, Privately printed, 1962.

Gurian, Waldemar. The Rise and Decline of Marxism. London: Burns, Oates & Washbourne, 1938.

Haberler, G. "Marxist Economics in Retrospect and Prospect." Marxist Ideology in the Contemporary World -- Its Appeals and Paradoxes. Edited by M. M. Drachkovitch. New York: Frederick A. Praeger, 1966. Pp. 113-25.

Habermas, Jürgen. Knowledge and Human Interests. Translated by Jeremy J. Shapiro. Boston: Beacon Press, 1971.

_____. Theory and Practice. Translated by John Viertel. Boston: Beacon Press, 1973.

Hacker, Andrew. The Study of Politics. 2nd edition. New York: McGraw-Hill Book Co., 1973.

Haile, Pennington. The Eagle and the Bear: The Philosophical Roots of Democracy and Communism. 2nd edition revised. New York: David McKay Co., 1965.

Haldane, John Burden Sanderson. "Marx." Science Advances. London: George Allen & Unwin, 1950. Pp. 14-6.

_____. "Marxist Philosophy." Adventures of a Biologist. New York: Harper & Brothers, 1940. Pp. 254-76.

_____. The Marxist Philosophy and the Sciences. Freeport, Long Island: Books for Libraries, 1969.

Hall, Vernon. "Marxism and Literature." A Short History of Literary Criticism. New York: New York University Press, 1965. Pp. 141-6.

Halle, Louis J. *The Ideological Imagination: Ideological Conflict in Our Time and Its Roots in Hobbes, Rousseau and Marx.* London: Chatts & Windus, 1972; Chicago: Quadrangle Books, 1972.

Hammen, Oscar J. *The Red "48"ers: Karl Marx and Friedrich Engels.* New York: Charles Schribner's Sons, 1969.

Hampsch, G. H. *The Theory of Communism: An Introduction.* New York: Philosophical Library, 1965.

Hansen, D. A. *An Invitation to Critical Sociology.* New York: Free Press, 1976.

Harrington, Michael. "Revolutions." *Is Law Dead?* Edited by E. V. Rostow. New York: Simon & Schuster, 1971. Pp. 336-62.

_____. *Socialism.* New York: Saturday Review Press, 1972.

Harris, A. L. "Marxian Right to the Whole Product." *Economic Essays in Honor of Wesley Clair Mitchell, by His Former Students.* New York: Columbia University Press, 1935. Pp. 147-98.

Hawkins, D. J. B. "The Philosophical Background of Marx and Engels." *Crucial Problems of Modern Philosophy.* Notre Dame, Ind.: University of Notre Dame Press, 1962. Pp. 96-109.

Heaton, H. "Economic Impact on History." *Interpretation of History.* Edited by J. R. Strayer. Princeton, N.J.: Princeton University Press, 1943. Pp. 85-117.

Heilbroner, R. L. "Inexorable World of Karl Marx." *The Worldly Philosophers.* New York: Simon & Schuster, 1953. Pp. 127-60.

Heimann, Eduard. *Reason and Faith in Modern Society: Liberalism, Marxism, and Democracy.* Middletown, Conn.: Wesleyan University Press, 1961.

Heiss, Robert. *Hegel, Kierkegaard, Marx.* Translated by E. B. Garside. Boston: Seymour Lawrence, 1975.

Held, V. "Marx, Sex, and the Transformation of Society." *Women and Philosophy.* Edited by C. C. Gould and M. W. Wartosky. Totowa, N.J.: G. P. Putnam's Sons, 1976. Pp. 168-84.

Henderson, William Otto. *Life of Friedrich Engels.* 2 vol. London: Frank Cass & Co., 1976.

Herod, Charles C. The Nation in the History of Marxian Thought. The Hague: Martinus Nijhoff, 1976.

Herreshoff, David S. American Disciples of Marx: From the Age of Jackson to the Progressive Era. Detroit: Wayne State University Press, 1967.

Hillquit, Morris. From Marx to Lenin. New York: Hanford Press, 1921.

Hobsbawm, Eric J. "Dr. Marx and the Victorian Critics." Labouring Men: Studies in the History of Labour. New York: Basic Books, 1964. Pp. 239-49.

_____. "Introduction." Karl Marx, Pre-Capitalist Economic Formations. Edited by E. J. Hobsbawm. New York: International Publishers Co., 1965. Pp. 9-65.

_____. "Karl Marx and the British Labour Movement." Revolutionaries: Contemporary Essays. New York: Pantheon Books, 1973. Pp. 95-108.

_____. "The Structure of Capital." Revolutionaries: Contemporary Essays. New York: Pantheon Books, 1973. Pp. 142-52.

Hodges, Donald Clark. Socialist Humanism: The Outcome of Classical European Morality. St. Louis: W. H. Green, 1974.

Hoffman, J. Marxism and the Theory of Praxis. New York: International Publishers Co., London: Lawrence & Wishart, 1975.

Hook, Sidney. From Hegel to Marx: Studies in the Intellectual Development of Karl Marx. Ann Arbor, Mich.: University of Michigan Press, 1962.

_____. "Karl Marx in Limbo." Political Power and Personal Freedom. New York: Criterion Books, 1959. Pp. 332-8.

_____. Marx and the Marxists: The Ambiguous Legacy. Princeton, N.J.: D. Van Nostrand Co., 1955.

_____. Reason, Social Myths, and Democracy. New York: John Day Co., 1940.

_____. Towards the Understanding of Karl Marx: A Revolutionary Interpretation. New York: John Day Co., 1933.

Hook, Sidney, ed. The Meaning of Marx: A Symposium. New York: Farrar & Rinehart, 1934.

Horowitz, David, ed. Marx and Modern Economics. London: Mac Gibbon & Kee, 1968; New York: Monthly Review Press, 1968.

Howard, Dick. The Development of the Marxian Dialectic. Carbondale, Ill.: Southern Illinois University Press,1972.

Howard, Michael Charles, and King, J. E. The Political Economy of Marx. Essex: Longman Group, 1975.

Howe, Irving. On the Nature of Communism and Relations with Communists. New York: League for Industrial Democracy, 1966.

Hudson, Geoffrey Francis. Fifty Years of Communism: Theory and Practice 1917-1967. London: Watts & Co., 1968.

Hulse, James W. The Forming of the Communist International. Stanford, Calif.: Stanford University Press, 1964.

Hunt, Richard N. The Political Ideas of Marx and Engels, I: Marxism and Totalitarian Democracy, 1818-1850. Pittsburgh: University of Pittsburgh Press, 1974.

Hunt, R. N. Carew. Marxism Past and Present. London: Geoffrey Bles, 1954.

_____. The Theory and Practice of Communism: An Introduction. Baltimore, Md.: Penguin Books, 1963.

Hyman, Stanley E. The Tangled Bank; Darwin, Marx, Frazer and Freud as Imaginative Writers. New York: Atheneum Publishers, 1962.

Hyppolite, Jean. Studies on Marx and Hegel. Translated by G. O'Neill. New York: Basic Books; London: Heinemann Education, 1969.

International Council for Philosophy and Humanistic Studies and International Social Science Council. Marx and Contemporary Scientific Thought. Atlantic Highlands, N.J.: Humanities Press, 1969.

International Social Science Council. Marx and Contemporary Scientific Thought/Marx et la pensee scientifique contemporaine. The Hague: Mouton & Co., 1970.

Jackson, John H. Marx, Proudhon, and European Socialism. New York: Collier Books, 1962.

Jackson, Thomas A. Dialectics: The Logic of Marxism. New York: Burt Franklin, 1971.

Jarrett, James L., and McMurrin, Sterling M. "Vitalism Thomism and Marxism: Introduction." Contemporary Philosophy: A Book of Readings. Edited by James L. Jarrett and Sterling M. McMurrin. New York: Henry Holt & Co., 1954. Pp. 486-9.

Jenkins, Mick. Frederich Engels in Manchester. Manchester, England: Lancashire & Cheshire Communist Party, 1964.

Johnson, O. M. Karl Marx: 40 Years After (1883-1923). New York: New York Labor News, n.d.

Jordan, Z. A. The Evolution of Dialectical Materialism: A Philosophical and Sociological Analysis. London, Melbourne: Macmillian & Co.; New York: St. Martin's Press, 1967.

Joseph, Horace W. The Labor Theory of Value in Karl Marx. New York: Oxford University Press, 1924.

Kagan, Henry E. Six Who Changed the World: Moses, Jesus Paul, Marx, Freud, Rinstein. New York: Thomas Yoseloff, 1963.

Kalin, Martin G. The Utopian Flight from Unhappiness: Freud Against Marx on Social Progress. Chicago: Nelson-Hall Co., 1974.

Kamenka, Eugene. The Ethical Foundations of Marxism. New York: Frederick A. Praeger; London: Routledge & Kegan Paul, 1962.

_____. "Marxism and Ethics." New Studies in Ethics. Vol. 2. Edited by W. D. Hudson. New York: St. Martin's Press, 1975.

_____. Marxism and Ethics. New York: St. Martin's Press, 1969.

Kautsky, Karl. The Class Struggle. Chicago: Charles H. Kerr & Co., 1910.

_____. The Dictatorship of the Proletariat. Ann Arbor, Mich.: University of Michigan Press, 1964.

_____. The Economic Doctrines of Karl Marx. New York: The Macmillan Co., 1925.

_____. Ethics and the Materialist Conception of History. Chicago: Charles H. Kerr & Co., 1907.

_____. Friedrich Engels: His Life, His Works, His Writings. Chicago: Charles H. Kerr & Co., n.d.

_____. The Social Revolution. Chicago: Charles H. Kerr & Co., 1908.

Kelsen, Hans. The Communist Theory of Law. New York: Frederick A. Praeger; London: Stevens & Sons, 1955.

Kenaflick, K. J. Michael Bakunin and Karl Marx. London: Freedom Press, 1948.

Keracher, J. Frederich Engels. Chicago: Charles H. Kerr & Co., n.d.

Kerr, Clark. Marshall, Marx and Modern Times: The Multi-dimensional Society. London: Cambridge University Press, 1969.

Kettle, Arnold. Karl Marx. London: George Weidenfield & Nicolson, 1968.

Kilroy-Silk, R. Socialism Since Marx. New York: Taplinger Publishing Co., 1972.

Kindersley, R. The First Russian Revisionists: A Study of "Legal Marxism" in Russia. Oxford: Clarendon Press, 1962.

Kline, G. L. "The Existentialist Rediscovery of Hegel and Marx." Phenomenology and Existentialism. Edited by Edward N. Lee and Maurice H. Mandelbaum. Baltimore, Md.: Johns Hopkins Press, 1967. Pp. 113-38.

Kolakowski, Leszek. The Alienation of Reason. Translated by Norbert Guterman. Garden City, N.Y.: Doubleday & Co., 1968.

_____. "Karl Marx and the Classical Definition of Truth." Revisionism: Essays on the History of Marxist Ideas. Edited by Leopold Labedz. New York: Frederick A. Praeger, 1962. Pp. 179-87.

_____. Marxism and Beyond. Translated by Jane Zielonko Peel. London: Pall Mall, 1969.

_____. Toward a Marxist Humanism: Essays on the Left Today. Translated by Jane Z. Peel. New York: Grove Press, 1968.

Koren, Henry J. Marx and The Authentic Man: A First Introduction to the Philosophy of Karl Marx. Pittsburgh: Duquesne University Press; Louvain, Belgium: E. Nauwelaerts, 1967.

Korsch, Karl. Karl Marx. New York: Russell & Russell, 1963.

_____. Marxism and Philosophy. New York: Monthly Review Press, 1971.

_____. Three Essays on Marxism. New York: Monthly Review Press, 1971.

Krader, Lawrence. The Asiatic Mode of Production: Sources, Development and Critique in the Writings of Karl Marx. Atlantic Highlands, N.J.: Humanities Press, 1975.

Kramnick, Isaac, ed. Essays in the History of Political Thought. Englewood Cliffs, N.J.: Prentice-Hall, 1969.

Kuhnelt-Leddihn, E. M. von. Leftism: From de Sade and Marx to Hitler and Marcuse. New Rochelle, N.Y.: Arlington House, 1974.

Labedz, Leopold, ed. Revisionism: Essays on the History of Marxist Ideas. New York: Frederick A. Praeger, 1962.

Labriola, Antonio. Essays on the Materialistic Conception of History. Translated by Charles H. Kerr. New York: Monthly Review Press, 1966.

Lachs, John. Marxist Philosophy: A Bibliographical Guide. Chapel Hill, N.C.: University of North Carolina Press, 1967.

Lafargue, Paul K. Karl Marx, His Life and Work. New York: International Publishers Co., 1943.

_____. Karl Marx, The Man. Translated by Henry Kuhn. New York: New York Labor News, 1947.

Lafargue, Paul, and Liebknecht, William. Karl Marx: His Life and Work: Reminiscences. New York: International Publishers Co., 1943.

Laidler, Harry W. "The Beginnings of Marxism." Social Economic Movements. New York: Thomas Y. Crowell Co., 1944. Pp. 121-9.

_____. "Communist Manifesto, and the Revolution of 1848." Social Economic Movements. New York: Thomas Y. Crowell Co., 1944. Pp. 130-44.

_____. History of Socialism: A Comparative Survey of Socialism, Communism, Trade Unionism, Cooperation, Utopianism, and Other Systems of Reform and Reconstruction. Updated and expanded edition. London: Routledge & Kegan Paul; New York: Thomas Y. Crowell Co., 1968.

_____. "Marx's Career after 1848." Social Economic Movements. New York: Thomas Y. Crowell Co., 1944. Pp. 145-59.

Lancaster, Lane W. "Karl Marx." Masters of Political Thought: Hegel to Dewey. Vol. 3. Boston: Houghton Mifflin Co., 1960. Pp. 160-202.

Landry, A. Marxism and the Woman Question. Toronto: Progress Books, 1943.

La Pira, G. et al. The Philosophy of Communism. New York: The Declan X. McMullen Co., 1952.

Larsson, R. Theories of Revolution, from Marx to the First Russian Revolution. Stockholm: Almqvist och Wiksell, 1970.

Laski, Harold J. "The Communist Manifesto." Essays in the History of Political Thought. Edited by I. Kramnick. Englewood Cliffs, N.J.: Prentice-Hall, 1969. Pp. 323-37.

_____. Communist Manifesto: Socialist Landmark. London: George Allen & Unwin, 1948.

_____. Harold J. Laski on the Communist Manifesto. New York: Pantheon Books, 1967.

_____. Karl Marx: An Essay. New York: League for Industrial Democracy, 1933.

_____. Marx and Today. London: Fabian Society, 1943.

Lefebvre, Henri. The Sociology of Marx. Translated by Norbert Guterman. New York: Pantheon Books, 1968.

Leff, Gordon. The Tyranny of Concepts: A Critique of Marxism. 2nd edition. University, Ala.: University of Alabama Press, 1969.

Lenin, Vladimir I. Karl Marx. Moscow: Foreign Languages Publishing House, 1953.

_____. Marx, Engels, Marxism. Moscow: Foreign Languages Publishing House, 1960.

_____. Selected Works. 3 vol. New York: International Publishers, 1968.

_____. The Teachings of Karl Marx. New York: International Publishers, 1964.

Leonhard, Wolfgang. Three Faces of Marxism: The Political Concepts of Soviet Ideology, Maoism and Humanist Marxism. New York: Holt, Rinehart & Winston, 1974.

Lerner, Max. "Engels and Marx - A Partnership." <u>Ideas are Weapons</u>. New York: Viking Press, 1939. Pp. 319-25.

Le Rossignol, James E. <u>From Marx to Stalin: A Critique of Communism</u>. New York: Thomas Y. Crowell Co., 1940.

Levi, Albert William. <u>Humanism and Politics: Studies in the Relationship of Power and Value in the Western Tradition</u>. Bloomington, Ind.: Indiana University Press, 1969.

Levine, Herbert M. <u>Communism and Democracy: Principles and Practices. An Introductory Study</u>. Dubuque, Iowa: Kendall/Hunt Publishing Co., 1971.

Levine, Norman. <u>The Tragic Deception: Marx contra Engels</u>. Santa Barbara: ABC-CLIO, 1975.

Levy, Hermann, et al. <u>Aspects of Dialectical Materialism</u>. London: C. A. Watts & Co., 1934.

Lewis, John. <u>The Life and Teaching of Karl Marx</u>. London: Lawrence & Wishart; New York: International Publishers Co., 1965.

_____. <u>Marxism and the Irrationalists</u>. London: Lawrence & Wishart, 1955.

_____. <u>Marxism and the Open Mind</u>. New York: Paine-Whitman Publishers; London: Routledge & Kegan Paul, 1957.

_____. <u>The Marxism of Marx</u>. Boston: Seymour Lawrence, 1972.

Ley, R. J. "Compassion and Absurdity: Brecht and Marx on the Truly Human Community." <u>Studies in German Literature of the Nineteenth and Twentieth Centuries</u>. Edited by Siegfried Mews. Chapel Hill, N.C.: University of North Carolina Press, 1971. Pp. 223-35.

Leys, W. A. R. "Historical 'Logic' of Hegel and Marx." <u>Ethics for Policy Decisions</u>. Englewood Cliffs, N.J.: Prentice-Hall, 1952. Pp. 135-49.

Lichtheim, George. "Freud and Marx." <u>Freud: The Man, His World, His Influence</u>. Edited by Jonathan Miller. Boston: Little, Brown & Co., 1972. Pp. 55-69.

_____. <u>From Marx to Hegel</u>. New York: Herder & Herder, 1971.

_____. <u>Marxism: An Historical and Critical Study</u>. 2nd edition revised. New York: Frederick A. Praeger; London: Routledge & Kegan Paul, 1964.

_____. The Origins of Socialism. New York: Frederick A. Praeger, 1969.

_____. A Short History of Socialism. New York: Frederick A. Praeger, 1970.

Liebknecht, Wilhelm Philipp Christian Martin Ludwig. Karl Marx: Biographical Memoirs. Westport, Conn.: Greenwood Press, 1968.

Lifshits, M. I. The Philosophy of Art of Karl Marx. New York: Critics Group, 1938.

Lindsay, Alexander Dunlap. Karl Marx's "Capital": An Introductory Essay. Westport, Conn.: Greenwood Press, 1973.

Lindsay, Jack. Marxism and Contemporary Science: or, Fullness of Life. London: Denis Dobson, 1949.

Lipshires, Sidney. Herbert Marcuse: From Marx to Freud, and Beyond. Cambridge, Mass.: Schenkman Publishing Co., 1974.

Livergood, N. D. Activity in Marx's Philosophy. New York: Universal Distributors; The Hague: Martinus Nijhoffs, 1968.

Lobkowicz, Nikolaus. Theory and Practice: The History of a Concept from Aristotle to Marx. Notre Dame, Ind.: University of Notre Dame Press, 1967.

Lobkowicz, Nikolaus, ed. Marx and the Western World. Notre Dame, Ind.: University of Notre Dame Press, 1967.

London, Kurt. "Marxism." Backgrounds of Conflict. New York: The Macmillan Co., 1945. Pp. 257-69.

Loria, Achille. Karl Marx. New York: Thomas Seltzer, 1920.

Lowe, Donald M. The Function of "China" in Marx, Lenin, and Mao. Berkeley, Calif.: University of California Press, 1966.

Löwith, Karl. From Hegel to Nietzsche. New York: Holt, Rinehart & Winston, 1964.

_____. "Man's Self Alienation in the Early Writings of Marx." Essays in the History of Political Thought. Edited by I. Kramnick. Englewood Cliffs, N.J.: Prentice-Hall, 1969. Pp. 338-53.

_____. "Marx." Meaning in History. Chicago: University of Chicago Press, 1949. Pp. 33-51.

_____. "Mediation and Immediacy in Hegel, Marx and Feuerbach." New Studies in Hegel's Philosophy. Edited by Warren E. Steinkraus. New York: Holt, Rinehart & Winstcn, 1971. Pp. 119-41.

Lozovsky, A. Marx and the Trade Union. New York: International Publishers Co., 1935.

Lukacs, Georg. History and Class Consciousness. Cambridge, Mass.: MIT Press, 1971.

_____. Tactics and Ethics: Political Essays, 1919-1929. Translated by Michael McColgan. New York: Harper & Row Publishers, 1975.

Lukes, S. "Alienation and Anomie." Philosophy, Politics and Society. 3rd series. Edited by P. Laslett and W. G. Runciman. New York: Oxford University Press, 1967.

Luxemburg, Rosa. Reform or Revolution. New York: Three Arrows Press, 1937.

_____. Rosa Luxemburg Speaks. Edited by Mary-Alice Waters. New York: Pathfinder Press, 1970.

_____. The Russian Revolution and Leninism or Marxism? Ann Arbor, Mich.: University of Michigan Press, 1961.

Macek, Josef. An Essay on the Impact of Marxism. Pittsburgh, Pa.: University of Pittsburgh Press, 1955.

McFadden, Charles J. The Metaphysical Foundations of Dialectical Materialism. Washington, D.C.: Catholic University of America, 1938.

MacGuire, John. Marx's Paris Writings. New York: Harper & Row, 1973.

MacIntyre, Alasdair C. Against the Self-images of the Age: Essays on Ideology and Philosophy. New York: Schocken Books, 1971.

_____. "Marx." Western Political Philosophers. Edited by Maurice W. Cranston. Chester Springs, Pa.: Dufour Editions, 1964. Pp. 99-108.

_____. Marxism: An Interpretation. London: SCM Press, 1953.

MacKenzie, Norman. Socialism: A Short History. London: Hutchinson's University Library, 1949.

McLeish, John. The Theory of Social Change: Four Views Considered. New York: Schocken Books; London: Routledge & Kegan Paul, 1969.

McLellan, David. Karl Marx. New York: Viking Press, 1975.

_____. Karl Marx: His Life and Thought. New York: Harper & Row Publishers, 1974.

_____. Marx Before Marxism. New York: Harper & Row Publishers, 1970; Middlesex, England: Penguin Books, 1972.

_____. The Thought of Karl Marx: An Introduction. London: Macmillan & Co.; New York: Harper & Row, 1972.

_____. The Young Hegelians and Karl Marx. London-Melbourne: Macmillan & Co.; New York: Frederick A. Praeger, 1969.

Macmurray, John. "The Early Development of Karl Marx's Thought." Christianity and the Social Revolution. Edited by John Lewis, Karl Polanyi and Donald Kitchin. London: Victor Gollancz, 1935. Pp. 209-36.

Mandel, Ernest. The Formation of the Economic Thought of Karl Marx: 1843 to "Capital." New York: Monthly Review Press, 1971.

_____. An Introduction to Marxist Economic Theory. New York: Pathfinder Press, 1973.

_____. Marxist Economic Theory. Translated by Brian Pearce. 2nd edition. New York: Monthly Review Press, 1969.

Mandel, Ernest, and Novack, George. The Marxist Theory of Alienation. New York: Pathfinder Press, 1970.

_____. On the Revolutionary Potential of the Working Class. New York: Pathfinder Press, 1969.

Manser, Anthony Richards. The End of Philosophy: Marx and Wittgenstein. Southampton: University of Southampton, 1973.

Manuilsky, D. Z. Engels in the Struggle for Revolutionary Marxism. Moscow: Co-operative Publishing Society of Foreign Workers in the U.S.S.R., n.d.

Marcus, L. Dialectical Economics. Lexington, Mass.: D. C. Heath & Co., 1975.

Marcus, Steven. *Engels, Manchester, and the Working Class.* New York: Random House, 1974.

Marcuse, Herbert. *Eros and Civilization.* Boston: Beacon Press, 1955.

_____. *One-Dimensional Man.* London: Routledge & Kegan Paul; Boston: Beacon Press, 1964.

_____. *Reason and Revolution.* 2nd edition. London: Routledge & Kegan Paul, 1955; Boston: Beacon Press, 1966.

_____. *Soviet Marxism: A Critical Analysis.* New York: Columbia University Press, 1958.

_____. *Studies in Critical Philosophy.* Translated by Joris de Bres. Boston: Beacon Press, 1973.

Marek, Franz. *Philosophy of World Revolution: A Contribution to an Anthology of Theories of Revolution.* Translated by D. Simon. New York: International Publishers Co., 1969.

Markovic, Mihailo. *The Contemporary Marx.* Nottingham, England: Spokesman Books, 1974.

_____. *From Affluence to Praxis.* Ann Arbor, Mich.: University of Michigan Press, 1974.

Martinet, Giles. *Marxism of Our Time, or the Contradictions of Socialism.* New York: Monthly Review Press, 1964.

Marxism and Modern Thought. New York: Harcourt, Brace & Co., 1935.

Masaryk, T. G. "Socialism." *Ideals of Humanity.* London: George Allen & Unwin, 1938. Pp. 20-34.

Mashruwala, K. G. *Gandhi and Marx.* Ahmedabad, India: Navajivan Publishing House, 1951.

Masur, Gerhard. "Founding and Destroying Fathers." *Prophets of Yesterday.* New York: The Macmillan Co., 1961. Pp. 38-105.

Mathewson, R. W. "Complete and Incomplete Men." *The Positive Hero in Russian Literature.* 2nd edition. Stanford, Calif.: Stanford University Press, 1975. Pp. 136-55.

_____. "Marxism, Realism, and the Hero." *The Positive Hero in Russian Literature.* 2nd edition. Stanford, Calif.: Stanford University Press, 1975. Pp. 115-35.

Mattick, Paul. *Marx and Keynes: The Limits of the Mixed Economy*. Boston: Porter E. Sargent, 1969.

Maxey, Chester C. "Challenge of Proletarianism." *Political Philosophies*. New York: The Macmillan Co., 1948. Pp. 564-94.

Mayer, Gustav. *Friedrich Engels: A Biography*. Translated by Gilbert and Helen Highet. Edited by R. H. S. Crossman. New York: Howard Fertig, 1969.

Mayer, Henry. *Marx, Engels and Australia*. Victoria, Australia: F. W. Cheshire, 1964.

Mayer, J. P. *Friedrich Engels*. New York: Rand Book Store, 1931.

Mayo, Henry B. *Democracy and Marxism*. New York: Oxford University Press, 1955.

_____. *Introduction to Marxist Theory*. New York: Oxford University Press, 1960.

Mazlish, B. "Marx." *The Riddle of History: The Great Speculators from Vico to Freud*. New York: Harper & Row, 1966. Pp. 221-306.

Mead, George Herbert. "Social Renaissance - Karl Marx and Socialism." *Movements of Thought in the Nineteenth Century*. Chicago: University of Chicago Press, 1936. Pp. 215-42.

Medvedev, Roy A. *On Socialist Democracy*. Translated by Ellen de Kadt. New York: Random House, 1975.

Meek, Ronald L. *Economics and Ideology and Other Essays: Studies in the Development of Economic Thought*. London: Chapman & Hall, 1967.

_____. "Some Notes on the Transformation Problem." *Essays in Economic Thought: Aristotle to Marshall*. Edited by Joseph J. Spengler and William R. Allen. Chicago: Rand McNally & Co., 1960. Pp. 470-83.

_____. *Studies in the Labour Theory of Value*. 2nd edition. London: Lawrence & Wishart, 1973.

Mehnert, Klaus. *Stalin versus Marx*. London: George Allen & Unwin, 1952.

Mehring, Franz. *Karl Marx: The Story of His Life*. Translated by E. Fitzgerald. Edited by Ruth and Heinz Norden. New Introduction by Max Shaftman. Ann Arbor, Mich.: University of Michigan Press, 1973.

Mendel, Arthur P. *Dilemmas of Progress in Tsarist Russia: Legal Marxism and Legal Populism*. Cambridge, Mass.: Harvard University Press, 1961.

Meszaros, Istvan. *Marx's Theory of Alienation*. New York: Harper & Row Publishers; London: Merlin Press, 1972.

Meyer, Alfred G. *Communism*. Revised and enlarged edition. New York: Random House, 1963.

_____. *Marxism Since the Communist Manifesto*. Washington, D.C.: Service Center for Teachers of History, 1961.

_____. *Marxism: The Unity of Theory and Practice*. Cambridge, Mass.: Harvard University Press, 1954.

Miliband, Ralph. *The State in Capitalist Society*. New York: Basic Books, 1969.

Miller, Alexander. *Christian Significance of Karl Marx*. Toronto: The Macmillan Co. of Canada, 1947.

Mills, C. Wright. *The Marxists*. New York: Dell Publishing, 1962.

Miranda, Jose Porfirio. *Marx and the Bible*. Translated by John Eagleson. Maryknoll, N.Y.: Orbis Books, 1974.

Mitrany, David. *Marx Against the Peasant*. Chapel Hill, N.C.: University of North Carolina Press, 1952.

_____. "Marx vs. the Peasant." *London Essays in Economics in Honor of Edwin Cannon*. Edited by T. E. Gregory and H. Dalton. London: George Routledge & Sons, 1927. Pp. 319-76.

Monnerot, Jules. *The Sociology and Psychology of Communism*. Translated by J. Degras and R. Rees. Boston: Beacon Press, 1953.

Moore, Barrington. "Strategy in Social Science." *Sociology on Trial*. Edited by Maurice Stein and Arthur Vidich. Englewood Cliffs, N.J.: Prentice-Hall, 1963. Pp. 66-95.

Moore, Stanley W. *The Critique of Capitalist Democracy: An Introduction to the Theory of State in Marx, Engels, and Lenin*. New York: Paine-Whitman Publishers, 1957.

_____. "Marxian Theories of Law in Primitive Society." *Culture in History: Essays in Honor of Paul Radin*. Edited by Stanley Diamond. New York: Columbia University Press, 1960. Pp. 642-62.

_____. *Three Tactics: The Background in Marx*. New York: Monthly Review Press, 1963.

Morishima, Michio. *Marx's Economics: A Dual Theory of Value and Growth*. Cambridge, England: University Press, 1973.

Moscow. Institut Marksizma-Leninizma. *Reminiscences of Marx and Engels*. Moscow: Foreign Languages Publishing House, 196-?.

Mosse, George L. "Marxism." *The Culture of Western Europe: The Nineteenth and Twentieth Centuries*. Chicago: Rand McNally & Co., 1961. Pp. 173-96.

Mukerji, Krishna P. *Marxism*. Colombo: Associated Newspapers of Ceylon, 1946.

Muller, Herbert J. "Social Sciences." *Science and Criticism*. New Haven, Conn.: Yale University Press, 1943. Pp. 173-238.

Mumford, L. "Marx: Dialectic of Revolution; Excerpt from 'The Condition of Man'." *Interpretations and Forecasts, 1922-72*. New York: Harcourt, Brace Jovanovich, 1973. Pp. 199-208.

Munson, Gorham B. "Propaganda of Socialism: The Communist Manifesto." *12 Decisive Battles of the Mind*. New York: Greystone Press, 1942. Pp. 89-118.

Murray, A. R. M. "Marxism, Communism, and Socialism." *Introduction to Political Philosophy*. New York: Philosophical Library, 1953. Pp. 181-205.

Murry, John M. *The Defense of Democracy*. London: Jonathan Cape, 1939.

_____. "Karl Marx." *Heroes of Thought*. New York: Julian Messner, 1938. Pp. 313-43.

_____. *Marxism*. New York: John Wiley & Sons, 1935.

_____. *The Necessity of Communism*. London: Jonathan Cape, 1933.

Myrdal, Gunner. "A Brief Note on Marx and 'Marxism'." *Against the Stream: Critical Essays on Economics*. New York: Pantheon Books, 1973. Pp. 308-16.

Nearing, S. A Warless World. New York: Vanguard Press, 1933.

Neill, Thomas P. "Marx: The Robot Dirties His Hands." Makers of the Modern Mind. Milwaukee, Wis.: Bruce Publishing Co., 1949. Pp. 284-319.

Neilson, Francis. "Centenary of the Communist Manifesto." Cultural Traditions and Other Essays. New York: Robert Schalkenbach Foundation, 1957. Pp. 149-62.

_____. "The Twilight of Marx." Cultural Traditions and Other Essays. New York: Robert Schalkenbach Foundation, 1957. Pp. 149-62.

Neumann, S. "Engels and Marx: Military Concepts of the Social Revolutionaries." Makers of Modern Strategy. Edited by E. M. Earle and others. Princeton, N.J.: Princeton University Press, 1943. Pp. 155-71.

Nicholson, Joseph S. The Revival of Marxism. New York: E. P. Dutton & Co., 1920.

Nicolaievsky, Boris Ivanovich, and Maenchen-Helfen, Otto. Karl Marx: Man and Fighter. Translated by Gwenda David and Eric Mosbacher. Revised edition. London: Allen Lane, 1973.

Nicolaus, Martin. "Foreword." Grundrisse. By Karl Marx. New York: Vintage Books, 1974. Pp. 7-66.

_____. "Proletariat and Middle Class in Marx: Hegelian Choreography and the Capitalist Dialectic." For a New America. Edited by James Weinstein and David W. Eakins. New York: Random House, 1970. Pp. 253-83.

Niebuhr, Reinhold. "Ideology and the Scientific Method." Christian Realism and Political Problems. New York: Charles Scribner's Sons, 1953. Pp. 75-94.

_____. "Marx and Engels on Religion." Faith and Politics. Edited by Ronald H. Stone. New York: George Braziller, 1968. Pp. 47-54.

_____. "Russia and Karl Marx." College Book of Essays. Compiled by J. A. Clark. New York: Henry Holt & Co., 1939. Pp. 422-8.

Nomad, Max. "The Teacher: Karl Marx, Who Sowed Dragon's Teeth." Apostles of Revolution. Boston: Little, Brown & Co., 1939. Pp. 76-145.

Nordlinger, Eric A., ed. Politics and Society: Studies in Comparative Political Sociology. Englewood Cliffs, N.J.: Prentice-Hall, 1970.

North, Gary. Marx's Religion of Revolution. Nutley, N.J.: Craig Press, 1968.

Nova, Fritz. Friedrich Engels: His Contributions to Political Theory. Ontario, Canada: Burns & MacEacherin; New York: Philosophical Library, 1968.

Novack, George E. Humanism & Socialism. New York: Pathfinder Press, 1973.

_____. An Introduction to the Logic of Marxism. 5th edition. New York: Merit Publishers, 1969.

_____. Pragmatism versus Marxism. New York: Pathfinder Press, 1975.

_____. Understanding History: Marxist Essays. New York: Pathfinder Press, 1972.

Nyberg, P. "The Communal Man: Marx." The Educated Man: Studies in the History of Educational Thought. Edited by Paul Nash, Andreas M. Kazamias and Henry J. Perkinson. New York: John Wiley & Sons, 1965. Pp. 227-303.

Odajynk, Walter. Marxism and Existentialism. Garden City, N.Y.: Doubleday Anchor, 1965.

Olafson, Frederick A., ed. Society, Law and Morality. Englewood Cliffs, N.J.: Prentice-Hall, 1961.

Olgin, Moissaye J. The Life and Teachings of Friedrich Engels. New York: Workers Library Publishers, 1936.

Ollman, Bertell. Alienation: Marx's Conception of Man in Capitalist Society. Cambridge, England: Cambridge University Press, 1971.

Orage, A. R. "Marx as Politician." Readers and Writers. London: George Allen & Unwin, 1922. Pp. 133-5.

_____. "Origins of Marx." Readers and Writers. London: George Allen & Unwin, 1922. Pp. 131-3.

O'Rourke, J. J. The Problem of Freedom in Marxist Thought. Netherlands: Reidel Publishing Co., 1974.

Osbert, Reuben. Freud and Marx. New York: Equinox Cooperative Press, 1937.

_____. Marxism and Psycho-Analysis. London: Barrie & Rockliff, 1965.

Ossowski, Stanislaw. Class Structure and Social Consciousness. New York: The Free Press of Glencoe, 1963.

Outline Study Course in Marxian Economics. Based on Vol. 1 of Capital. Chicago: International Council Correspondence, 1937.

Ozinga, James R. Communism: A Tarnished Promise: The Story of an Idea. Columbus, Ohio: Charles E. Merrill Publishing Co., 1975.

Paci, Enzo. The Function of the Sciences and the Meaning of Man. Translated by Paul Piccone and James E. Hansen. Evanston, Ill.: Northwestern University Press, 1972.

Pannekoek, Anton. Marxism and Darwinism. Translated by Nathan Weiser. Chicago: Charles H. Kerr & Co., 1912.

Pappenheim, Fritz. The Alienation of Modern Man. New York: Monthly Review Press, 1968.

Parkes, Henry B. Marxism: An Autopsy. Chicago: University of Chicago Press, 1964.

Parsons, Howard L. Humanism and Marx's Thought. Springfield, Ill.: C. C. Thomas Publishers, 1971.

_____. The Young Marx and the Young Generation. Toronto: Progress Books, 1968.

Pascal, Roy. Karl Marx: His Apprenticeship to Politics. London: Labour Monthly, 1943.

_____. Karl Marx, Political Foundations. London: Labour Monthly, 1943.

Payne, Robert. Marx. New York: Simon & Schuster; London: W. H. Allen & Co., 1968.

Payne, Robert, ed. The Unknown Karl Marx. New York: New York University Press, 1971; London: University of London Press, 1972.

Perchik, Lev. M. Karl Marx. New York: International Publishers Co., 1934

Peterson, Arnold. Karl Marx and Marxian Science. New York: New York Labor News Co., 1943.

_____. Karl Marx and Marxism: A Universal Genius, His Discoveries, His Traducers. New York: New York Labor News Co., 1933.

_____. Marxism vs. Anti-Marxism. New York: New York Labor News Co., 1931.

_____. Reviling of the Great. New York: New York Labor News Co., 1949.

Petrovic, Gajo. Marx in the Mid-Twentieth Century. New York: Doubleday & Co., 1967.

Petulla, Joseph M. Christian Political Theology: A Marxian Guide. Maryknoll, N.Y.: Orbis Books, 1972.

Plaine, Henry L., ed. Darwin, Marx, and Wagner. Columbus, Ohio: Ohio State University Press, 1962.

Plamenatz, John. From Marx to Stalin. London: Batchworth Press, 1953.

_____. German Marxism and Russian Communism. Reprint of 1954 edition. New York: Harper & Row Publishers, 1965.

_____. Ideology. New York: Frederick A. Praeger, 1970.

_____. Karl Marx's Philosophy of Man. New York: Oxford University Press, 1975.

_____. Man and Society. Volume 2, Bentham through Marx. New York: McGraw Hill, 1963.

Plekhanov, Georgil V. Essays in the History of Materialism. New York: Howard Fertig, 1967.

_____. Fundamental Problems of Marxism. New York: International Publishers Co., 1969.

Poggi, Gianfranco. Images of Society: Essays on the Sociological Theories of Tocqueville, Marx and Durkheim. Stanford, Calif.: Stanford University Press; London: Oxford University Press, 1972.

Polanyi, Karl. Origins of Our Time: The Great Transformation. Originally published as The Great Transformation. London: Victor Gollancz, 1945.

Polin, Raymond. Marxian Foundations of Communism: An Introduction to the Study of Communist Theory. Chicago: H. Regnery Co., 1966.

Pollard, Sidney. *The Idea of Progress: History and Society*. Baltimore, Md.: Penguin Books, 1968.

Popper, Karl R. *The Open Society and Its Enemies: Volume Two*. Princeton, N.J.: Princeton University Press, 1971.

Porter, Eugene O. *Fallacies of Karl Marx*. El Paso, Texas: Texas Western College Press, 1962.

Portus, Garhet Vere. *Marx and Modern Thought*. Sydney: Worker's Educational Association of N.S.W., 1921.

Postan, M. M. "Karl Marx." *Great Democrats*. Edited by A. B. Brown. London: Nicholson & Watson, 1934. Pp. 435-52.

Postgate, Raymond William. *Karl Marx*. London: Hamish Hamilton, 1933.

_____. *Revolution from 1789 to 1906*. Magnolia, Mass.: Peter Smith, n.d.

Poulantzas, N. "Political Ideology and Scientific Research." *Scientific Research and Politics*. Edited by L. Dencik. Lund, Sweden: Student Literatur, 1969.

Prawer, Siegbert Soloman. *Karl Marx and World Literature*. New York: Oxford University Press, 1976.

Prenant, Marcel. *Biology and Marxism*. London: Lawrence & Wishart, 1940.

Randall, J. H. Jr. *The Career of Philosophy*. 2 vols. New York: Columbia University Press, 1970.

Read, Herbert E. *Anarchy and Order*. Boston: Beacon Press, 1971.

Regnier, M. *Hegelianism and Marxism*. Translated by Barbara Reid. Trumbull: Greater Bridgeport Region, Planning Agency, 1963.

Reid, David C. *Capital and Profits*. Stockbridge, Mass.: Stockbridge Socialist Press, 1912.

Rexroth, Kenneth. "Karl Marx: The Communist Manifesto." *Classics Revisited*. Chicago: Quadrangle Books, 1968. Pp. 243-8.

Riazanov, David. *Karl Marx and Friedrich Engels*. Translated by Joshua Kunitz. New York: Monthly Review Press, 1974.

Riazanov, David, ed. Karl Marx, Man, Thinker and Revolutionist. London: Martin Lawrence, 1927.

Riddle, George A. R., 1st Baron. "The Real Karl Marx." More Things that Matter. London: Hodder & Stoughton, 1925. Pp. 70-8.

Riis, Sergius Martin. Karl Marx, Master of Fraud. New York: Robert Speller & Sons, 1962.

Roberts, Leo, and Carson, Edward. Dialectical Materialism: History, Theory and Practice. New York: International Publishers Co., 1938.

Roberts, Paul Craig, and Stephenson, M. A. Marx's Theory of Exchange, Alienation and Crisis. Stanford: Hoover Institite Press, 1973.

Robinson, Joan. An Essay on Marxian Economics. 2nd edition. New York: St. Martin's Press, 1967.

———. Marx, Marshall, and Keynes. Delhi: Delhi School of Economics, University of Delhi, 1955.

———. On Re-reading Marx. Cambridge, England: Students' Bookshops, 1953.

Rogin, Leo. "Karl Marx." The Meaning and Validity of Economic Theory. New York: Harper & Brothers, 1956. Pp. 332-410.

Rosenberg, Harold. "Criticism - Action." Act and the Actor: Making the Self. New York: World Publishing Co., 1970. Pp. 135-51.

———. "Marxism; Critism and/or Action." The Radical Papers. Edited by Irving Howe. New York: Doubleday & Co., 1966. Pp. 73-85.

———. "The Pathos of the Proletariat." Act and the Actor: Making the Self. New York: World Publishing Co., 1970. Pp. 14-57.

———. "Politics of Illusion." Discovering the Present. Chicago: University of Chicago Press, 1973. Pp. 316-28.

———. "Politics of Illusion." Liberations. Edited by I. H. Hassan. Middletown, Conn.: Wesleyan University Press, 1971. Pp. 117-28.

———. "Resurrected Romans." Tradition of the New. New York: Horizon Press, 1959. Pp. 154-77.

Rosenburg, Arthur. Democracy and Socialism. Boston: Beacon Press, 1965.

Rossiter, Clinton. Marxism; The View from America. New York: Harcourt, Brace & Co., 1960.

Rotenstreich, Nathan. Basic Problems of Marx's Philosophy. New York: Liberal Arts Press, 1966.

Rothberg, A., ed. Anatomy of a Moral: The Political Essays of Milovan Djilas. New York: Frederick A. Praeger, 1959.

Roubiczek, Paul. "Marxism." Misinterpretation of Man. New York: Charles Scribner's Sons, 1947. Pp. 166-98.

Rowse, A. L. "Karl Marx." Some Makers of the Modern Spirit. Edited by John Macmurray. London: Methuen & Co., 1933. Pp. 166-78.

_____. "The Literature of Communism: Its Theory." End of an Epoch. New York: The Macmillan Co., 1947. Pp. 224-36.

_____. "Marx and Russian Communism." End of an Epoch. New York: The Macmillan Co., 1947. Pp. 253-73.

Rubel, Maximilien. "The Relationship of Bolshevism to Marxism." Revolutionary Russia. Conference on the Russian Revolution, Harvard University. Edited by Richard Pipes. Cambridge, Mass.: Harvard University Press, 1968. Pp. 301-25.

Rubel, Maximilien, and Manale, Margaret. Marx Without Myth: A Chronological Study of His Life and Work. New York: Harper & Row Publishers, 1975.

Rubin, Isaak Il'ich. Essays on Marx's Theory of Value. Translated by Milos Samardzija and Fredy Perlman. Detroit, Mich.: Black & Red, 1972.

Rubinov, Isaac Max. Was Marx Wrong. New York: Marx Institute of America, 1914.

Rühle, Otto. Karl Marx: His Life and Work. New York: The Blakiston Co., 1943.

Russel, B. A. W. R. 3rd Earl. "Dialectical Materialism." Freedom versus Organization. New York: W. W. Norton & Co., 1934. Pp. 188-200.

_____. "Karl Marx." History of Western Philosophy. New York: Simon & Schuster, 1945. Pp. 782-90.

——————. "Marx and Engels." Freedom versus Organization. New York: W. W. Norton & Co., 1934. Pp. 176-87.

——————. "Politics of Marxism." Freedom versus Organization. New York: W. W. Norton & Co., 1934. Pp. 211-21.

——————. "Theory of Surplus Value." Freedom versus Organization. New York: W. W. Norton & Co., 1934. Pp. 201-10.

Russell, B. A. W. R.; Dewey, John; Cohen, Morris; Hook, Sidney; and Eddy, Sherwood. The Meaning of Marx: A Symposium. New York: Farrar & Rinehart, 1934.

Saar, Robert J. The Fallacy of Communism. Boston, Mass.: Meador Publishing Co., 1956.

Sabine, George H. Marxism. Ithica, N.Y.: Cornell University Press; London: Oxford University Press, 1958.

Sacks, K. "Engels Revisited: Women, the Organization of Production, and Private Property." Toward an Anthropology of Women. Edited by Rayna R. Reiter. New York: Monthly Review Press, 1975. Pp. 211-34.

Salert, Barbara. Revolutions and Revolutionaries: Four Theories. Amsterdam: Elsevier, 1976.

Salter, Frank Reyner. Karl Marx and Modern Socialism. London: Macmillan & Co., 1921.

Salvadori, Massimo, ed. Modern Socialism. New York: Walker & Company, 1968.

Sampson, R. V. "Marxism." Progress in the Age of Reason. Cambridge, Mass.: Harvard University Press, 1956. Pp. 204-25.

Samuelson, Paul A. "Karl Marx as a Mathematical Economist." Trade, Stability and Macro-economics: Essays in Honor of Lloyd Metzler. Edited by G. Horwich and P. A. Samuelson. New York: Academic Press, 1974. Pp. 269-307.

Sanchez Vazquez, Adolfo. Art and Society: Essays in Marxist Aesthetics. Translated by Maro Riofrancos. New York: Monthly Review Press, 1973.

Sanderson, John. An Interpretation of the Political Ideas of Marx and Engels. New York: Fernhill House; London: Longmans Group, 1969.

Sargent, Lyman T. Contemporary Political Ideologies: A Comparative Analysis. Homewood, Ill.: Dorsey Press, 1972.

Savage, Katharine. Marxism and Communism. London: The Bodley Head, 1968.

──────. The Story of Marxism and Communism. New York: Henry Z. Walck, 1969.

Schact, Richard. Alienation. Garden City, N.Y.: Doubleday & Co., 1970.

Schaff, Adam. Marxism and the Human Individual. New York: McGraw-Hill Book Co., 1970.

──────. A Philosophy of Man. New York: Monthly Review Press, 1963.

──────. "Studies of the Young Marx: A Rejoinder." Revisionism. Edited by Leopold Labedz. New York: Frederick A. Praeger, 1962. Pp. 188-94.

Schlesinger, Rudolf. Marx: His Time and Ours. London: Routledge & Kegan Paul, 1950.

Schmidt, Alfred. The Concept of Nature in Marx. Translated by Ben Fowkes. London: NLB, 1971.

Schnittkind, Henry T., and Schnittkind, Dana A. "Karl Marx." Living Biographies of Famous Men. Garden City, N.Y.: Garden City Publishing Co., 1944. Pp. 173-82.

Schumpeter, Joseph A. Capitalism, Socialism and Democracy. 2nd edition. New York: Harper & Brothers, 1947.

──────. "Communist Manifesto in Sociology and Economics." Essays. Cambridge, Mass.: Addison-Wesley Publishing Co., 1951. Pp. 282-95.

──────. 10 Great Economists from Marx to Keynes. London: George Allen & Unwin, 1952.

Schwarzschild, Leopold. The Red Prussian: The Life and Legend of Karl Marx. New York: Grosset & Dunlap, 1958.

Scott, J. W. Karl Marx on Value. New York: The Macmillan Co., 1920.

Seaward, Caroline. Karl Marx. London: Wayland Publishers, 1974.

Sée, Henri Eugene. The Economic Interpretation of History. Translated by Melvin M. Knight. New York: Burt Franklin, 1968.

Seligman, Edwin R. A., and Waton, Harry. Debate: "Is the Failure of Socialism Due to the Fallacies of Marxian Theory?" Affirmative: Edwin R. A. Seligman. Negative: Harry Waton. New York: Marx-Engels Institute, 1922.

Sellars, Roy Wood. Social Patterns and Political Horizons. Nashville, Tenn.: Aurora Publishers, 1970.

Shah, C. G. Marxism, Gandhism, Stalinism. Bombay, India: Popular Prakashan, 1963.

Shaw, George B. Bernard Shaw and Karl Marx. New York: Random House, 1930.

Sherman, Howard J. Radical Political Economy; Capitalism and Socialism from a Marxist-Humanist Perspective. New York: Basic Books, 1972.

Shoul, B. "Karl Marx and Say's Law." Essays in Economic Thought: Aristotle to Marshall. Edited by Joseph Spengler and William R. Allen. Chicago: Rand McNally & Co., 1960. Pp. 454-69.

Shroyer, T. The Critique of Domination: The Origins and Development of Critical Theory. New York: George Braziller, 1973.

Sibley, Mulford Q. Political Ideas and Ideologies: A History of Political Thought. New York: Harper & Row, 1970.

Sikes, Earl R. "Karl Marx and Scientific Socialism." Contemporary Economic Systems. New York: Henry Holt & Co., 1940. Pp. 52-91.

Silberner, Edmund. Friedrich Engels and the Jews. New York: Conference on Jewish Relations, 1949.

Simkhovitch, Vladimir G. Marxism Versus Socialism. New York: Henry Holt & Co., 1913.

Simon, Brian, ed. The Challenge of Marxism. London: Lawrence & Wishart, 1963.

Sloan, Pat. Marx and the Orthodox Economists. Totowa, N.J.: Rowman & Littlefield; Oxford, England: Blackwell, 1973.

Slochower, H. "Clash and Congruence between Marx and Freud." No Voice is Wholly Lost. New York: Creative Age Press, 1945. Pp. 309-18.

_____. "The Marxist Idea of the Universal Man." No Voice is Wholly Lost. New York: Creative Age Press, 1945. Pp. 263-77.

Smith, V. E. "The Dialectical World of Marxism." Idea-Men of Today. St. Paul, Minn.: Bruce Publishing Co., 1950. Pp. 185-212.

Smulkstys, Julius. Karl Marx. New York: Twayne Publishers, 1974.

Somerville, John. The Philosophy of Marxism: An Exposition. New York: Random House, 1967.

Spargo, John. Karl Marx His Life and Work. New York: B. W. Huebsch, 1910.

_____. The Marx He Knew. Chicago: Charles H. Kerr, 1909.

_____. Sidelights on Contemporary Socialism. New York: B. W. Huebsch, 1911.

Spinka, Matthew. "Karl Marx and Dialectical Materialism." Christian Thought from Erasmus to Berdyaev. Englewood Cliffs, N.J.: Prentice-Hall, 1962. Pp. 168-79.

Spratt, Philip. A New Look at Marx. London: Phoenix House, 1957.

Sprigge, Cecil Jackson Squire. Karl Marx. New York: The Macmillan Co., 1957.

Stark, Werner. The Sociology of Knowledge. Chicago, Ill.: The Free Press of Glencoe, 1958.

Stekloff, G. M. The History of the First International. Translated by Eden and Cedar Paul. New York: International Publishers Co., 1927

Stepanova, Evgeniia Akimovna. Friedrich Engels. Moscow: Novosti Press Agency Publishing House, 1970.

_____. Karl Marx: Short Biography. Translated by J. Gibbons. 2nd revised edition. Moscow: Foreign Languages Publishing House, 1960.

Stockhammer, Morris, ed. Karl Marx Dictionary. New York: Philosophical Library, 1965.

Stojanovic, Svetozar. Between Ideals and Reality: A Critique of Socialism and Its Future. Translated by Gerson S. Sher. New York: Oxford University Press, 1973.

Strachey, John. The Nature of Capitalist Crisis. New York: Covici, Friede, 1935.

Strand, T. A. Equality Defined: The Theory of Trinity or Tri-ism as the Argument Against the Idealism in the Concept of Communism. New York: William-Frederick Press, 1952.

Struik, D. J., ed. The Birth of the Communist Manifesto. New York: International Publishers, 1971.

Suda, J. P. Manu, Marx, and Gandhi. Meerut, India: Jai Prakash Nath & Co., 1967.

Sweezy, Paul M. "The Communist Manifesto after 100 Years." Present as History. New York: Monthly Review Press, 1953. Pp. 3-29.

_____. "Karl Marx and the Industrial Revolution." Events, Ideology and Economic Theory. Edited by Robert V. Eagly. Detroit, Mich.: Wayne State University Press, 1968. Pp. 107-19.

_____. The Theory of Capitalist Development: Principles of Modern Political Economy. New York: Monthly Review Press, 1968.

Sweezy, Paul M., ed. Karl Marx and the Close of His System, by Eugen von Bohm-Bawerk, and Bohm-Bawerk's Criticism of Marx by Rudolf Hilferding: Together with an Appendix Consisting of an Article by Ladislaus von Bortkiewicz. New York: Augustus M. Kelly, 1949.

Swingewood, A. Marx and Modern Social Theory. New York: John Wiley & Son, 1975.

Sztompka, Piotr. System and Function: Toward a Theory of Society. New York: Academic Press, 1974.

Talmon, J. L. The Origins of Totalitarian Democracy. London: Martin Secker & Warburg, 1952. Also published as The Rise of Totalitarian Democracy. Boston: The Beacon Press, 1952.

_____. Political Messianism, the Romantic Phase. London: Martin Secker & Warburg, 1960.

Taylor, George Robert Sterling. "Karl Marx." Leaders of Socialism. New York: Duffield & Green, 1910. Pp. 57-66.

Taylor, Overton H. Classical Liberalism, Marxism, and the Twentieth Century. Cambridge, Mass.: Harvard University Press, 1960.

_____. "Schumpeter and Marx: Imperialism and Social Classes in the Schumpeterian System." Economics and Liberalism: Collected Papers. Cambridge, Mass.: Harvard University Press, 1955. Pp. 257-93.

_____. "The Socialist Tradition, and Karl Marx's Vision of the History and Destiny of Mankind." Classical Liberalism, Marxism and the Twentieth Century. Cambridge, Mass.: Harvard University Press, 1960. Pp. 29-62.

Telford, Shuley. Economic and Political Peace. 2nd edition. Portland Oregon: William & Richards, 1972.

Terray, Emmanuel. Marxism and "Primitive" Societies. Translated by Mary Klopper. New York: Monthly Review Press, 1972.

Thalheimer, August. Introduction to Dialectical Materialism. New York: Covici Friede, 1936.

Thomas, Clive Yolande. Dependence and Transformation: The Economics of the Transition to Socialism. New York: Monthly Review Press, 1974.

Thomas, Wendell. "German Views: Kent; Marx and Engels." On the Resolution of Science and Faith. New York: Island Press, 1946. Pp. 63-71.

Tillich, Paul. "The Breakdown of the Universal Synthesis." Perspectives on 19th and 20th Century Protestant Theology. Edited by Carl E. Braaten. New York: Harper & Row Publishers, 1967. Pp. 136-207.

_____. "Marx's View of History: A Study in the History of the Philosophy of History." Culture in History: Essays In Honor of Paul Radin. Edited by S. Diamond. New York: Columbia University Press, 1960. Pp. 631-41.

_____. Political Expectation: Essays by Paul Tillich on Political, Social and Economic Issues. Edited by J. L. Adams. New York: Harper & Row Publishers, 1971.

Timasheff, N. S. "Karl Marx: Communist Manifesto." Great Books: A Christian Appraisal. Edited by Harold C. Gardiner. New York: The Devin-Adair Co., 1949. Pp. 104-8.

Toennies, F. J. Karl Marx: His Life and Teachings. Translated by C. P. Loomis and I. Paulus. East Lansing, Mich.: Michigan State University Press, 1974.

Trattner, Ernest R. "Marx: Theory of the Economic Interpretation of History." Architects of Ideas. New York: Carrick & Evans, 1938. Pp. 241-71.

Trevor-Roper, H. R. "Karl Marx and the Study of History." *Men and Events: Historical Essays*. New York: Harper & Brothers, 1957. Pp. 285-98.

Trotsky, Leon. *The New Course*. Ann Arbor, Mich.: University of Michigan Press, 1965.

_____. *Permanent Revolution and Results and Prospects*. New York: Pioneer Publications, 1962.

_____. *The Revolution Betrayed*. New York: Merti Publications, 1937.

_____. *Terrorism and Communism*. Ann Arbor, Mich.: University of Michigan Press, 1961.

Tsanoff, Radoslav A. "Ethics of Socialism." *Moral Ideals of Our Civilization*. New York: E. P. Dutton & Co., 1942. Pp. 541-52.

Tsuru, S. *Essays on Marxian Economics*. Tokyo: Nihon Gakujutsu Kaigi, 1956.

_____. Keynes versus Marx: The Methodology of Aggregates." *Post Keynesian Economics*. Edited by K. Kurihara. New Brunswick, N.J.: Rutgers University Press, 1954. Pp. 320-44.

Tucker, Robert C. *The Marxian Revolutionary Idea*. New York: W. W. Norton & Co., 1969.

_____. *Philosophy and Myth in Karl Marx*. 2nd edition. Cambridge, England: Cambridge University Press, 1972.

Turner, Denys. *On the Philosophy of Marx*. Atlantic Highlands, N.J.: Humanities Press, 1968.

Turner, John Kenneth. *Challenge to Karl Marx*. New York: Reynal & Hitchcock, 1941.

Ulam, Adam B. *The Unfinished Revolution: An Essay on the Sources of Influence of Marxism and Communism*. New York: Random House, 1960.

Untermann, Ernest. *Marxian Economics*. Chicago: Charles H. Kerr, 1907.

Untermeyer, Louis. "Karl Marx." *Makers of the Modern World*. New York: Simon & Schuster, 1955. Pp. 26-33.

van Leeuwen, A. T. *Critique of Earth*. New York: Charles Scribner's Sons, 1975.

_____. *Critique of Heaven*. New York: Herder & Herder, 1971.

Varga, E. *The Great Crisis and Its Political Consequences*. New York: Howard Fertig, 1974.

Veblen, Thorstein B. "The Socialist Economics of Karl Marx and His Followers." *The Place of Science in Modern Civilization*. New York: Viking Press, 1919. Pp. 409-56.

_____. "Veblen on Marx." *The Development of Economic Thought*. Edited by Henry W. Spiegel. New York: John Wiley & Sons, 1952. Pp. 313-28.

Venable, Vernon. *Human Nature: The Marxian View*. New York: Alfred A. Knopf, 1945.

Vetterli, Richard, and Fort, W. E. Jr. *The Socialist Base of Modern Totalitarianism*. Berkeley, Calif.: McCutchan Publishing Corp., 1968.

Vigor, P. H. "Marx and Modern Capitalism." *Political Ideas*. Edited by David Thomson. New York: Basic Books, 1966. Pp. 176-88.

Voeglin, Eric. "Marx: The Genesis of Gnostic Socialism." *From Enlightenment to Revolution*. Edited by John Hallowell. Durham, N.C.: Duke University Press, 1975. Pp. 273-302.

_____. "Marx: Inverted Dialects." *From Enlightenment to Revolution*. Edited by John Hallowell. Durham, N.C.: Duke University Press, 1975. Pp. 240-72.

von Bohm-Bawerk, E. *Karl Marx and the Close of His System*. New York: Augustus M. Kelly, 1949.

Vygodskii, Vitalii Solomonovich. *The Story of a Great Discovery: How Karl Marx Wrote Capital*. Translated by Christopher S. V. Salt. Revised by Maurice Dobb, Peter Hess and Wolfgang Winkler. Turnbridge Wells, England: Abacus Press, 1974.

Waddington, K. *Outlines of Marxist Philosophy*. London: Lawrence & Wishart, 1974.

Walton, D., and Hall, S., eds. *Situating Marx: Evaluations and Departures*. London: Chaucer Publishing Co., 1972.

Walton, Paul, and Gamble, Andrew. *From Alienation to Surplus Value*. London: Sheed & Ward, 1972.

Ward, John W. "Mill, Marx, and Modern Individualism." Red, White and Blue. New York: Oxford University Press, 1969. Pp. 213-26.

Warner, R. S. "The Methodology of Marx's Comparative Analysis of Modes of Production." Comparative Methods in Sociology. Edited by Ivan Vallier. Berkeley, Calif.: University of California Press, 1971. Pp. 49-74.

Waton, Harry. The Philosophy of Marx. New York: The Marx Institute, 1921.

Weldon, T. D. The Vocabulary of Politics. New York: Johnson Reprint Corp., 1970.

Westmeyer, Russell E. "Karl Marx." Modern Economics and Social Systems. New York: Farrar & Rinehart, 1940. Pp. 97-105.

Wetter, Gustav A. Dialectical Materialism. Translated by Peter Heath. New York: Frederick A. Praeger, 1959.

White, Hayden V. "The Philosophical Defense of History in the Metonymical Mode." Metahistory. Baltimore, Md.: Johns Hopkins University Press, 1973. Pp. 281-330.

Wicksteed, Phillip Henry. "The Marxian Theory of Value." The Common-Sense of Political Economy. 2nd edition. Vol. II. Edited by Lionel Robbins. London: Routledge & Kegan Paul, 1933. Pp. 705-24.

Wiles, P. J. D. The Political Economy of Communism. Cambridge, Mass.: Harvard University Press, 1963.

William, Maurice. The Social Interpretation of History. Published by the author, 89 Norman Avenue, Brooklyn, N.Y., 1920.

Williams, Raymond. "Marxism and Culture." Culture and Society, 1780-1950. New York: Columbia University Press, 1958. Pp. 265-84.

Williams, Roger L., ed. The Commune of Paris, 1871. New York: John Wiley, 1969.

Williams, William Appleton. "Karl Marx's Challenge to America; Excerpt from 'The Great Evasion'." History as a Way of Learning. New York: New Viewpoints, 1973. Pp. 345-65.

_____. The Great Evasion. Chicago, Ill.: Quadrangle Books; Ontario, Canada: Burns & MacEachern, 1968.

Wilson, Edmund. "Marx, Engels, and Bakunin." Readings for Opinion. Edited by Earle R. Davis and William C. Hummel. Englewood Cliffs, N.J.: Prentice-Hall, 1960. Pp. 382-6.

_____. "Marxism and Literature." Literary Opinion in America. Vol. 2. Edited by Morton D. Zabel. New York: Harper & Row Publishers, 1962. Pp. 693-705.

_____. To the Finland Station: A Study in the Writing and Acting of History. Garden City, N.Y.: Doubleday & Co., 1947.

_____. The Triple Thinkers. New York: Oxford University Press, 1948.

Wittfogel, Karl August. Oriental Despotism: A Comparative Study of Total Power. New Haven, Conn.: Yale University Press, 1957.

Wittke, C. F. "Marx and Weitling." Essays in Political Theory, Presented to George H. Sabine. Edited by Milton R. Konvitz and Arthur E. Murphy. Ithaca, N.Y.: Cornell University Press, 1948. Pp. 179-93.

Wolfe, Bertram D. "A Century of Marx and Marxism." Darwin, Marx, and Wagner. Edited by H. L. Plaine. Columbus, Ohio: Ohio State University Press, 1962. Pp. 93-115.

_____. "French Socialism, German Theory and the Flaw in the Foundation of the Socialist Internationals." Essays in Russian and Soviet History. Edited by John S. Curtiss. New York: Columbia University Press, 1963. Pp. 177-97.

_____. Marx and America. New York: John Day, 1934.

_____. Marxism, One Hundred Years in the Life of a Doctrine. New York: Dial Press, 1965.

Wolfson, Murray. Karl Marx. New York: Columbia University Press, 1971.

_____. A Reappraisal of Marxian Economics. New York: Columbia University Press, 1966.

Wood, Ellen M. Mind and Politics: An Approach to the Meaning of Liberal Socialist Individualism. Berkeley, Calif.: University of California Press, 1972.

Wright, David M. The Trouble with Marx. New Rochelle, N.Y.: Arlington House, 1967.

Zeitlin, Irving M. _Ideology and the Development of Sociological Theory_. Englewood Cliffs, N.J.: Prentice-Hall, 1968.

──────. _Marxism: A Re-examination_. Princeton, N.J.: D. Van Nostrand Co., 1967.

Zitta, Victor. _Georg Lukacs' Marxism: Alienation, Dialectics, Revolution: A Study in Utopia and Ideology_. New York: Humanities Press, 1965.

Zwerman, William L. _New Perspectives on Organization Theory: An Empirical Reconsideration of the Marxian and Classical Analyses_. Westport, Conn.: Greenwood Press, 1970.

ARTICLES ON MARX AND ENGELS

Abdel-Malek, Anouar. "Marxism and the Sociology of Civilizations." Diogenes 64(1968): 91-116.

Abrahamson, Mark; Taylor, Howard F.; Kessin, Kenneth; and Ima, Kenji. "The Self or the Collectivity: Simulation of a Marxian Hypothesis." Social Forces 47(1969): 299-304.

Achminov, Herman. "Marxism: Dogma or Guide?" Institute for the Study of the USSR. Bulletin 6 No. 10(1959): 11-22.

_____. "The Perennial Problem of Revisionism." Institute for the Study of the USSR. Bulletin 6(July 1959): 3-12.

Acton, H. B. "Marx, Engels, and Marxism." Review article. Political Studies 12(1964): 235-7.

_____. "The Marxist Outlook." Philosophy 22(1947): 208-30.

_____. "The Materialist Conception of History." Proceedings of the Aristotelian Society 52(1951-52): 207-24.

_____. "On Some Criticisms of Historical Materialism.' The Aristotelian Society: Supplement 44(1970): 143-56.

_____. "Remarks on J. and M. Miller's Review of The Illusion of the Epoch." Soviet Studies 7(1956): 409-11.

Adam, Hussein. "Black Thinkers and the Need to Confront Karl Marx." Pan African Journal 4(1971): 75-102.

Adamiak, Richard. "Marx, Engels and Duehring." Journal of the History of Ideas 35(1974): 98-112.

_____. "The Withering Away of the State: A Reconsideration." Journal of Politics 32(1970): 3-18.

Addis, Laird. "Freedom and the Marxist Philosophy of History." Philosophy of Science 33(1966): 101-17.

Adelman, Frederick J. "Freedom and Marxism." Studies in Soviet Thought 10(1970): 1-12.

Adoratski, V. "Introduction to Marx and Engels." Labour Monthly 15(1933): 163-9.

Adorno, Theodore W. "Is Marx Obsolete?" Diogenes 64(1968): 1-16.

Agar, H. "John Strachey, Marx, and the Distributist Ideal." American Review 5(1935): 168-84.

Agrawal, N. N. "Marx and Engels on the National Question." Indian Journal of Political Science 16(1955): 243-76.

Ai, Ssu-Ch'I. "Engels Affirmed the Identity of Thought and Being." Chinese Studies in Philosophy 4(1971): 83-104.

Akhavi, S. "Egypt's Socialism and Marxist Thought: Some Preliminary Observations on Social Theory and Metaphysics." Comparative Studies in Society and History 17(1975): 190-211.

Alexander, R. J. "Marx, Lenin and the Developing Countries." New Politics 9(1971): 87-95.

Alexander, S. S. "Mr. Keynes and Mr. Marx." Review of Economic Studies 7(1940): 123-35.

Allen, Derek P. H. "Is Marxism a Philosophy?" Journal of Philosophy 71(1974): 601-13.

──────. "The Utilitarianism of Marx and Engels." American Philosophical Quarterly 10(1973): 189-99.

Andelson, R. V. "Nicholas Berdyaev's Critique of Marxism." American Journal of Economics and Sociology 21(1962): 271-84.

Andrew, Edward. "Marx's Theory of Classes: Science and Ideology." Canadian Journal of Political Science 8(1975): 454-66.

──────. "A Note on the Unity of Theory and Practice in Marx and Nietzsche." Political Theory 3(1975): 305-16.

──────. "Work and Freedom in Marcuse and Marx." Canadian Journal of Political Science 3(1970): 241-56. Reply with rejoinder, W. Luss 4(1971): 398-404.

Anton, Anatole. "Commodities and Exchange: Notes for a Interpretation of Marx." Philosophy and Phenomenological Research 34(1974): 355-85.

Apostol, P. "Marxism and the Structure of the Future." Futures 4 No. 3(1972): 201-10.

Apresian, Z. G. "An Appraisal of the Work Done in the 1930's on the Foundations of Marxist Esthetics." Soviet Studies in Philosophy 5(1967): 39-50.

Aptheker, H. "Marxism and Religion." Religion in Life 37 (1968): 89-98.

Arendt, Hannah. "History and Immortality." Partisan Review 24 No. 1(1957): 11-35.

_____. "Reflections on Violence." Journal of International Affairs 23(1969): 1-35.

Aron, Raymond, et al. "The Diffusion of Ideologies." Confluence March 1953, pp. 1-65; June 1953, pp. 1-108; September 1953, pp. 69-141.

Arora, P. "Marx: Utopian or Scientist?" Political Quarterly 38(1967): 301-14.

Ash, William. "Marxism and the Negro Revolt." Monthly Review 18(May 1966): 19-30.

_____. "Marxist Ethics and European Traditions." Science & Society 30(1966): 326-34.

Ashcraft, Richard. "Lewis Feuer and the Intellectuals." New Politics 8(1970): 49-58.

_____. "Marx and Weber on Liberalism as Bourgeois Ideology." Comparative Studies in Society and History 14(1972): 130-68.

Avineri, Shlomo. "From Hoax to Dogma." Encounter 28(March 1967): 30-2.

_____. "The Hegelian Origins of Marx's Political Thought." Review of Metaphysics 21(1967): 33-56.

_____. "How to Save Marx from the Alchemists of Revolution." Political Theory 4(1976): 35-44.

_____. "The Instrumentality of Passion in the World of Reason: Hegel and Marx." Political Theory 1(1973): 388-98. Comment by Judith N. Shklar, pp. 399-404.

_____. "Marx and Jewish Emancipation." Journal of the History of Ideas 25(1964): 445-50.

_____. "Marx and Modernization." Review of Politics 31 (1969): 172-88.

_____. "Marx and the Intellectuals." Journal of the History of Ideas 28(1967): 269-78.

_____. "Marx's Vision of Future Society and the Problem of Utopianism." Dissent 20(1973): 323-31.

_____. "The Non-European World in Marx's Philosophy of History." Iyyun 19(1968): 12-27.

Axelos, Kostas. "Marx, Freud, and the Undertakings of Thought in the Future." Diogenes 72(1970): 96-111.

Bailey, Cyril. "Karl Marx on Greek Atomism." Classical Quarterly 22(1928): 205-6.

Bailey, G. "Monument of Tolerance." New York Times Magazine 5 August 1951, p. 12+.

Bailey, Sydney D. "The Revision of Marxism." Quarterly Review 291(1953): 177-85.

_____. "The Revision of Marxism." Review of Politics 16(1954): 452-62.

Bajt, A. "A Postmortem Note on the 'Transformation Problem'." Soviet Studies 21(1970): 371-4.

_____. "Labour as Scarcity in Marx's Value Theory: An Alternative Explanation." History of Political Economy 3(1971): 152-69.

Balassa, B. A. "Karl Marx and John Stuart Mill." Weltwirtschaftsliches Archiv 83(1959): 147-64.

Balbus, Isaac D. "The Concept of Interest in Pluralist and Marxian Analysis." Politics & Society 1(1971): 151-77.

_____. "The Negation of the Negation: Theory of Capitalism Within and Historical Theory of Social Change." Politics & Society 3(1972): 49-63.

Bandyopadhyay, Pradeep. "One Sociology or Many: Some Issues in Radical Sociology." Sociological Review 19(1971): 5-30.

Barbalet, J. M. "Political Science, The State, and Marx." Politics 9(1974): 69-73.

Barnhart, J. E. "Anthropological Nature in Feuerbach and Marx." Philosophy Today 11(1967): 265-75.

Baron, Samuel H. "Marx's Grundrisse and the Asiatic Mode of Production." Survey 21(1975): 128-47. Reply by M. Sawer, pp. 223-4.

Bartlett, F. H. "Marx and Freud: Reply to J. Rapaport." Science & Society 5(1941): 376-86.

Bartlett, Francis H., and Shodell, James. "Fromm, Marx and Alienation." Science & Society 27(1963): 321-6.

Bash, Harry H. "Determinism and Avoidability in Socio-Historical Analysis." Ethics 74(1964): 186-200.

Bauman, Zygmunt. "Marx and the Contemporary Theory of Culture." Co-existence 5(1968): 161-71.

_____. "Marx and the Contemporary Theory of Culture." Social Science Information/Information sur les Sciences Sociales 7(1968): 19-34.

_____. "Modern Times Modern Marxism." Social Research 34(1967): 399-415.

Baumol, W. J. "The Transformation of Values: What Marx 'Really' Meant (An Interpretation)." Journal of Economic Literature 12(1974): 51-62.

_____. "Values vs. Prices: What Marx 'Really' Meant." American Economist 17(1973): 63-71.

Baumol, William J.; Morishima, Michio; and Samuelson, Paul A. "Colloquium: On Marx, the Transformation Problem and Opacity." Journal of Economic Literature 12(1974): 51-77.

Baylen, J. O. "Marx's Dispatches to Americans about Russia and the West, 1853-1856." South Atlantic Quarterly 56 (1957): 20-6.

Becker, James F. "Social Imbalance and the Marxian System." Kyklos 15(1962): 635-54.

Beitscher, Jane K., and Hunt, E. K. "Insights into the Dissolution of the Feudal Mode of Production: A Case Study of the Limousin." Science & Society 40(1976): 57-71.

Bell, Daniel. "One Road from Marx: On the Vision of Socialism, and the Fate of Workers' Control in Socialist Thought." World Politics 11(1959): 491-512.

_____. "The Rediscovery of Alienation: Some Notes Along the Quest for the Historical Marx." Journal of Philosophy 56(1959): 933-52.

Bell, David R. "Marx, Sartre, and Marxism." Manchester Literary and Philosophical Society, Memoirs and Proceedings 104(1961-62): 47-64.

Bell, S. "Ricardo and Marx." Journal of Political Economy 15(1907): 112-7.

Bendix, Reinhard. "Inequality and Social Structure: A Comparison of Marx and Weber." American Sociological Review 39(1974): 149-61.

_____. "Socialism and the Theory of Bureaucracy." Canadian Journal of Economics and Political Science 16 (1950): 501-14.

_____. "Social Stratification and the Political Community." Archives Européenes de Sociologie 1(1960): 181-212.

_____. "Tradition and Modernity Reconsidered." Comparative Studies in Society and History 9(1967): 292-346.

Bennett, F. A. Review of Philosophy of Art of Karl Marx, by M. Lifshits. Sociological Review 22(1974): 625-9.

Bense, M. "The Paris Manuscripts of Young Marx." Aussenpolitik 2(1951): 556-60.

Benson, J. Kenneth. "Theories of Stratification: A Comparison of Marx and Parsons." Proceedings of the Southwest Sociological Association 13(1963): 7-13.

Benson, Lee. "Group Cohesion and Social and Ideological Conflict: A Critique of Some Marxian and Tocquevillan Theories." American Behavioral Scientist 16(1973): 741-67.

Berdahl, Robert M. "New Thoughts on German Nationalism." American Historical Review 77(1972): 65-80.

Berdyaev, N. "Spiritual Dualism and Daily Bread." Translated by D. A. Lowrie. American Scholar 7(1938): 223-9.

Berger, M. "Engels' Theory of the Vanishing Army: A Key to the Development of Marxist Revolutionary Tactics." Historian 37(1975): 421-35.

Berki, R. N. "On Marxian Thought and the Problem of International Relations." World Politics 24(1971): 80-105.

Berland, Oscar. "Radical Chains: The Marxian Concept of Proletarian Mission." Studies on the Left 6 No. 5(1966): 27-51. Reply, pp. 51-60.

Bernard, L. L. "Higher Criticism of Karl Marx." Forum 49 (1913): 202-16.

Bernstein, Richard J. "The Challenge of Scientific Materialism." Iyyun 18(1967): 1-21.

Bernstein, S. "From Utopianism to Marxism." Science & Society 14(1950): 58-67.

Bernstein, S., ed. "Centenary of Marxism." Science & Society 12(1948): 1-196.

Bernstein, Samuel. "Marx in Paris, 1848; A Neglected Chapter." Science & Society 3(1939): 323-55.

Bestor, Arthur Eugene. "Evolution of the Socialist Vocabulary." Journal of the History of Ideas 9(1948): 259-302.

Beteille, Andre. "Class and Caste: A Rejoinder." Man in India 46(1966): 172-6.

Bhaduri, A. "On the Significance of Recent Controversies on Capital Theory: A Marxian View." Economic Journal 79 (1969): 532-9.

Bigo, P. "Enigma of Marxism." International Philosophy Quarterly 5(1965): 637-46.

Birnbaum, Norman. "Conflicting Interpretations of the Rise of Capitalism: Marx and Weber." British Journal of Sociology 4(1953): 125-41.

_____. "The Crisis in Marxist Sociology." Social Research 35(1968): 348-80.

_____. "The Idea of Industrial Society." Sociological Review Monograph 8(1964): 5-14.

Biswas, A. K. "On the Marxian Notion of Value." Arthaniti 2(1958): 1-22.

Bittelman, Alexander. "Frederich Engels." Political Affairs August 1950, pp. 51-65.

Bladen, V. W. "Centenary of Marx and Mill." Journal of Economic History Supplement 8(1948): 32-41.

Blake, J. "Political Economy of Labor." Science & Society 24(1960): 193-206.

Blake, William N. "Karl Marx's Concept of Education." Philosophy of Education: Proceedings 24(1965): 179-85.

Blakeley, Thomas J. "The Salient Features of the Marxist-Leninist Theory of Knowledge." Boston College Studies in Philosophy 1(1966): 155-74.

Blanchette, Oliva. "History and Nature in Karl Marx." Philosophical Forum (Boston) 2(Fall 1970): 24-35.

_____. "International Symposium on Marx and the Western World." International Philosophical Quarterly 7(1967): 129-37.

Blaug, M. "Technical Change and Marxian Economics." Kyklos 13(1960): 495-512.

Bloom, S. F. "Karl Marx and the Jews." Jewish Social Studies 4(1942): 3-16.

——————. "Man of His Century: A Reconsideration of the Historical Significance of Karl Marx." Journal of Political Economy 51(1943): 494-505.

——————. "The 'Withering Away' of the State." Journal of the History of Ideas 7(1946): 113-21.

Bloy, M. B. "Culture and Counter-Culture." Commonweal 89 (January 1969): 493-6.

Blum, Alan F. "Reading Marx." Sociological Inquiry 43 (1973): 23-34.

Bober, M. M. "Marx and Economic Calculation." American Economic Review 36(1946): 344-57.

——————. "Outline of Marxism." Education 60(1940): 410-5.

Boh, Ivan. "Marxist Dialectic and Formal Logic." Proceedings of the Catholic Philosophical Association 40(1966): 77-85.

Bonar, James. "Frederick Engels." Economic Journal 5 (1895): 490-2.

——————. "Frederick Engels." Quarterly Journal of Economics 10(1895): 95-7.

Borchert, D. M. "Marx and Christ: The Question of Violence." Christian Century 14 January 1974, pp. 65-9.

Borden, Morton. "Some Notes on Horace Greeley, Charles Dana and Karl Marx." Journalism Quarterly 34(1957): 457-65.

Borden, Morton, ed. "Five Letters of Charles A. Dana to Karl Marx." Journalism Quarterly 36(1959): 314-6.

Borkenau, Franz. "Marx's Prophecy in the Light of History: Balance Sheet after a Century." Commentary 7(1949): 430-6.

Bose, Arun. "Marx on Value, Capital, and Exploitation. History of Political Economy 3(1971): 298-334.

Bose, Nirmal Kumar. "Class and Caste." Man in India 45 (1965): 265-74.

Bosmajian, Haig A. "A Rhetorical Approach to the 'Communist Manifesto'." Dalhousie Review 43(1963): 457-68.

Bottomore, T. B. "The Ideas of the Founding Fathers." European Journal of Sociology 1(1960): 33-49.

———. "Karl Marx: Sociologist or Marxist?" Science & Society 30(1966): 11-24.

———. "Some Reflections on the Sociology of Knowledge: Marx." British Journal of Sociology 7(1956): 52-4.

Bowles, Robert E. "The Marxian Adaptation of the Ideology of Fourier." South Atlantic Quarterly 54(1955): 185-93.

Braverman, Harry. "Marx in the Modern World: New Issues in Socialist Economics." American Socialist 5(May 1958): 10-5.

Braybrooke, David. "Diagnosis andRemedy in Marx's Doctrine of Alienation." Social Research 25(1958): 325-45.

Brenkert, George G. "Schacht on Marx's Concept of Alienation." Studies in Soviet Thought 13(1973): 311-20.

Brewster, Ben. "Introduction to 'Notes on Machines'." Economy and Society 1(1972): 235-43.

Brogan, C. "Mill and Marx." National Review 1 March 1974, pp. 258-60.

Bronfenbrenner, Martin. "A Harder Look at Alienation." Ethics 83(1973): 267-82.

———. "'Das Kapital' for the Modern Man." Science & Society 29(1965): 419-38.

———. "Marx, Samuelson and Their Latest Critics." Journal of Economic Literature 11(1973): 58-63.

———. "Marxian Influences in 'Bourgeois' Economics." American Economic Review Papers and Proceedings 57 (1967): 624-35. Discussion by E. D. Domar, D. F. Gordon and H. S. Gordon, pp. 636-41.

———. "The Vicissitudes of Marxian Economics." History of Political Economy 2(1970): 205-24.

Brown, Bruce. "The French Revolution and the Rise of Social Theory." Science & Society 30(1966): 385-432.

Brown, W. J. "According to St. Marx." Spectator 178(1947): 711-2.

_____. "From Marx to Marriage." Spectator 180(1948): 367-8.

Buchanan, Scott. "Surplus Value." Virginia Quarterly Review 13(1937): 86-105.

Bullit, Margaret M. "Toward a Marxist Theory of Aesthetics: The Development of Socialist Realism in the Soviet Union." Russian Review 35(1976): 53-76.

Burgher, George. "Marxism and Normative Judgements." Science & Society 23(1959): 253-62.

Burns, C. D. "Karl Marx and Revolution." English Review 31(1920): 244-53.

Burrage, Michael. "Two Approaches to the Study of Mass Media." Archives Européenes de Sociologie 10(1969): 238-53.

Burrow, J. W. "The Many Faces of Karl Marx." Horizon 11 (Winter 1969): 52-7.

Cadogan, Peter. "Harney and Engels." International Review of Social History 10(1965): 66-104.

Campbell, R. W. "Marx, Kantorovich and Novozhilov: Stoimost vs. Reality." Slavic Review 20(1961): 402-18.

"Capital: Adam Smith, Karl Marx, and P. D. Leake." Chartered Accountant Students Society Joint Transactions 1932-1933, Published 1934, pp. 106-20.

"Capitalists and Workers." International Socialist Review 18(1917): 104-10.

Carlebach, Julius. "The Problem of Moses Hess's Influence on the Young Marx." Leo Baech Institute Yearbook 18 (1973): 27-40.

Carleton, W. G. "The Conservative Myth." Antioch Review 27(1967): 379-97.

Carritt, Edgar F. "A Discussion of Dialectical Materialism." Labour Monthly 15(1933): 324-29+.

Carroll, Michael P. "Engels on the Subjugation of Women: Some Cross-Cultural Tests." Pacific Sociological Review 18(1975): 223-41.

Carver, Terrell. "Marx and Hegel's Logic." Political Studies 24(1976): 57-68.

_____. "Marx's Commodity Fetishism." <u>Inquiry</u> 18(1975): 39-63.

Carver, T., and Thomas, P., eds. "Marx and Marx Studies." <u>Political Studies</u> 24(1976): 1-102.

Catephores, G. "Marxian Alienation - A Clarification." <u>Oxford Economic Papers</u> 24(1972): 124-36.

Caton, Hiram. "Marx's Sublation of Philosophy into Praxis." <u>Review of Metaphysics</u> 26(1972): 233-59.

"Centenary of Marx's Capital." <u>Science & Society</u> 31(1967): 385-540.

Chaloner, W. H., and Henderson, W. O. "Marx/Engels and Racism." <u>Encounter</u> 45(July 1975): 18-23.

Chamberlain, Gary Lee. "The Man Marx Made." <u>Science & Society</u> 27(1963): 302-20.

Chamberlin, W. H. "Karl Marx, the False Prophet." <u>American Mercury</u> 46(January 1939): 60-8.

Chang, Te-Chun. "On Whether There is Identity between Erroneous Thinking and Existence." <u>Chinese Studies in Philosophy</u> 3(1972): 336-75.

Chappell, John E. "Marxism and Geography." <u>Problems of Communism</u> 14(November-December 1965): 12-22.

"The Chartist Movement." <u>Labour Monthly</u> 11(1929): 721-30.

Child, Arthur. "The Concept of Class Interest." <u>Ethics</u> 80 (1970): 279-95.

Christiansen, Jens. "Marx and the Falling Rate of Profit." <u>American Economic Review</u> 66 No. 2(1976): 20-6.

Ciolkosz, Adam. "Karl Marx and the Polish Insurrection of 1863." <u>Polish Review</u> 10 No. 4(1965): 8-51.

Clarke, J. J. "The End of History: A Reappraisal of Marx's Views on Alienation and Human Emancipation." <u>Canadian Journal of Political Science</u> 4(1971): 367-80.

Clifford-Vaughan, M. "Social Change and Legal Norms." <u>Proceedings of the Aristotelian Society</u> 67(1966-67): 103-10.

Cohen, Gerald A. "Bourgeois and Proletarians." <u>Journal of the History of Ideas</u> 29(1968): 211-30.

_____. "Karl Marx and the Withering Away of Social Science." Philosophy & Public Affairs 1(1972): 182-203.

_____. "Marx's Dialectic of Labor." Philosophy & Public Affairs 3(1974): 235-61.

_____. "On Some Criticisms of Historical Materialism." Aristotelian Society: Supplement 44(1970): 121-42.

_____. "The Workers and the Word: Why Marx Had the Right to Think He Was Right." Praxis 4(1968): 376-90.

Cohen, Morris. "Causation and its Application to History." Journal of the History of Ideas 3(1942): 12-29.

Cohn, E. "Engels Formula for Estimating the Costs of Producing an Individual: A Note." Journal of Political Economy 78(1970): 778-82.

"Cola di Rienzi by Frederick Engels: The Discovery of a Previously Unknown Manuscript." Encounter 43(November 1974): 61-5.

Cole, G. D. H. "What Has Happened to Marxism?" New Republic 17 March 1952, pp. 13-5; 24 March 1952, pp. 9-11. Discussion 31 March 1952, pp. 2+.

Coleman, James; Mouledous, Joseph C.; and Mouledous, Elizabeth C. "Implications of the Findings of Alienation, Criticism of the Concept of Alienation and Reply." American Journal of Sociology 70(1964): 82-4.

Collinet, Michel. "The Idea of Progress in the Nineteenth Century." Diogenes 33(1961): 98-116.

Collins, Henry. "Karl Marx, the International and the British Trade Union Movement." Science & Society 26(1962): 400-21.

Collins, Kins. "Marx on the English Agricultural Revolution: Theory and Evidence." History and Theory 6(1967): 351-81.

Colp, Ralph, Jr. "The Contacts between Karl Marx and Charles Darwin." Journal of the History of Ideas 35(1974): 329-38.

Combellack, C. R. S. "Two Critics of Society, (Marx and Thoreau)." Pacific Spectator 3(1949): 440-5.

"Comment: Marx on Russia." 20th Century 151(1952): 470-2.

Commons, J. R. "Karl Marx and Samuel Gompers." Political Science Quarterly 41(1926): 281-6.

_____. "Marx Today: Capitalism and Socialism." Atlantic 136(1925): 682-93.

Comstock, R. "Marxist Critique of Religion: A Persisting Ambiguity." American Academy of Religion, Journal 44 (1976): 327-42.

Comyn, Marian. "My Recollections of Karl Marx." 19th Century and After 91(1922): 161-9.

Conklin, F. "Some Aspects of the Marxian Philosophy of God." New Scholasticism 28(1954): 38-57.

Cooper, B. "Recent Studies on Marx." Political Science Reviewer 2(Fall 1972): 185-216.

Copleston, Frederick C. "Words and Marx." Heythrop Journal 9(1968): 5-16.

Cork, Jim. "John Dewey, Karl Marx, and Democratic Socialism." Antioch Review 9(1949): 435-52.

Cornforth, Maurice. "Thinking with Marx." Heythrop Journal 10(1969): 180-6.

Coser, Lewis A. "Marxist Thought in the First Quarter of the 20th Century." American Journal of Sociology 78(1972): 173-201.

Cousins, J. M. "Some Problems in the Concept of the "Proletariat'." Mens en Maatschappij 46(1971): 198-224.

Cowley, M. "Footnotes to the Life of Marx." New Republic 26 February 1936, pp. 79-80.

Coyne, E. J. "Karl Marx, 1818-1883." Studies 22 March 1933, pp. 113-28.

Cramer, F. H. "Definitions of Freedom: Marx vs. Schopenhauer." Forum 112(October 1949): 193-9.

Cranston, M. "The Ideology of Althusser." Problems of Communism 22(March-April 1973): 53-63.

Crocker, Lawrence. "Marx's Concept of Exploitation." Social Theory and Practice 2(1972): 201-15.

Crosby, John F. "Evolutionism and the Ontology of the Human Person: Critique of the Marxist Theory of the Emergence of Man." Review of Politics 38(1976): 208-43.

Cross, Truman B. "Young Marx, Marxism: Viktor Chernov's Use of 'The Theses of Feuerbach'." Journal of the History of Ideas 32(1971): 600-6.

Csiksentmihalyi, Mihaly. "Marx: A Socio-Psychological Evaluation." Modern Age 11(1967): 272-82.

Cunningham, Frank. "Practice and Some Muddles about the Methodology of Historical Materialism." Canadian Journal of Philosophy 3(1973): 235-48.

Daley, H. E. "A Marxian-Malthusian View of Poverty and Development." Population Studies 25(1971): 25-37.

Danielou, J. "Marxist History and Sacred History." Review of Politics 13(1951): 503-13.

Daniels, Robert Vincent. "Fate and Will in the Marxian Philosophy of History." Journal of the History of Ideas 21(1960): 538-52.

"Das Kapital: A Centenary Appreciation." American Economic Review 57(1967): 597-641.

Davies, J. C. "A Note on Political Motivation." Western Political Quarterly 12(1959): 410-6.

Davis, D. E. "Marxism and People's Wars." Orbis 15(1972): 1194-205.

Davis, Horace B. "Imperialism and Labor: An Analysis of Marxian Views." Science & Society 26(1962): 26-45.

_____. "Nations, Colonies and Social Classes: The Position of Marx and Engels." Science & Society 29(1965): 26-43.

Davis, J. C. "Utopia and History." Historical Studies 13 (1968): 165-76.

Dawson, G. W. "Man in the Marxian Kingdom of Freedom: A Critique." Archiv für Rechts - und Sozial-philosophie 59 (1973): 357-73.

Daya. "Surplus Value, Profit and Exploitation. An Attempt at an Analysis of Some Concepts in Marxian Economy." Review of Economic Studies 22(1954-55): 96-108.

de Brunhoff, Suzanne. "Controversies in the Theory of Surplus Value: A Reply to John Eatwell." Science & Society 38(1974-75): 478-81. Comment by David Laibman, pp. 482+.

De Gorge, Richard T. "Read Marx Instead." Problems of Communism 22(January-February 1973): 72-3.

De'Jouvenel, Bertrand. "The Crisis of the Communist Mind." Orbis 1(1957: 77-96.

Delgado, L. "The Materialist Conception of Economics." Aryan Path 26 No. 7(1955): 297-301.

Della Volpe, G. "The Marxist Critique of Rousseau." New Left Review 59(1970): 101-9.

Demaitre, Edmund. "Man and God in Marx." Problems of Communism 19(November 1970): 49-53.

_____. "The New Marxism of the West." Communist Affairs 5(November-December 1967): 3-9.

_____. "The Origins of National Communism." Studies in Comparative Communism 2(1969): 1-20.

_____. "Wonders of Marxology." Problems of Communism 15(July 1966): 29-35.

de Schweintz, Karl, Jr. "On the Determinism of the Marxian System." Social Research 29(1962): 37-49.

De Sola Pool, I. "Some Facts about Values." P.S. (Newsletter, American Political Science Association) 3(1970): 102-6.

Deutscher, Issac, et al. "Marxism and Non-violence." Liberation 14(July 1969): 10-6.

de Weerd, Hans. "Karl Marx on Russian Policy." Ukrainian Review 3 No. 2(1956): 19-24.

Dewey, E. W., and Miller, D. L. "Veblen's Materialism versus Marxian Materialism." Southwestern Social Science Quarterly 35(September 1954): 165-74.

Dewey, John. "Karl Marx and Democratic Socialism." Antioch Review 9(1949): 435-52.

Dickinson, H. D. "The Falling Rate of Profit in Marxian Economics." Review of Economic Studies 24(February 1957): 120-30.

Diggins, John P. "Getting Hegel out of History: Max Eastman's Quarrel with Marxism." American Historical Review 79(1974): 38-71.

_____. "Thoreau, Marx, and the 'Riddle' of Alienation." Social Research 39(1972): 571-98.

Dirscherl, D. A. "Karl Marx's Critique of God." American Benedictine Review 16(1965): 210-8.

Djilas, M. "On Alienation: Thoughts on a Marxist Myth." Encounter 36(May 1971): 8-15.

Dobb, Maurice. "Marx on Pre-Capitalist Economic Formations." Science & Society 30(1966): 319-25.

_____. "Marx's Capital and its Place in Economic Thought." Science & Society 31(1967): 527-40.

Dobriansky, Lev E. "Marx and the Prison House of Nations." Ukrainian Quarterly 19(1963): 227-36.

Doherty, John F. "Karl Marx: Seed of the Prophets." Philippine Studies 9(1961): 611-26.

_____. "Marx and the Sociology of Chance." Philippine Studies 11(1963): 536-47.

Domhoff, G. W. "Historical Materialism, Cultural Determinism, and the Origin of the Ruling Class." Psychoanalytic Review 56(1969): 271-87.

Doniela, W. V. "Dialectic: An Introduction." Politics 9 No. 11(1974): 74-82.

Dos Santos, Theotonio. "The Concept of Social Classes." Science & Society 34(1970): 166-93.

Dotson, Floyd. "Marx and Engels on the Family: Retrospect with a Moral." American Sociologist 9 No. 4(1974): 181-6.

Douglas, P. H. "Karl Marx the Prophet." World Tomorrow 15 March 1933, pp. 225-7.

Dozier, H. D. "Henry Ford and Karl Marx." Atlantic 147 (March 1931): 288-95.

Dreyer, J. S. "Evolution of Marxist Attitude Toward Marginalist Technique." History of Political Economy 6(1974): 48-75. Reply by F. D. Wolff, 7(1975): 270-2.

Drobnitskii, O. G. "Marxist Philosophy and the Problem of Value." Soviet Studies in Philosophy 5(Spring 1967): 14-24.

Drucker, H. M. "The Marx Industry Today." Political Studies 21(1973): 385-7.

_____. "Marx's Concept of Ideology." Philosophy 47 (1972): 152-61.

Duffield, J. "The Value Concept in Capital in Light of Recent Criticism." Science & Society 34(1970): 293-302. Reply by D. C. Hodges, pp. 342-6.

Duffy, A. E. P. "The Eight Hour Day Movement in Britain, 1836-1893." Manchester School of Economic and Social Studies 36(1968): 203-22.

Dunayevskaya, Raya. "A New Revision of Marxian Economics." American Economic Review 34(1944): 531-7.

Dunham, Barrows. "On Teaching Marxist Epistemology." Philosophy of Science 29(1962): 365-8.

Dunman, J. "Marxist and Christian Concept of Man." Science & Society 32(1968): 278-87.

Dupré, Louis. "Dialectical Philosophy Before and After Marx." New Scholasticism 46(1972): 488-511.

_____. "Recent Literature on Marx and Marxism." Journal of the History of Ideas 35(1974): 703-14.

_____. Review of For Marx, by L. Althusser and Reading Capital, by E. Balibar. Commonweal 10 December 1971, pp. 260-2.

Dupré, L., and Page, B. "Marx and Religion." Commonweal 26 April 1968, pp. 171-80.

Dutt, R. P. "Karl Marx: 1818-1883." Labour Monthly 15 (1933): 133-62.

_____. "Marxism in Caricature." Review of What Marx Really Meant by G. D. H. Cole and Karl Marx: A Study in Fanaticism by E. H. Carr. Labour Monthly 16(1934): 432-9.

_____. "Note on the Falsification of Engels' Preface to Marx's Class Struggle in France." Labour Monthly 15 (1933): 771-7.

Dvorkin, I. "Karl Marx: The 120th Anniversary of Marx's Birth." Illustrated Sovietland May 1938, pp. 2-5+.

Dworkin, Gerald. "Marx and Mill: A Dialogue." Philosophy and Phenomenological Research 26(1966): 403-14.

Dyer, Phillip W. "The Conception of the State in the Philosophy of Marx and Engels." Journal of Thought 7 (1972): 147-55.

Eames, S. Morris. "Social Planning and Individual Freedom." Praxis 4(1968): 59-72.

Eastman, L. "Mao, Marx, and the Future Society." Problems of Communism 18(May-June 1969): 21-6.

Eastman, M. "Against the Marxian Dialectic." New Republic 21 February 1934, pp. 35-9. Discussion, 28 February 1934, pp. 63-7 and 28 March 1934, pp. 188+.

Easton, Loyd D. "Alienation and Empiricism in Marx's Thought." Social Research 37(1970): 402-27.

_____. "Alienation and History in the Early Marx." Philosophy and Phenomenological Research 22(1961): 193-205.

_____. "August Willich, Marx and Left-Hegelian Socialism." Cahiers de l'Institute de Science Economique Applique Serie S 10(1965): 101-37.

_____. Review of The Social and Political Thought of Karl Marx, by S. Avineri. Commentary 46(November 1968): 114-6.

Eatwell, John. "Controversies in the Theory of Surplus Value: Old and New." Science & Society 38(1974): 281-303. Discussion, pp. 478-87.

Eckstein, Paul. "On Karl Marx and Max Weber." Science & Society 34(1970): 346-8.

Elias, Norbert. "Sociology of Knowledge: New Perspectives." Sociology 5(1971): 149-68.

Elliott, C. F. "The Populist and the Legal Marxist: Another View." Australian Journal of Politics and History 11 (1965): 163-9.

_____. "'Qui Custodiet Sacra?' Problems of Marxist Revisionism." Journal of the History of Ideas 28(1967): 71-86.

Elliott, John E. "Marx and Contemporary Models of Socialist Economy." History of Political Economy 8(1976): 151-84.

_____. "Professor Robert's Marx: On Alienation and Economic Systems." Journal of Economic Issues 9(1975): 471-500. Reply and rejoinder, pp. 530-42.

Elliott, W. Y. "Modern State: Karl Marx and Mr. Laski." Southern Review 1(1935): 209-20.

Ellis, T. L., Jr. "Marx and Deutsch on Value." Southern Atlantic Quarterly 72(1973): 131-42.

Ellwood, C. A. "Marx's Economic Determinism in Light of Modern Psychology." American Journal of Sociology 17 (1911): 35-46.

Ensor, R. C. K. "What Marxism Is." Spectator 5 May 1933, pp. 636-7.

Erlich, A. "Notes on Marxian Model of Capital Accumulation." American Economic Review Papers and Proceedings 57(1967): 599-615, 636-41.

Eubanks, Cecil L. "The Marxist's Theory of Knowledge: Preliminary Thoughts on a Functional Interpretation." LSU Journal of Sociology 1 No. 1(1971): 58-73.

Evans, Charles. "A New Philosophical Interpretation of Marx." Social Research 40(1973): 177-91.

Evans, Michael. "Marx Studies." Political Studies 18(1970): 528-35.

_____. "More Marx Studies." Political Studies 22(1974): 218-23.

_____. "Two Translations of Marx." Government and Opposition 7(1972): 243-7.

Evenitsky, A. "Marx's Model of Expanded Reproduction." Science & Society 27(1963): 159-75.

_____. "Monopoly Capitalism and Marx's Economic Doctrines." Science & Society 24(1960): 134-49.

Ewing, C. "De Maistre and Marx in the Modern World." Southwestern Social Science Quarterly 29(June 1948): 1-14.

Falk, Heinrich. "Can Spirit Come from Matter." International Philosophical Quarterly 7(1967): 541-55.

Fallenbuchl, Z. M. "The Communist Revolutions and Marx's Theory of Historical Development." University of Windsor Review 1(1965): 208-20.

Fan-Hung. "Keynes and Marx on the Theory of Capital Accumulation, Money, and Interest." Review of Economic Studies 7(October 1939): 28-41.

Fedorov, E. K., and Novik, I. B. "Man and His Natural Environment." Soviet Studies in Philosophy 12(Fall 1973): 3-24.

Feenberg, A. "Lukacs and the Critique of 'Orthodox' Marxism." Philosophical Forum 3(1972): 422-67.

_____. "Marxist Theory and Socialist Society: A Dilemma."
Newsletter on Comparative Studies of Communism 6 No. 3
(1973): 2-31.

Fellner, William. "Marxian Hypotheses and Observable Trends
Under Capitalism: A 'Modernised' Interpretation."
Economic Journal 67 No. 265(1957): 16-25.

Ferraro, Joseph W. "Marxism and Thomism: Some Reflections
on the Basis for a Dialogue." International Philosophical
Quarterly 10(March 1970): 75-101.

Fetscher, Irving. "Karl Marx on Human Nature." Social Research 40(1973): 443-67.

_____. "New Tendencies in Marxist Philosophy." East
Europe 16(May 1967): 9-14.

Feuer, Lewis S. "The Conversion of Karl Marx's Father."
Jewish Journal of Sociology 14 No. 2(1972): 149-66.

_____. "The Influence of the American Communist Colonies
on Engels and Marx." Western Political Quarterly 19
(1966): 456-74.

_____. "Is the 'Darwin-Marx Correspondence' Authentic?"
Annals of Science 32 No. 1(1975): 1-12.

_____. "John Stuart Mill and Marxian Socialism." Journal
of the History of Ideas 10(1949): 297-304.

_____. "Karl Marx and the Promethean Complex." Encounter
31 No. 183(1968): 15-32.

_____. "The New Marxism of the Intellectuals." New
Leader 51(November 1968): 7-11.

_____. "The North American Origin of Marx's Socialism."
Western Political Quarterly 16(1963): 53-67.

_____. "Ralph Waldo Emerson's Reference to Karl Marx."
New England Quarterly 33(1960): 378-9.

_____. "The Social Roots of Einstein's Theory of Relativity." Annals of Science 27 No. 3(1971): 277-98.

Fichter, Joseph H. "Marx Evaluates Labor." Commonweal 26
May 1939, pp. 118-20.

Fiorenza, Francis P. "Dialectical Theology and Hope, III."
Heythrop Journal 10(1969): 26-42.

Firth, Raymond. "The Sceptical Anthropologist? Social Anthropology and Marxist Views on Society." Proceedings of the British Academy 58(1972): 177-214.

Fletcher, John G. "Spengler, Marx, and Keyserling: Three Visions of History." Living Age 15 October 1927, pp. 723-7.

Foner, Philip S. "Marx's Capital in the United States." Science & Society 31(1967): 461-6.

_____. "Two Neglected Interviews with Karl Marx." Science & Society 36(1972): 3-28.

Foner, Philip S., ed. "Samuel Gompers to Frederick Engels: A Letter." Labor History 11(Spring 1970): 207-11.

Foster, W. Z. "Marxism and the American Working Class." Political Affairs 32 No. 10(1953): 1-19.

Frank, J. "Economic Basis of Liberal Values: Review of Marxism, An Autopsy, by H. B. Parker." Southern Review 7(1941): 21-39.

Franklin, Mitchell. "On Hegel's Theory of Alienation and its Historic Force." Tulane Studies in Philosophy 9 (1960): 50-100.

Fraser, John. "Marxists and Intellectuals." Science & Society 35(1971): 257-85.

Freistadt, Hans. "Dialectical Materialism: A Friendly Interpretation." Philosophy of Science 23(1956): 97-110.

Friedman, Daniel J. "Marx's Perspective on the Objective Class Structure." Polity 6(1974): 318-44.

Friedman, J. "Marxism, Structuralism, and Vulgar Materialism." Man 9(1974): 444-69.

Friesen, Abraham. "The Marxist Interpretation of the Reformation." Archiv für Reformationsgeschichte 64 (1973): 34-55.

"From Marx to Khrushchev." British Survey 186(1964): 10-20.

Fromm, Erich. "Marx's Contribution to the Knowledge of Man.' Praxis 5(1969): 55-64.

_____. "Marx's Contribution to the Knowledge of Man." Social Science Information/Information sur les Sciences Sociales 7 No. 3(1968): 7-18.

Fuller, F. E. "The Moral Challenge of the Communist Manifesto." _American Scholar_ 17 No. 1(1948): 11-7.

Furnberg, F. "The Doctrine of Marx is All-Powerful." _Communist International_ 15(1938): 557-9.

Gagern, Michael. "The Puzzling Pattern of the Marxist Critique of Feuerbach." _Studies in Soviet Thought_ 11 (1971): 135-58.

Gandhi, Madan G. "Marx and the Search for Humanism." _Political Science Review_ 14(1975): 65-76.

Ganguli, B. N. "Karl Marx on Quesnay." _Indian Economic Review_ 7 No. 2(1972): 129-69.

Gardis, R. "Marxism and Religion, Are They Compatible?" _Menorah Journal_ 25(1937): 20-32.

Gauber, H. R. "Darwin and _Das Kapital_." _Isis_ 52(1961): 582+.

Geltman, M. "Little Known Chapter in American History: Column for Horace Greeley's Tribune." _National Review_ 5 October 1965, pp. 865-7.

Gerratana, Valentino. "Marx and Darwin." _New Left Review_ 82(1973): 60-82.

Geymonat, Ludovico. "Neopositivist Methodology and Dialectical Materialism." _Science & Society_ 37(1973): 178-94.

Giddens, Anthony. "Marx, Weber, and the Development of Capitalism." _Sociology_ 4(1970): 289-310.

Gilbert, Alan. "Avineri's Marx: An Exchange Salvaging Marx from Avineri." _Political Theory_ 4(1976): 9-34.

Gilbert, F. "Intellectual History: Its Aims and Methods." _Daedalus_ 100(Winter 1971): 80-97.

Gilman, Stuart, and Saeger, Richard. "Marx and the Religious: The Gnostic Perspective." _Philosophy Today_ 17 (1973): 12-20.

Girardin, J. C. "On the Marxist Theory of the State." _Politics & Society_ 4 No. 2(1974): 193-224.

Glass, James M. "Marx, Kafka and Jung: The Appearance of Species-Being." _Politics & Society_ 2 No. 2(1972): 255-71.

_____. "The Philosopher and the Shaman: The Political Vision as Incantation." _Political Theory_ 2(1974): 181-96.

_____. "Plato, Marx, and Freud: The Vision of Eros and Transcendance." Psychiatry 37(1974): 147-57.

Glichsberg, C. I. "The Decline of Literary Marxism." Antioch Review 1(1941): 452-62.

Glinskaja, Alicia. "Ethical Questions in the First Volume of Karl Marx's Das Kapital." Studia Filosofia 4(1970): 47-60.

Goldway, David. "Appearance and Reality in Marx's Capital." Science & Society 31(1967): 428-47.

Gollin, G. "The Sociology of Saint-Simon: Monument or Steping-stone?" Journal of the History of the Behavioral Sciences 6(1970): 188-96.

Gollin, Gillian Lindt. "Theories of the Good Society: Four Views on Religion and Social Change." Journal for the Scientific Study of Religion 9(1970): 1-16.

Gordon, Bertram M. "Two Modern Movements and Revolution: Fascism and Marxism -- A Comparison." Duquesne Review 18(Spring 1973): 3-18.

Gordon, D. F. "What Was the Labor Theory of Value?" American Economic Review Papers and Proceedings 49(1959): 462-72.

Gordon, S. "Why Does Marxian Exploitation Theory Require a Labor Theory of Value?" Journal of Political Economy 76 (1968): 137-40.

Goth, William. "The Marx Chamberlain Made." Science & Society 28(1964): 208-13.

Gottheil, Fred M. "Increasing Misery of the Proletariat: An Analysis of Marx's Wage and Employment Theory." Canadian Journal of Economics and Political Science 28 (1962): 103-13.

Gough, I. "Marx's Theory of Productive and Unproductive Labour." New Left Review 76(1972): 47-72.

Gouldner, Alvin W. "Marxism and Social Theory." Theory and Society 1(1974): 17-35.

_____. "The Metaphoricality of Marxism and the Context-freeing Grammer of Socialism." Theory and Society 1 (1974): 387-414.

_____. "Romanticism and Classicism: Deep Structures in Social Science." Diogenes 82(1973): 88-107.

Gouthier, David P. "The Philosophy of Revolution." University of Toronto Quarterly 32(1963): 126-41.

Green, Andre'. "Sexuality and Ideology in Marx and Freud." Human Context 6(1974): 362-84.

Greenbaum, Fred. "John Dewey Views Karl Marx." Social Science 42 No. 4(1967): 195-204.

Greenberg, L. M. "The Commune of 1871 as a Decentralist Reaction." Journal of Modern History 41(1969): 304-18.

Greenleaf, R. "History, Marxism, and Henry Adams." Science & Society 15(1951): 193-208.

Greenspan, Stanley P. "Some Theoretical Contributions Made by Marx, Weber, and Durkheim to the Field of Industrial Sociology." Journal of Educational Sociology 36(1963): 213-8.

Gregor, A. James. "Classical Marxism and the Totalitarian Ethic." Journal of Value Inquiry 2(1968): 58-72.

_____. "Giovanni Gentile and the Philosophy of the Young Karl Marx." Journal of the History of Ideas 24(1963): 213-30.

_____. "The Impact of Darwinism on the Materialist Conception of History." Revue Internationale de Sociologie 3(December 1967): 74-89.

_____. "Marx, Feuerbach and the Reform of the Hegelian Dialectic." Science & Society 29(1965): 66-80.

_____. "Marxism and Ethics: A Methodological Inquiry." Philosophy and Phenomenological Research 28(1968): 368-84.

Grimes, C. E., and Simmons, C. E. D. "A Re-assessment of Alienation in Karl Marx." Western Political Quarterly 23 (1970): 266-75.

Grosshans, Henry. "Mazzini, Marx, and'the Paris Commune." Research Studies 31 No. 4(1963): 141-56.

Grossman, H. "Evolutionist Revolt Against Classical Economics." Journal of Political Economy 51(1943): 506-22.

Groves, R. "Marx and the Labour Parliament of 1854." Labour Monthly 12(1930): 172-6.

Gruenwald, Oskar. "Marxist Humanism." Orbis 18(1974): 888-916.

Grunberg, Ludwig. "Value-Revaluation and the Axiological Perspective in Philosophy." Journal of Value Inquiry 3 (Summer 1969): 100-12.

Guendling, J. E. "Dialectics of Nature, A Quest for Empirical Status." Southern Journal of Philosophy 5 (Winter 1967): 238-52.

Gupta, K. C. "Marxist Dialectics." Calcutta Review 128 (August 1953): 157-63.

Gurian, Waldemar. "The Communist Manifesto: A Hundred Years After." Commonweal 10 September 1948, pp. 516-9.

Gustafsson, Bo G. "Friedrich Engels and the Historical Role of Ideologies." Science & Society 30 (1966): 257-74.

_____. "Rostow, Marx, and the Theory of Economic Growth." Science & Society 25 (1961): 229-44.

Guthrie, E. F. "Historical Materialism and its Sociological Critics." Social Forces 29 (1941): 172-84.

Habermas, Jürgen. "The Place of Philosophy in Marxism." Insurgent Sociologist 5 No. 2 (1975): 41-8.

Hacker, Helen Mayer. "Marx, Weber and Pareto on the Changing Status of Women." American Journal of Economics and Sociology 12 (1953): 149-62.

Hacker, L. M. "Mistakes of Karl Marx." Vital Speeches 21 (1955): 1140-4.

Haenisch, Walter. "Karl Marx and the Democratic Association of 1847." Science & Society 2 (1937): 83-102.

Hager, K. "Marx's Theoretical Predictions and Our Time." World Marxist Review 18 (March 1975): 91-9.

Hahn, F. "The Winter of Our Discontent." Economica 40 (1973): 322-30.

Haines, H. "Politics and Protest: Hegel and Social Criticism." Political Science Quarterly 86 (1971): 406-28.

Haldane, J. B. S. "Engels." Labour Monthly 27 (1945): 235-6.

Hale, W. H. "When Karl Marx Worked for Horace Greeley." American Heritage 8 (April 1957): 20-5+.

Hall, B. "Another View of Marx: A Closer Look at Bakuninism." New Politics 7 (Winter 1968): 78-85.

Halle, L. J. "Marx: His Death and Resurrection." Encounter 34(January 1970): 75-9.

———. "Marx's Religious Drama." Encounter 25(October 1965): 29-37.

Hallett, John. "Karl Marx: 50 Years After." Fortune 139 (1933): 311-21.

Hammen, Oscar J. "Alienation, Communism and Revolution in the Marx-Engels 'Briefwechsel'." Journal of the History of Ideas 33(1972): 77-100.

———. "Capitalizing on Das Kapital." South Atlantic Quarterly 60(Winter 1961): 19-28.

———. "Marx and the Agrarian Question." American Historical Review 77(1972): 679-704. Reply with rejoinder 78(1973): 194-6.

———. "Spectre of Communism in the 1840's." Journal of the History of Ideas 14(1953): 404-20.

———. "The Young Marx, Reconsidered." Journal of the History of Ideas 31(1970): 109-20.

Hampsch, George H. "Dignity, Social Power and Classless Society." Philosophy Forum (Dekalb) 10(December 1971): 277-91.

———. "The Marxist Notion of Social Class." Duquesne Review 9 No. 1(1963): 25-42.

Hancock, Roger N. "Marx's Theory of Justice." Social Theory and Practice 1(Spring 1971): 65-72.

Hansen, A. H. "The Technological Interpretation of History." Quarterly Journal of Economics 36(1921-22): 78-83.

Hare, P. G. "Skilled Labour in the Marxist System: A Comment." Bulletin of the Conference of Socialist Economists 9(Autumn 1974): 1-3.

Harley, J. H. "New Social Democracy and Marx." Contemporary 80(1901): 723-33.

Harrington, Michael. "Marx Who?" Review of The Marxian Revolutionary Idea, by R. C. Tucker. New Republic 26 July 1969, pp. 29-31.

Harris, Abram L. "Economic Evolution: Dialectical and Darwinian." Journal of Political Economy 42(1934): 34-79.

_____. "John Stuart Mill's Theory of Progress." (Compared to Marx) Ethics 66 No. 3(1956): 157-75.

_____. "Pure Capitalism and the Disappearance of the Middle Class." Journal of Political Economy 47(1939): 328-56.

_____. "The Social Philosophy of Karl Marx." Ethics 58 No. 3 Pt. 2(1948): 42 p.

_____. "Utopian Elements in Marx's Thought." Ethics 60 No. 2(1950): 79-99.

Harris, Donald J. "On Marx's Scheme of Reproduction and Accumulation." Journal of Political Economy 80(1972): 505-22.

Harris, J. A. "A Marxist Approach to the Labor Theory of Value." Science & Society 35(1971): 339-43.

Harris, John. "The Marxist Conception of Violence." Philosophy & Public Affairs 3(1974): 192-220.

Harrison, A. "Marx and Materialism, Reply to Hyndman and Bax." English Review 19(1915): 216-24.

Harrison, Royden. "E. S. Beesly and Karl Marx." International Review of Social History 4(1959): 208-38.

_____. "Marx, Engels and the British Response to the Commune." Massachusetts Review 12(1971): 463-77.

Harrison, Royden, and Abramsky, Chemin. "'The Man of Earthquakes': A Neglected Interview with Karl Marx." Bulletin of the Society for the Study of Labour History 12(1966): 21-5.

Hartmann, Klaus. "Praxis: A Ground for Social Theory." Journal of the British Society for Phenomenology 1(May 1970): 47-58.

Harvey, David. "Population, Resources, and the Ideology of Science." Economic Geography 50(1974): 256-77.

Haupt, Heinz-Gerhard, and Leibfried, Stephen. "Marxian Analysis of Politics or Theory of Social Change?: Toward a Marxian Theory of the Political Domain." Politics & Society 3 No. 1(1972): 33-48.

Hawton, Hector. "Marxism and Humanism." Humanist 31(1971): 19-20.

Hay, J. M., and Jackson, T. A. "A Discussion of Dialectical Materialism." Labour Monthly 15(1933): 503-11.

Hazelrigg, Lawrence E. "Class Property, and Authority: Dahrendorf's Critique of Marx's Theory of Class." Social Forces 50(1972): 473-86.

Heilbroner, Robert L. "Do Machines Make History?" Technology and Culture 8(1967): 335-45.

_____. "Marxism, Psychoanalysis and the Problem of a Unified Theory of Behavior." Social Research 42(1975): 414-32.

Heimann, Eduard. "Atheist Theocracy." Social Research 20 (1953): 311-31.

_____. "Marxism and Underdeveloped Countries." Social Research 19(1952): 322-45.

_____. "Marxism: 1848 and 1948." Journal of Politics 11 (1959): 523-31.

_____. "What Marx Means Today." Social Research 4(1937): 33-51.

Heinen, H. D. "Cultural Materialism, Marx, and the Hegelian Monkey." Current Anthropology 16(1975): 450-6.

Henchy, James A. "The Communist Theory of Law." Studies 46 (1957): 411-20.

Hellerich, G. "Some Educational Implications of Karl Marx's Communism." Educational Forum 34(1970): 471-8.

Henderson, W. O., and Chaloner, W. H. "Friederich Engels and the England of the 1840's." History Today 6(1956): 448-56. Discussion pp. 616+, 855.

Henry, Michel. "Introduction to the Thought of Marx." Philosophy Today 15(1971): 186-203.

_____. "Productive Forces and Subjectivity: Socialism as Marx Saw It." Translated by S. Pleasance. Diogenes 88 (1974): 77-99.

Herberg, W. Review of Marxism: The Unity of Theory and Practice, by A. G. Meyer. Commonweal 4 February 1955, pp. 482-4.

Hernandez, Angel. "The Development of Marx's Economic Thought." New Left Review 72(1972): 93-104. Reply by E. Mandel, pp. 104-8.

Hershlag, Z. Y. "Theory of Stages of Economic Growth in Historical Perspective." Kyklos 22(1969): 661-87.

Hill, C. "English Civil War Interpreted by Marx and Engels." Science & Society 12(1948): 130-56.

Hinners, Richard. "The Ideological Turn and Its Problem for the History of Philosophy." Proceedings of the American Catholic Philosophical Association 43(1969): 130-8.

Hirst, Paul Q. "Marx and Engels on Law, Crime and Morality." Economy and Society 1(1972): 28-56.

Hirszowicz, M. "Marxist Approach." International Social Science Journal 18(1966): 11-21.

Hobsbawn, Eric J. "Karl Marx's Contribution to Historiography." Diogenes 64(1968): 37-56.

Hochfeld, Julian. "The Concept of Class Interest." Polish Sociological Bulletin 16(1967): 5-14.

Hodgen, M. T. "Karl Marx and the Social Scientists." Scientific Monthly 72(April 1951): 252-8.

Hodges, Donald Clark. "Anatomy of Exploitation." Science & Society 24(1960): 228-45. Erratum, p. 360.

_____. "Bakunin's Controversy with Marx." American Journal of Economics and Sociology 19(1960): 259-74.

_____. "Classical Economics and Marx's Theory of Social Class." Indian Journal of Social Research 2 No. 2(1961): 91-5.

_____. "Class, Stratum and Intelligentsia." Science & Society 27(1963): 49-61.

_____. "The Detente between Marxism and Linguistic Philosophy." Praxis 3(1967): 578-91.

_____. "Dialectical Materialism and Social Research." Indian Sociological Bulletin 2 No. 4(1965): 206-14.

_____. "The Dual Character of Marxian Social Science." Philosophy of Science 29(1962): 333-49.

_____. "Engels' Contribution to Marxism." Socialist Register 1965, pp. 297-310.

_____. "Foundations of a Sociology of Labour." Indian Journal of Social Research 3 No. 2(1962): 35-43.

_____. "The 'Intermediate Classes' in Marxian Theory." Social Research 28(1961): 23-36.

_____. "Marx's Concept of Egoistic Man." Praxis 4(1968): 363-75.

_____. "Marx's Concept of Value and Critique of Value Fetishism." Science & Society 34(1970): 342-6.

_____. "Marx's Contribution to Humanism." Science & Society 29(1965): 173-91.

_____. "Marx's General Law of Capitalist Development." Cahiers de l'Institut de Science Economique Appliquee 176 Serie S 10(1966): 121-38.

_____. "Marx's Theory of Value." Philosophy and Phenomenological Research 33(1972): 249-58.

_____. "The Method of Capital." Science & Society 31 (1967): 505-14.

_____. "Moral Progress from Philosophy to Technology." Philosophy and Phenomenological Research 28(1968): 430-6.

_____. "Occam's Razor and Value Fetishism in Marx's Sociology of Labor." American Journal of Economics and Sociology 24(1965): 193-200.

_____. "On Marx's Contribution to Economic Sociology." Indian Journal of Social Research 5 No. 2(1964): 129-40.

_____. "The Role of Classes in Historical Materialism." Science & Society 23(1959): 16-26.

_____. "The Unity of Marx's Thought." Science & Society 28(1964): 316-23.

_____. "The Value Judgement in 'Capital'." Science & Society 29(1965): 296-311.

_____. "The Young Marx, A Reappraisal." Philosophy and Phenomenological Research 27(1966): 216-29.

Hodges, H. A. "Communism." Journal of the Royal United Service Institution 100 No. 597(1955): 11-9.

Hodgson, Geoff. "Marxian Epistemology and the Transformation Problem." Economy and Society 3(1974): 357-92.

Hoffman, R. "Marx and Proudhon; A Reappraisal of Their Relationship." Historian 29(1967): 409-30.

Hoffman, R. J. "The Marxian Philosophy of History." American Review 1936, pp. 507-15.

Hogan, Horner. "The Basic Perspective of Marxism-Leninism." Studies in Soviet Thought 7(1967): 297-317.

Holesovsky, Vaclav. "Rediscoveries of Karl Marx." Massachusetts Review 9(1968): 487-500.

Holmes, J. H. "Henry George and Karl Marx: A Plutarchian Experiment." American Journal of Economic Sociology 6 (1947): 159-67.

Holmes, Roger. "Marxism and the Nature of Groups." British Journal of Sociology 21(1970): 273-84.

Holmes, W. "Theory of Alienation as Sociological Explanation: Its Advantages and Limitations." Sociology 10(1976): 207-24.

Hook, Sidney. "The Baptism of Aristotle and Marx." Nation 9 April 1938, pp. 415-7.

_____. "Communist Manifesto 100 Years After." New York Times Magazine 1 February 1948, pp. 6+.

_____. "Dialectic in Social and Historical Inquiry." Journal of Philosophy 36(1939): 365-78.

_____. "The Enlightenment and Marxism." Journal of the History of Ideas 29(1968): 93-108.

_____. "For Louis Althusser." Encounter 41(October 1973): 86-92.

_____. "Marx and Darwinism." New Republic 29 July 1931, p. 290.

_____. "Marx and Freud: Oil and Water." Open Court 42 (January 1958): 20-5.

_____. "The Marxian Dialectic." New Republic 22 March 1933, pp. 150-4.

_____. "Marx's Second Coming." Problems of Communism 15 (July 1966): 26-9.

_____. "Myth and Fact in the Marxist Theory of Revolution and Violence." Journal of the History of Ideas 34(1973): 271-80.

_____. "The Philosophy of Dialectical Materialism." Journal of Philosophy 25(1928): 113-24, 141-55.

_____. "Prussian Blue and Russian Red." Review of The Red Prussian: The Life and Legend of Karl Marx, by Leopold Schwartzschild. Saturday Review of Literature 31 May 1947, pp. 13-4.

_____. "What Is Dialectic?" Journal of Philosophy 26 (1929): 85-99, 113-23.

_____. "What Is Living and What Is Dead in Marxism." Southern Review 6(1940): 293-316.

_____. "What Is Materialism?" Journal of Philosophy 31 (1934): 235-42.

_____. "What's Left of Karl Marx." Saturday Review 6 June 1959, pp. 12-4+.

Horowitz, David. "Marxism and Its Place in Economic Science." Berkeley Journal of Sociology 16(1971-72): 46-59.

_____. "Marxism and Its Place in Economic Science." Maxwell Review 11(Winter 1974-75): 12-8.

Hoselitz, Bert F. "The Dynamics of Marxism: What Remains Valid?" Modern Review 3(Summer 1949): 11-23.

_____. "Karl Marx on Secular and Social Development: A Study in the Sociology of Nineteenth-Century Social Science." Comparative Studies in Society and History 6 No. 2(1964): 142-63.

_____. "Socialism, Communism and International Trade." Journal of Political Economy 57(1949): 227-41.

Howard, Dick. "On Deforming Marx: The French Translation of 'Grundrisse'." Science & Society 33(1969): 358-65.

Huberman, Leo, and Sweezy, Paul M. "The Communist Manifesto After 100 Years." Monthly Review 1(August 1949): 102-20.

Hudson, G. F. "Mao, Marx, and Moscow." Foreign Affairs 37 (1959): 561-72.

Hunt, R. N. Carew. "Criticism and Self-criticism." Occidente 11 No. 1(1955): 34-43.

_____. "The Ethics of Marxism." Nineteenth Century and After 145(1949): 108-17.

Hyman, Stanley E. "After the Great Metaphors." American Scholar 31(1962): 236-56.

_____. "Capital as Literature." Kenyon Review 23(1961): 590-610.

_____. "The Marxist Criticism of Literature." Antioch Review 7(1947): 541-68.

Hyndman, H. M. "Coming Triumph of Marxist Socialism." English Review 19(February 1915): 290-304.

Hyndman, H. M., and Bax, R. B. "Socialism, Materialism, and the War." English Review 19(December 1914): 52-69.

Hyppolite, Jean. "The 'Scientific' and the 'Ideological' in a Marxist Perspective." Diogenes 64(1968): 27-36.

Iggers. G. G. "The New Historiography in Historical Perspective." Australian Journal of Politics and History 17 (1971): 44-55.

Ignatow, Assen. "The Old and New Marxism." Studies in Soviet Thought 14(1974): 93-8.

Il'ichev, L. F. "Engels' Struggle Against Agnosticism." Soviet Studies in Philosophy 10(Summer 1971): 27-42.

"In the Light of Marxism." Labour Monthly 7(1925): 482-8.

Irvine, W. "G. B. Shaw and Karl Marx." Journal of Economic History 6(May 1946): 53-72.

Israel Joachim. "The Principle of Methodological Individualism and Marxian Epistemology." Acta Sociologica 14 No. 3 (1971): 145-50.

_____. "Remarks Concerning Some Problems of Marxist Class Theory." Acta Sociologica 13 No. 1(1970): 11-29.

Itoh, M. "Study of Marx's Theory of Value." Science & Society 40(1976): 307-40.

Jackman, M. R., and Jackman, R. W. "Interpretation of the Relation Between Objective and Subjective Social Status." American Sociological Review 38(1973): 569-82.

Jackobson, N. P. "Marxism and Religious Materialism." Journal of Religion 25(1949): 95-113.

Jackson, T. A. "Marx and Engels on Ireland: With Excerpts from Letters." Labour Monthly 14(1932): 643-8, 710-5, 76--75; 15(1933): 53-60.

Jacoby, Russell. "The Politics of Subjectivity: Notes on Marxism, the Movement, and Bourgeois Society." Telos 6 (1971): 116-26.

James, C. L. R. "The Commune in 1971." Massachusetts Review 12(1971): 432-4.

Jaroshevskij, Tadeus M. "The Problem of Man's Individuality and Its Development in the Philosophy of Karl Marx." Studia Filosofia 4(1970): 61-110.

Jasinska, A. "The Need For and Principles of Systematizing the Teachings of Karl Marx." Polish Sociological Bulletin 1 No. 13(1966): 6-18.

──────. "The Need For and Principles of Systematizing the Teachings of Karl Marx." Quality and Quantity 5(1971): 265-79.

Jaspers, K. "Importance of Nietzsche, Marx and Kierkegaard in the History of Philosophy." Translated by S. Goodman. Hibbert Journal 49(1951): 226-34.

Jauss, H. R. "Idealist Embarrassment: Observations on Marxist Aesthetics." New Literary History 7(Autumn 1975): 191-208.

Jay, Martin. "Frankfurt School's Critique of Marxist Humanism." Social Research 39(1972): 285-305.

Jemnitz, J. "Engels and the Problems of the International Labour Movement in the 1890's." Acta Historica 17(1971): 225-54.

Johnson, Oakley C. "Karl Marx and the United States." Mainstream 16(May 1963): 3-19.

Johnson, Orace. "The 'Last Hour' of Senior and Marx." History of Political Economy 1(1969): 359-69.

Johnston, William M. "Karl Marx's Verse of 1836-1837 as a Foreshadowing of His Early Philosophy." Journal of the History of Ideas 28(1967): 259-68.

Johnstone, Monty. "The Paris Commune and Marx's Conception of the Dictatorship of the Proletariat." Massachusetts Review 12(1971): 447-62.

Johri, S. K. "The Social Thought of Karl Marx and Gandhi." Indian Journal of Social Research 4 No. 2(1963): 75-9.

Jones, Llewellyn. "What Did Marx Really Mean?" Christian Century 5 April 1933, pp. 456-8.

Joseph, H. W. B. "Karl Marx's Theory of Value." Economic Review 20(1910): 51-66.

Kalab, Milos. "The Marxist Conception of the Sociological Method." Quality and Quantity 3(1969): 5-22.

Kalecki, M. "The Marxian Equations of Reproduction and Modern Economics." Social Science Information/Information sur les Sciences Sociales 7 No. 6(1968): 73-9.

Kamenka, Eugene. "Baptism of Karl Marx." Hibbert Journal 56(1958): 340-51.

_____. "Marx in Stereotype." Problems of Communism 19 (September 1970): 61-2.

_____. "The Primitive Ethic of Karl Marx." Australasian Journal of Philosophy 35 No. 2(1957): 75-96.

Kapchenko, N. "Engels on Working-Class Foreign Policy." International Affairs 12(December 1970): 16-23.

Kara, K. "On the Marxist Theory of War and Peace." Journal of Peace Research 1(1968): 1-27.

"Karl Marx: Life and Ideas of the Rebel Whose 'ism' Interpreted by Stalin, Helps Nurture Soviet Policy." Fortune May 1946, pp. 140-8.

"Karl Marx's CAPITAL; Some Pointers on Its Contents on the Occasion of Its 70th Anniversary." Communist 16(1938): 934-45.

Kauder, Emil. "The Intellectual Sources of Karl Marx." Kyklos 21(1968): 269-88.

Kaufman, Arnold S. "On Alienation." Inquiry 8 No. 2(1965):

Kaufmann, M. "Karl Marx and the International." Leisure Hour 27: 788, 821. n.d.

Kavolis, Vytautas. "Art Content and Economic Reality." American Journal of Economics and Sociology 24(1965): 321-8.

Kazhdan, A. P. "Engels on the Origins of Christianity." Soviet Studies in Philosophy 10(Summer 1971): 81-102.

Kedrov, B. M. "Engels' Great Book." Soviet Studies in Philosophy 10(Summer 1971): 3-26.

Kellner, Douglas. "Introduction to 'On the Philosophical Foundation of the Concept of Labor'." Telos 16(1973): 2-8.

Kelly, G. A. "A Note on Alienation." Political Theory 1 (1973): 46-50. Comment by B. Ollman, pp. 51-3.

Kelsen, H. "Foundations of Democracy: Marxian Doctrine that Democracy is Possible Only Under a Socialist Economic System." Ethics 66 No. 1 Pt. 2(1955): 68-75.

──────. "Foundations of Democracy: Redefinition of Democracy." Ethics 66 No. 1 Pt. 2(1955): 71-5.

Kelso, L. O. "Karl Marx: The Almost Capitalist." American Bar Association Journal 43(1957): 235-8, 275-9.

Kemp, T. "Aspects of the Marxist Theory of the State." Indian Journal of Social Research 5 No. 2(1964): 111-28.

Kiernan, V. G. "Marx and India." Socialist Register 1967, pp. 159-89.

──────. "On the Development of a Marxist Approach to Nationalism." Science & Society 34(1970): 92-8.

Kiker, B. F. "Historical Roots of the Concept of Human Capital." Journal of Political Economy 74(1966): 481-99. Reply by E. Cohen, 78(1-70): 778-82.

Kimio, Shiozawa. "Marx's View of Asian Society and His 'Asiatic Mode of Production'." Developing Economics 4 (1966): 299-315.

Kirchenmann, Peter. "Problems of Information in Dialectical Materialism." Studies in Soviet Thought 8(1968): 105-21.

Kishkovsky, A. "Marxism and Religion." Bulletin of the Institute for the Study of the USSR. 3 No. 4(1956): 21-9.

Klare, Karl E. "The Critique of Everyday Life: Marxism, and the New Left." Berkeley Journal of Sociology 16(1971-72): 15-45.

Kleene, G. A. "Bernstein vs. Old-School Marxism." Annals of the American Academy of Political Science 18(1901): 391-419.

Klehr, Harvey. "Marxist Theory in Search of America." Journal of Politics 35(1973): 311-31.

Kline, George L. "Was Marx an Ethical Humanist?" Studies in Soviet Thought 9(1969): 91-103.

Kloskowska, Antonina. "The Conception of Culture According to Karl Marx." Polish Sociological Bulletin 21(1970): 5-16.

Kobliakov, V. P. "On the Truth of Moral Judgements." Soviet Studies in Philosophy 7(Fall 1968): 49-59.

Kohak, Erazim. "The Humanization of Power." Humanist 31 (January-February 1971): 20-2.

Kojeve, Alexandre. "Hegel, Marx and Christianity." Interpretation Summer 1970, pp. 21-42.

Kolakowski, Leszek. "Marxist Philosophy and National Reality: Natural Communities and Universal Brotherhood." Round Table 253(January 1974): 43-56.

Kolman, E. "Marx and Darwin." Labour Monthly 13(1931): 702-5.

Kopnin, P. V. "Dialectical Materialism and Metaphysics." International Philosophical Quarterly 6(1966): 33-44.

Korac, Veljko. "The Phenomena of Theoretical Anti-Humanism." Praxis 5(1969): 430-4.

Korsch, K. Review of Human Nature: The Marxian View, by V. Venable. Journal of Philosophy 42(1945): 712-8.

Kovaly, Pavel. "Is it Possible to Humanize Marxism?" Studies in Soviet Thought 11(1971): 276-93.

Kovel, Joel. "The Marxist View of Man and Psychoanalysis." Social Research 43(1976): 220-46.

Kozlov, G. "The Triumph of the Theory of Scientific Communism." Problems of Economics (Moscow) 1(November 1958): 6-17.

Kozr-Kowalski, Stanislaw. "Marx's Theory of Classes and Social Strata and Capital: Fragment of the Work: Marx's Theory of Classes and the World Today." Polish Sociological Bulletin 21(1970): 17-32.

_____. "Weber and Marx." Polish Sociological Bulletin 17(1968): 5-17.

Krader, Lawrence. "Marxist Anthropology: Principles and Contradictions. New Perspectives in the Science of Man. Part 1: Society, Individual and Person." International Review of Social History 20(1975): 236-72.

114

_____. "The Works of Marx and Engels in Ethnology Compared." International Review of Social History 18 (1973): 223-75.

Krelle, W. "Marx as a Growth Theorist." German Economic Review 9 No. 2(1971): 122-33.

Kresic, Andrija. "The Proletariat and Socialism in the Works of Marx and in the World Today." Praxis 5(1969): 371-86.

Krieger, L. "Marx and Engels on Historians." Journal of the History of Ideas 14(1953): 381-403.

_____. "The Uses of Marx for History." Political Science Quarterly 75(1960): 355-78.

Ku, Chin-P'ing. "The Struggle of Marx and Engels Against 'Genuine Socialism'." Chinese Studies in Philosophy 4 (Summer 1973): 73-98.

Kubat, D. "Marx and Ceszkowski." American Slavic and East European Review 20(1961): 114-7.

Kuczynski, Jurgen. "Population Theories and Marxism." Labour Monthly 46(1964): 232-6.

Kuhn, William F. "Fifty Years After." Thought 8(1933-34): 459-70.

Kumagai, H. "Ricardo, Marx, Keynes and the Relationship between Wage Rate and Prices." Osaka Economic Papers 6 (1957): 1-15.

Kupers, Terry. "Historical Materialism and Scientific Psychology." Science & Society 37(1973): 81+.

Kuptsov, V. I., and Teredhov, M. P. "The Concept of Determinism in Marxist Philosophy." Soviet Studies in Philosophy 9(Winter 1970-71): 278-92.

Kurtz, Paul W. "Humanism and the Freedom of the Individual." Humanist 29(January-February 1969): 14-9.

_____. "Technology and Marxist Ideology and Dogma." Social Studies 50(1959): 50-8.

Kuvacic, Ivan. "The World as an Objective Being." Pacific Philosophy Forum 6(December 1967): 54-62.

Kuzimov, I. "Frederick Engels and the Economic Theory of Socialism." International Affairs (USSR) 11(November 1970): 26-32.

Kuznecov, K. T. "The Political and Philosophical Ideas of Karl Marx During the First Period of His Activity (1842-43)." Voprosy Filosofii 5(1953): 107-17.

Kuznetsov, B. G. "The 'Dialectics of Nature' and Dialectics in 'Capital'." Soviet Studies in Philosophy 10(Summer 1971): 43-62.

Lafargue, Paul. "Karl Marx at Home: The Titan of the Poor Was a Gentle, Considerate Father; His Son-in-law Describes Some Little Known Aspects of Marx's Personality; His Deep Love for Engels." New Masses 6 May 1941, pp. 13-4.

Laibman, D. "Values and Prices of Production: The Political Economy of the Transformation Problem." Science & Society 37(1973-74): 404-36.

Lam, Elizabeth P. "Does Macmurry Understand Marx?" Journal of Religion 20(1940): 47-65.

Lane, A. D. "The Machine Minders." New Society 13 No. 331 (1969): 163-4.

Lange, O. R. "Marxian Economics and Modern Economic Theory." Review of Economic Studies 2(1934-35): 189-201.

_____. "Marxian Economics in the Soviet Union." American Economic Review 35(1945): 127-33.

Langslet, Lars Roar. "Young Marx and Alienation in Western Debate." Inquiry 6(1963): 1-2.

Laroui, Abdallah. "Marx and the Intellectual From the Third World: Or the Problem of Historical Retardation Once Again." Diogenes 64(1968): 118-40.

Laskey, M. J. "In Defence of Utopianism." 20th Century 149 (January 1951): 21-7.

Lauer, Quentin. "Marxism: Philosophy of Freedom." Thought 38 No. 148(1963): 22-38.

Lazarus, Louis. "List of Marx/Engels Articles in the New York Daily Tribune." Tamiment Institute Library Bulletin August 1963, pp. 4-20. Supplements, November 1963, pp. 7-10; May 1964, pp. 20-1.

_____. "Marx and Engels; American Manuscripts and Imprints, 1846-1898: A List of Materials in the Taimiment Institute Library." Taimiment Institute Library Bulletin January 1963, pp. 2-25. Errata, November 1963, p. 6.

Le Baron, Bentley. "Marx on Human Emancipation." Canadian Journal of Political Science 4(1971): 559-70.

_____. "What is Law - Beyond Scholasticism." Logique et Analyse 14 (March-June 1971): 77-83.

Lebowitz, M. A. "Marx's Falling Rate of Profit: A Dialectical View." Canadian Journal of Economics 9(1976): 232-54.

Lee, Harold N. "A Criticism of the Marxian Interpretation of History." Tulane Studies in Philosophy 1(1952): 95-106.

Leiss, William. "Critical Theory and its Future." Political Theory 2(1974): 330-50.

_____. "Technological Rationality: Notes on 'Work and Freedom in Marcuse and Marx'." Canadian Journal of Political Science 4(1971): 398-9. Reply, pp. 400-3.

Lenin, V. I. "Friedrich Engels." Labour Monthly 17(1935): 498-505.

Leontief, Wassily. "The Significance of Marxian Economics for Present-day Economic Theory." American Economic Review 28(March 1938): 1-9.

Lerner, A. P. "Marxism and Economics: Sweezy and Robinson." Journal of Political Economy 53(1945): 79-87.

Letiche, J. M. "Das Kapital: A Centenary Appreciation." American Economic Review Papers and Proceedings 57(1967): 597-8.

Levin, Michael. "Marxism and Romanticism: Marx's Debt to German Conservatism." Political Studies (Oxford) 22 (1974): 400-13.

Levine, Norman. "Anthropology in the Thought of Marx and Engels." Studies in Comparative Communism 6 Nos. 1-2 (1973): 7-26.

_____. "Humanism Without Eschatology." Journal of the History of Ideas 33(1972): 281-98.

_____. "Marxism and Engelism: Two Differing Views of History." Journal of the History of the Behavioral Sciences 9 No. 3(1973): 217-39.

_____. "Marxism and Engelism: Two Differing Views of History." Maryland Historian 3 No. 2(1972): 137-55.

Lewis, A. B. "Mills of Marx Grind Slowly." Christian Century 13 May 1936, pp. 699-701.

Lewis, J. D. "Individual and the Group in Marxist Theory." International Journal of Ethics 47(October 1936): 45-56.

Lewis, J. D., ed. "Marxism, Revolution, and Democracy: 1848 and 1948." Journal of Politics 11(1949): 518-65.

Lewis, John. "Marxism and its Critics." Marxist Quarterly 2(October 1955): 203-16.

_____. "The Uniqueness of Man and the Dialectic of History." Praxis 6(1970): 93-9.

Lichtheim, George. "Class and Hierarchy: A Critique of Marx." European Journal of Sociology/Archives Européenes de Sociologie 5 No. 1(1964): 101-11.

_____. "The Concept of Ideology." History and Theory 4 No. 2(1965): 164-95.

_____. "From Pascal to Marx." New Statesman 4 September 1964, pp. 322-3.

_____. "Marx and the Asiatic Mode of Production." St. Anthony's Papers 14(1963): 86-112.

_____. "Marxism and Marxology: The Fundamentals of a Doctrine." Problems of Communism 15(July-August 1966): 14-25.

_____. "Marxist Doctrine in Perspective." Problems of Communism 7 No. 6(1958): 32-7.

_____. "The Origins of Marxism." Journal of the History of Philosophy 3(1965): 96-105.

_____. "Social Democracy and Communism: 1918-1968." Studies in Comparative Communism 3 No. 1(1970): 5-30.

_____. "Transmutation of a Doctrine." Problems of Communism 15(July 1966): 14-25. Reply by W. C. Gausmann, pp. 98-9.

_____. "Western Marxist Literature." Survey 50(January 1964): 119-28.

Lichtman, Richard. "Marx's Theory of Ideology." Socialist Revolution 5 No. 1(1975): 45-76.

118

_____. "Symbolic Interactionism and Social Reality: Some Marxist Queries." Berkeley Journal of Sociology 15(1970): 75-94.

Lidtke, Vernon L. "German Social Democracy and German State Socialism, 1876-1884." National Review of Social History 9(1964): 202-25.

Lipset, Seymour Martin. "Ideology and No End. The Controversy Till Now." Encounter (Great Britain) 39 No. 6(1973): 17-22.

Lischer, R. "Lutheran Shape of Marxian Evil." Religion in Life 42(1973): 549-58.

Little, C. J. "Karl Marx, 1818-1883." Chautauguan 10:694. n.d.

Lobkowicz, Nicholas. "Is the Soviet Notion of Practice Marxian?" Studies in Soviet Thought 6(1966): 25-36.

_____. "Karl Marx's Attitude Towards Religion." Review of Politics 26(1964): 319-52.

Lohse, Bernhard. "The Marxist Interpretation of Luther and Muentzer." Australian Journal of Politics and History 19 (1973): 343-52.

Lovett, R. M. "Karl Marx." New Republic 24 July 1929, pp. 265-6.

Lowe, Donald M. "Marx and China, A Disparity of Two Worlds: A Review Article." China Quarterly 41(1970): 114-21.

Lowenthal, Richard. "Social Transformation and Democratic Legitimacy." Social Research 43(1976): 246-75.

Löwith, K. "Man's Self-alienation in the Early Writings of Marx." Social Research 21(1954): 204-30.

Lubasz, Heinz. "Marx's Conception of the Revolutionary Proletariat." Praxis 5(1969): 288-90.

_____. "Marx's Initial Problematic: The Problem of Poverty." Political Studies 24(1976): 24-42.

Lucas, John, and Meacham, Standish. "Engels, Manchester and the Working Class: A Discussion." Victorian Studies 18 (1975): 461-72.

Ludz, Peter C. "Marxism and Systems Theory in a Bureaucratic Society." Social Research 42(1975): 661-74.

McBride, William Leon. "The Concept of Justice in Marx, Engels, and Others." Ethics 85 No. 3(1975): 204-18.

McCoy, Charles N. R. "The Logical and the Real in Political Theory: Plato, Aristotle, and Marx." American Political Science Review 48(1954): 1058-66.

MacDonald, H. M. "Marx, Engels, and the Polish National Movement." Journal of Modern History 13(1941): 321-34.

Macdonell, J. "Karl Marx and German Socialism." Fortnightly Review 23: 382+. n.d.

McGill, V. J. "Notes on Theory and Practice in Marxist Philosophy." Philosophy and Phenomenological Research 5 (1944-45): 217-41.

McGovern, Arthur F. "Marx's Path to Communism." America 4 May 1968, pp. 596-8.

_____. "Young Marx on the Role of Ideas in History." Philosophy Today 15(Fall 1971): 204-16.

_____. "The Young Marx on the State." Science & Society 34(1970): 430-66.

McInnes, Neil. "Alien Marx." Encounter 40(June 1973): 63-5.

_____. "From Marx to Marcuse." Survey 16(1971): 138-55.

_____. "The Young Marx and the New Left." Journal of Contemporary History 6 No. 4(1971): 141-59.

Maciver, A. M. "Karl Marx." Sociological Review 14(1922): 325-8.

McLean, Edward B. "Marxism Considered as an Absolute Radicalism and the Effects of Marxist Political Behavior." Politico 32(1967): 548-66.

_____. "Marx's Political Theory and the Negation of Politics." International Review of History and Political Science 5(1968): 52-74.

McLellan, David. "Marx and the Missing Link." Encounter 35 (November 1970): 35-45.

_____. "Marx's View of the Unalienated Society." Review of Politics 31(1969): 459-65.

McMurtry, John. "Making Sense of Economic Determinism." Canadian Journal of Philosophy 3(December 1973): 249-61.

Magrass, Yale R. "With Words Like Bats . . . Inferences from B. Ollman's Alienation." Human Factor 11 No. 1 (1972): 45-51.

Magri, L. "What is a Revolutionary Party?" New Left Review 60(1970): 97-128.

Mahowald, Mary B. "Marx's Gemeinschaft: Another Interpretation." Philosophy and Phenomenological Research 33 (1973): 472-88.

Maital, S. "Is Marxian Growth Crisis-Ridden?" History of Political Economy 4(1972): 113-26.

Malecki, Edward S. "Theories of Revolution and Industrialized Societies." Journal of Politics 35(1973): 948-85.

Mallock, W. H. "Missing Essential in Economic Science." 19th Century and After 65(March 1909): 435-52.

Mamut, L. S. "Karl Marx on the State as the Political Organization of Society." Voprosy Fifosofii 7(1968): 29-39.

_____. "Questions of Law in Marx's 'Capital'." Soviet Law and Government 6(Spring 1968): 3-10.

Mandel, David. "Traditions in Political Analysis and the Problem of 'What' is in People's Heads." The Human Factor 11 No. 1(1972): 32-44.

Mandic, Oleg. "A Marxist Perspective on Contemporary Religious Revivals." Social Research 37(1970): 237-58.

_____. "The Marxist School of Sociology: What is Sociology in a Marxist Sense?" Social Research 34(1967): 435-56.

Manuel F. E. "In Memoriam: Critique of the Gotha Program, 1875-1975." Daedalus 105(Winter 1976): 59-77.

Marcuse, Herbert. "Contributions to a Phenomenology of Historical Materialism." Telos 4(1969): 3-34.

_____. "On the Philosophical Foundation of the Concept of Labor in Economics." Telos 8(1973): 9-37.

_____. "The Realm of Freedom and the Realm of Necessity: A Reconsideration." Praxis 5(1969): 20-5.

_____. "Recent Literature on Communism." World Politics 6(1954): 515-25.

_____. "Re-examination of the Concept of Revolution."
Diogenes 64(1968): 17-26.

_____. "Re-examination of the Concept of Revolution."
New Left Review 56(1969): 27-34.

Marcuse, L. "Heine and Marx: A History and a Legend."
Germanic Review 30(1955): 110-24.

Markovic, Mihailo. "The Basic Characteristics of Marxist Humanism." Humanist 29(January-February 1969): 19-23.

_____. "The Concept of Revolution." Praxis 5(1969): 41-54.

_____. "Critical Social Theory in Marx." Praxis 6 (1970): 283-97.

_____. "Economism on the Humanization of Economics."
Praxis 5(1969): 451-75.

_____. "Marx and Critical Scientific Thought." Praxis 4(1968): 391-403.

_____. "Marxism vs. Technology." Dialogue 1(Spring 1968): 31-6.

_____. "Marxist Humanism and Ethics." Inquiry 6(1963): 18-34.

_____. "Marxist Humanism and Ethics." Science & Society 27(1963): 1-22.

Markus, Gyorgy. "Marxist Humanism." Science & Society 30 (1966): 275-87.

Marshall, D. "War of Machines; Partisans of the Modern World." Catholic World 144(January 1937): 397-402.

Martin, J. "Socialism and the Class War." Quarterly Journal of Economics 23(1908-1909): 512-7.

Martin, K. "Marxism Reviewed." Political Quarterly 18 (1947): 240-9.

Martin, Neil A. "Marxism, Nationalism, and Russia." Journal of the History of Ideas 29(1968): 231-52.

"Marx and the Modern World." Labour Monthly 4(1923): 195-200.

"Marx in Print." Times Literary Supplement 9 May 1968, p. 481.

"Marx on Public Schools." America 93(1955): 385-6.

Masters, R. D. Review of The Social and Political Thought of Karl Marx, by S. Avineri. Saturday Review 5 April 1969, pp. 31-3+.

Matrai, L. "Three Antagonists of Hegel: Feuerbach, Kierkegaard, Marx." Danish Yearbook of Philosophy 8(1971): 115-34.

Mattick, P. "Marx and Keynes." Cahiers de l'Institut de Science Economique Appliquée 121, Ser. S. No. 5(January 1962): 113-216.

─────. "Samuelson's 'Transformation' of Marxism into Bourgeois Economics." Science & Society 36(1972): 258-73.

Mayer, Carl. "Max Weber's Interpretation of Karl Marx." Social Research 42(1975): 701-19. Reply by H. R. Wagner, pp. 720-8.

Mayer, H. "Marx, Engels and the Politics of the Peasantry." Cahiers de l'Institut de Science Economique Appliquée 102, Ser. S. No. 3(June 1960): 91-152.

─────. "Notes on Marxism and the State." Public Administration (Sydney) 11 No. 3(1952): 129-42.

Mayo, H. B. "Marxism as a Philosophy of History." Canadian Historical Review 34(1953): 1-17.

─────. "Marxist Theory and Scientific Methods." Canadian Journal of Economics and Political Science 18(1952): 487-99.

Mazlish, Bruce. "The Tragic Farce of Marx, Hegel and Engels: A Note." History and Theory 11(1972): 335-7.

Medalie, Richard J. "The Communist Theory of State." American Slavic and East European Review 18(1959): 510-25.

Meek, R. L. "Marginalism and Marxism." History of Political Economy 4(1972): 499-511.

─────. "Marx's Doctrine of Increasing Misery." Science & Society 26(1962): 422-41.

─────. "Some Notes on the Transformation Problem." Economic Journal 66(1956): 94-107.

Megill, Kenneth A. "The Community in Marx's Philosophy." Philosophy and Phenomenological Research 30(1970): 382-93.

_____. "On Marx's Method." Southern Journal of Philosophy 9(Spring 1971): 61-96.

Mehl, Rober. "Hope of the Marxist." Ecumenical Review 6 (1954): 214-28.

Mehta, V. R. "Marxism with a Human Face." Political Science Review 14(1975): 128-36.

Meillassoux, Claude. "From Reproduction to Production." Economy and Society 1 No. 1(1972): 93-105.

Meisel, James H. "A Question of Affinities: Pareto and Marx." Cahiers Vilfredo Pareto 5(1965): 165-74.

"Memories of Marx." Living Age 342(March 1932): 83-4.

Menczer, B. "Centenary of the Communist Manifesto." Contemporary Review 172(December 1947): 354-9.

Mendel, A. P. "Rise and Fall of Scientific Socialism." Foreign Affairs 45(October 1966): 98-111.

Mewes, Horst. "On the Concept of Politics in the Early Works of Marx." Social Research 43(1976): 276-94.

Meyer, Alfred G. "The Aufhebung of Marxism." Social Research 43(1976): 199-219.

Mihajlov, Mahajlo. "Djilas Versus Marx: The Theory of Alienation." Survey 18 No. 2(1972): 1-13.

Miliband, Ralph. "Marx and the State." Socialist Register 1965, pp. 278-96.

Miller, D. "Ideology and the Problem of False Consciousness." Political Studies 20(1972): 432-47.

Miller, J., and Miller, M. "A New Stage in the English Study of Marxism." Soviet Studies 7 No. 3(1956): 275-95.

Miller, R. W. "Consistency of Historical Materialism." Philosophy & Public Affairs 4(1975): 390-409.

Miller, Richard. "Rawls and Marxism." Philosophy & Public Affairs 3(1974): 167-91.

Minoguchi, Tokijiro. "Marxian Theories of Social Classes." Hitotsubashi Journal of Social Studies 5 No. 1(1969): 44-58.

Mins, Henry F. "Marxists and Non-Marxists: 'Theoretical Schemes' and 'Political Creeds'." Science & Society 30 (1966): 25-31.

_____. "Marx's Doctoral Dissertation." Science & Society 12(1968): 157-69.

Mishra, Ramesh. "Marx and Welfare." Sociological Review 23 (1975): 287-313.

Mitias, Michael H. "Marx and the Human Individual." Studies in Soviet Thought 12(1972): 245-54.

Molnar, Thomas. "Marxist Revisionism: A Commentary." Modern Age 16(1972): 301-8.

_____. "The Western Marxists." Survey 20(1974): 154-8.

Molner, Miklos. "Bakunin and Marx." The Review (Belgium) 5 No. 3(1963): 70-84.

Moore, Carlos. "Were Marx and Engels White Racists?: The Prolet-Aryan Outlook of Marxism." Berkeley Journal of Sociology 19(1974-75): 125-53. Reply by J. L. Himmelstein, pp. 157-66; addendum by C. Mack, pp. 167-70.

Moore, John W. "Freud, Marx, and Tomorrow." Kinesis 4 (Fall 1971): 31-41.

Moore, S. "The Metaphysical Argument in Marx's Labour Theory of Value." Cahiers de l'Institut de Science Economique Appliquée 140 Ser. S. No. 7(aout 1963): 73-98.

Moore, Stanley. "Marx and Lenin as Historical Materialists." Philosophy & Public Affairs 4(1974): 171-94.

_____. "Marx and the Origin of Dialectic Materialism." Inquiry 14(1971): 420-9.

_____. "Marx and the State of Nature." Journal of the History of Philosophy 5(1967): 133-48.

_____. "Utopian Themes in Marx and Mao: A Critique for Modern Revisionists." Monthly Review 21(June 1969): 33-44.

Mor, A. "Marx's Concept of Alienation." Iyyun 19(January 1968): 28-50.

Morais, H. M. "Marx and Engels on America." Science & Society 12(1948): 3-21.

Moravia, A. "Communism and Art." Confluence 2 No. 2(1953): 31-47.

Morawski, Stefan. "The Aesthetic Views of Marx and Engels." Journal of Aesthetics and Art Criticism 28(1970): 301-14.

Morel, Georgeo. "The Meaning of Karl Marx." America 28 October 1967, pp. 464-8.

Moreno, J. L. "Sociometry and Marxism: The Experimental Method in Science." Sociometry 12(1949): 106-43.

Morgan, Ivor. "Marx's 'Grundrisse': Notes of a Victorian Futurologist." Australian Quarterly 44 No. 1(1972): 87-91.

Morishima, M. "The Fundamental Marxian Theorem: A Reply to Samuelson." Journal of Economic Literature 12(1974): 71-4.

_____. "Marx in the Light of Modern Economic Theory." Econometrica 42(1974): 611-32.

Morishima, M., and Catephores, G. "Is There an Historical Transformation Problem?" Economic Journal 85(1975): 309-28.

Morishima, M., and Seton, F. "Aggregation in Leontief Matrices and the Labour Theory of Value." Econometrica 29 (1961): 203-20.

Moroziuk, Russel P. "The Role of Atheism in Marxian Philosophy." Studies in Soviet Thought 14(1974): 191-212.

Morris, Jacob. "Some Comments on Marx's Value Theory." Science & Society 36(1972): 341-3.

_____. "Unemployment and Unproductive Employment." Science & Society 22(1958): 193-206.

Morris, Jacob, and Lewin, Haskell. "The Skilled Labor Reduction Problem." Science & Society 37(1973-74): 454-72.

Moudel, Arthur P. "The Rise and Fall of Scientific Socialism." Foreign Affairs 45(October 1966): 98-111.

Mouzelis, N. "Social and System Integration - Some Reflections on a Fundamental Distinction." British Journal of Sociology 25(1974): 395-409.

Mueller, Gustav E. "The Hegel Legend of 'Thesis-Antithesis-Synthesis'." Journal of the History of Ideas 19(1958): 411-14.

Mühlestein, H. "Marx and the Utopian Wilhelm Weitling." Translated by H. F. Mins. Science & Society 12(1948): 113-29.

Muhll, G. E. von der. "Marxism, Ideologies, and the Intellectuals." Indian Political Science Review 2 Nos. 3-4 (1968): 121-31.

Mukerji, D. P. "Rationality in Economic Science and the Contributions of Robbins, Keynes, Marx and Schumpeter." Indian Journal of Economics 35(April 1955): 295-317.

Munro, Thomas. "The Marxist Theory of Art History: Socio-Economic Determinism and the Dialectical Process." Journal of Aesthetics and Art Criticism 18(1960): 430-45.

Murphy, J. G. "Marxism and Retribution." Philosophy & Public Affairs 2 No. 3(1973): 217-43.

Nairn, Tom. "The Modern Janus." New Left Review 94(1975): 3-29.

Naqvi, K. A. "Schematic Presentation of Accumulation in Marx." Indian Economic Review 5(February 1960): 13-22.

Narskii, I. S. "The Logic of Marx's 'Capital'." Soviet Studies in Philosophy 7(Spring 1969): 14-23.

_____. "On the Problem of Contradiction in Dialectical Logic." Soviet Studies in Philosophy 6(Spring 1968): 3-10.

Nasser, A. G. "Marx's Ethical Anthropology." Philosophy and Phenomenological Research 35(1975): 484-500.

Nearing, Scott. "Marx's Contribution to Social Advance." World Tomorrow 15 March 1933, pp. 250-2.

Needleman, Martin, and Needleman, Carolyn. "Marx and the Problem of Causation." Science & Society 33(1969): 322-39. Reply by C. Lamont, 34(1970): 236-7.

Neill, Roger Brian. "The 'New Materialism' and the Sociology of Knowledge." Insurgent Sociologist 4 No. 2(1974): 37-54.

Neill, T. P. "Marx and the Modern Mind." Catholic World 164 (February 1947): 395-401.

Nell, E., and Nell, O. "On Justice under Socialism." Dissent 19(1972): 483-91.

Nettl, J. P. "The Early Marx and Modern Sociology." Praxis 4(1968): 346-63.

_____. "The Early Marx and Modern Sociology." Studies in Comparative Communism 2 No. 2(1969): 48-73.

Nicolaus, Martin. "Proletariat and Middle Class in Marx: Hegelian Choregraphy and the Capitalist Dialectic." Studies on the Left 7 No. 1(1967): 22-49.

_____. "The Unknown Marx." New Left Review 48(1968): 41-61.

Niebuhr, R. "The Anomaly of European Socialism." Yale Review 42 No. 2(1952): 161-7.

_____. "Marxism in Eclipse." Spectator 4 June 1943, pp. 518-9.

Nielsen, Kai. "Alienation and Self-Realization." Philosophy 48(January 1973): 21-33.

_____. "Humanism and Atheism." Religious Humanism 4 (Winter 1970): 29-33.

Niemeyer, Gerhart. "Two Socialisms: Of Marx and the Welfare State." Modern Age 6(Fall 1962): 367-77.

Nisbet, Robert A. "The Decline and Fall of Social Class." Pacific Sociological Review 2 No. 1(1959): 11-7.

Nomad, M. "Karl Marx, The Myth and the Man." Scribner's Magazine 93(March 1933): 151-4+.

Novak, Michael. "The Absolute Future." Commonweal 85 (1967): 400-2.

Nowak, Leszek. "The Problem of Explanation in Karl Marx's 'Capital'." Polish Sociological Bulletin 2 No. 22(1970): 47-64.

_____. "Value, Idealization, Valuation." Quality and Quantity 8 No. 2(1974): 107-19.

Nulle, Stebelton H. "Progress: The Necessary Myth." Antioch Review 26(1966): 371-83.

"Obituary of Karl Marx." Academy 23: 205. n.d.

Oculi, Okello. "On Marx's Attitude to Colonialism." African Review 4(1974): 459-72. Rejoinder by Kivesi Botchwey, pp. 473-80.

Ogurtsov, P. "Perspectives on Practice as a Philosophical Category." Soviet Studies in Philosophy 7(Summer 1968): 26-45.

Ohara, K. "Veblen to Marx." Keizai Kenkyu 9 No. 2(1958): 97-103.

Okishio, Nobuo. "A Mathematical Note on Marxian Theorems." Weltwirtschaftliches Archiv 91 No. 2(1963): 287-98.

Olafson, F. A. "Existentialism, Marxism, and Historical Justification." Ethics 65(1955): 126-34.

Ollevier, M. "English Excerpts of Karl Marx Poetry." Review of Reviews (London) 83(May 1933): 46.

Ollman, Bertell. "Is There a Marxian Ethic? The Fact-Value Distinction." Science & Society 35(1971): 156-68.

_____. "Marxism and Political Science: Prolegomenon to a Debate on Marx's Method." Politics & Society 3(1973): 491-510. Comment by Isaac D. Balbus, pp. 511-6 and Joseph O'Malley, pp. 517+.

_____. "Marx's Use of 'Class'." American Journal of Sociology 73(1968): 573-80.

_____. "Toward Class Consciousness Next Time: Marx and the Working Class." Politics & Society 3(1972): 1-24.

Olssen, E. A. "Marx and the Ressurection." Journal of the History of Ideas 29(1968): 131-40.

O'Malley, Joseph J. "History and Man's 'Nature' in Marx." Review of Politics 28(1966): 508-27.

_____. "Marx's 'Economics' and Hegel's Philosophy of Right: An Essay on Marx's Hegelianism." Political Studies 24(1976): 43-56.

_____. "Methodology in Karl Marx." Review of Politics 32(1970): 219-30.

O'Neill, John. "Alienation, Class Struggle and Marxian Anti-Politics." Review of Metaphysics 17(1964): 462-71.

_____. "Authority, Knowledge and the Body Politic." Southern Journal of Philosophy 8(1970): 255-64.

_____. "The Concept of Estrangement in the Early and Later Writings of Karl Marx." Philosophy and Phenomenological Research 25 No. 1(1964): 64-84.

_____. "For Marx Against Althusser." Human Context 6 No. 2(1974): 385-98.

_____. "Marxism and Mythology." Ethics 77(October 1966): 38-49.

"On Marx." Symposium. Social Research 43(Summer 1976): 199-321.

Opp, Karl Dieter. "Dogmatic Trends in Marxist Sociology." Quality and Quantity 8(1974): 283-93.

Ostermann, Robert. "Have You Met Karl Marx?" Catholic World 172(February 1951): 326-33.

Pachter, Henry M. "The Idea of Progress in Marxism." Social Research 41(1974): 136-61.

Papovic, M. "Two Kinds of Revisionism." East Europe 8 (November 1959): 54-6.

Parker, H. B. "Some Marxist Fallacies." Southern Review 4(1939): 474-88.

Parkin, Frank. "System Contradiction and Political Transformation." Archives Européenes de Sociologie 13(1972): 45-62.

Parsons, Howard L. "The Background of the Student Movement in Marx's Time." Telos 5(1970): 196-201.

_____. "The Influence of Marx's Thought in the United States." Praxis 3(1967): 264-75.

_____. "The Prophetic Mission of Karl Marx." Journal of Religion 44(1964): 52-72.

_____. "Value and Mental Health in the Thought of Marx." Philosophy and Phenomenological Research 24(1964): 355-65.

_____. "The Young Marx and the Young Generation." Horizons: The Marxist Quarterly 27(1968): 17-74.

Pascal, Roy. "Karl Marx, 1842-1942: His Apprenticeship to Politics." Labour Monthly 1942, 31 p.

Pascal, R., and Pascal, F. "Hegel's Philosophy of Right and His Importance for Marx." Labour Monthly 25(1943): 285-8.

Pastusiak, L. "A Marxist Approach to the Study of International Relations." East European Quarterly 3(1969): 285-93.

Patel, S. J. "Marxism and Recent Economic Thought." Science & Society 11(1947): 52-65.

Patten, S. N. "Economic Marx." Annals of the American Academy of Political and Social Science 44(1912): 19-25.

Patterson, Tim. "Notes on the Historical Application of Marxist Cultural History." Science & Society 39(1975): 257-91.

Paul, Leslie. "Marxism: A Religion That Denies God." *Commonwealth Empire Review* April 1950, pp. 20-4.

Pavlov, Deyan. "A Tentative Marxist Interpretation of the Problem of Values." *Journal of Value Inquiry* 7(Summer 1973): 148-52.

Pearce, G. J. M. "Marxism." *Church Quarterly Review* 145 (October 1947): 66-79.

Pelikan, J. "Marxist Heresy - A Theological Evaluation." *Religion in Life* 19(1950): 356-66.

Perlo, Victor. "Marxian Commodity-Flow Diagrams for State Monopoly Capitalism." *Science & Society* 39(1975-76): 417-35.

Peterson, William. "Marx versus Malthus: The Men and the Symbols." *Population Review* 1 No. 2(1957): 21-32.

Petrovic, Gajo. "The Development and Essence of Marx's Thought." *Praxis* 4(1968): 330-45.

_____. "Man as Economic Animal and Man as Praxis." *Inquiry* 6(1964): 35-56.

_____. "Marxism versus Stalinism." *Praxis* 3(1967): 55-69.

_____. "Marx's Theory of Alienation." *Philosophy and Phenomenological Research* 23(1963): 419-26.

Petrus, Joseph A. "Marx and Engels on the National Question." *Journal of Politics* 33(1971): 797-825.

Pettee, G. S. "Failure of Marxism." *Journal of Social Philosophy* 6(1941): 101-36.

Phipps, William E. "Humanism in Marx's Early Manuscripts." *Religious Humanism* 2(Summer 1968): 118-21.

Piccone, Paul. "Gramsci's Hegelian Marxism." *Political Theory* 2(1974): 32-45.

_____. "The Problem of Consciousness." *Telos* 5(1970): 178-87.

Pickles, W. "Marx and Proudhon." *Politica* 3(1938): 236-60.

Pilling, Geoffrey. "The Law of Value in Ricardo and Marx." *Economy and Society* 1(1972): 281-307.

Plamenatz, John. "Deviations from Marxism." *Political Quarterly* 21(1950): 40-55.

Plasek, Wayne. "Marxist and American Sociological Conceptions of Alienation: Implications for Social Problems Theory." Social Problems 21(1974): 316-28.

Polanyi, Michael. "The Magic of Marxism." Bulletin of Atomic Scientists 12 No. 6(1956): 211-14, 32. Reply with rejoinder, H. Freistadt, 13(1957): 39-40.

──────. "Scientific Outlook: Its Sickness and Cure." Science 15 March 1957, pp. 480-4.

Pollitt, Harry. "Karl Marx." Labor Monthly 21(1939): 239-46.

Ponomarev, B. "The 45th Anniversary of the Death of Friedrich Engels." Communist International 10(1940): 655-75.

Popescu, Oreste. "Periodization in the History of Economic Thought." International Social Science Journal 17(1965): 607-34.

Popper, Karl. "What is Dialectic?" Mind 49(1940): 403-26.

Poulantzas, N. "Marxist Political Theory in Great Britain." New Left Review 43(1967): 57-74.

Powick, G., and Zelt, J. "Friedrich Engels and Topical Questions of Proletarian Internationalism." German Foreign Policy 10 No. 2(1971): 98-107.

Pranger, R. J. "Marx and Political Theory." Review of Politics 30(1968): 191-209.

Primbs, Edward R. J. "Truth in Science and Labor." Science & Society 26(1962): 276-92.

Prinz, Arthur M. "Background and Ulterior Motive of Marx's 'Preface' of 1859." Journal of the History of Ideas 30 (1969): 437-50.

──────. "New Perspectives on Marx as a Jew." Leo Baeck Institute. Yearbook 15(1970): 107-24.

Rader, Melvin. "Marx's Interpretation of Art and Aesthetic Value." British Journal of Aesthetics 7(July 1967): 237-49.

Rapaport, Anatol. "A View of the Intellectual Legacy of Karl Marx." Social Science Information/Information sur les Sciences Sociales 7 No. 4(1968): 7-26.

Rapaport, J. "Marxism and Psychoanalysis: A Critique of Bartlett's Position." Science & Society 5(1941): 260-8.

Rappard, W. E. "Karl Marx and Labor Legislation." Quarterly Journal of Economics 27(1913): 530-5.

Rasmussen, David M. "Between Autonomy and Sociality." Cultural Hermeneutics 1(April 1973): 3-45.

Ratner, S. "Development of Dewey's Evolutionary Materialism." His Estimate and Evaluation of Marx's Teachings. Social Research 20(1953): 139-46.

Regnier, Marcel. "Hegelianism and Marxism." Social Research 34(1967): 31-46.

Reid, J. P. "Marx on the Unity of Man." Thomist 28(1964): 259-301.

Renshaw, Patrick. "The First International, 1864." History Today 14(1964): 863-9.

Resis, Albert. "Das Kapital Comes to Russia." Slavic Review 29(1970): 219-37.

Restuccia, Paul. "Marx on Alienation and Private Property." Praxis 6(1970): 215-22.

Review of Capital, by Karl Marx. Athenaeum 18 September 1897, p. 385.

Review of The Condition of the Working Class in England in 1844, by Friedrich Engels. Spectator 3 September 1892, p. 326; and Westminster Review 137(June 1892): 702-3.

Review of Revolution and Counter-Revolution, by Friedrich Engels. Dial 1 November 1896, p. 257.

Review of Socialism; Utopian and Scientific, by Friedrich Engels. Dial 16 May 1893, p. 314; and Westminster Review 138(October 1892): 445-6.

Rexroth, Kenneth. "The Works of Marx." Saturday Review 17 September 1966, pp. 62+.

Rhodes, J. M. "Dionysian and Promethean Humanism." Modern Age 14(1970): 174-89.

Riazanov, D. "Karl Marx on China." Labour Monthly 8(1926): 86-92.

_____. "Relations of Marx with Blanqui." Labour Monthly 10(1928): 492-7.

Roberts, Paul C. "Marx's Classification of Economic Systems and the Soviet Economy." Soviet Studies 23 No. 1(1971): 96-102. Comment by Alec Nove, pp. 103-5.

Roberts, Paul C., and Stephenson, Matthew A. "Alienation and Central Planning in Marx." Slavic Review 27(1968): 470-80.

_____. "A Note on Marxian Alienation." Oxford Economic Papers 22(1970): 438-42.

Robinson, Joan. "Marx on Unemployment." Economic Journal 51(1941): 234-48.

_____. "Marxism; Religion and Science." Monthly Review 14(1962): 423-31.

Rodinson, Maxime. "Marxist Sociology and Marxist Ideology." Diogenes 64(1968): 57-90.

Rogers, Arthur K. "Class Consciousness." Ethics 27(1917): 334-49.

Rogin, L. Review of Essay on Marxian Economics, by J. Robinson. American Economic Review 34(1944): 124-34.

Ropers, Richard. "Mead, Marx and Social Psychology." Catalyst 7(Winter 1973): 42061.

Rosdolsky, Roman. "Worker and Fatherland: A Note on a Passage in the 'Communist Manifesto'." Science & Society 29(1965): 330-7.

Rosen, Zvi. "The Influence of Bruno Baer on Marx's Concept of Alienation." Social Theory and Practice 1 No. 2(1970): 50-60.

Rosenberg, Bernard. "Veblen and Marx." Social Research 15 (1948): 99-117.

Rosenberg, Harold. "Marxism: Criticism and/or Action." Dissent 21(1974): 199-206.

_____. "The Pathos of the Proletariat." Kenyon Review 11(1949): 595-629.

Rosenberg, Nathan. "Karl Marx and the Economic Role of Science." Journal of Political Economy 82(1974): 713-28.

Rosenbloom, Richard S. "Men and Machines." Technology and Culture 5(1964): 489-511.

Rossiter, C. "Why Marx Failed Here." Saturday Evening Post 20 August 1960, pp. 32-3+.

Rotenstreich, Nathan. "On Radicalism." Philosophy of the Social Sciences 4(1974): 169-82.

_____. "The Ontological Status of History." American Philosophical Quarterly 9(1972): 49-58.

_____. "Theory and Practice in Marx." Iyyun 19(1968): 1-11.

Rothman, Stanley. "Marx Transformed?" Problems of Communism 18(November 1969): 58-60.

_____. "Marxism and the Paradox of Contemporary Political Thought." Review of Politics 24(1962): 212-32.

_____. "The Old Marx and the New: An Analysis." Social Order 12(1962): 459-64.

_____. "Understanding Marxism." Problems of Communism 15(July 1966): 51-4. Reply by T. Draper, November 1966, pp. 97-8.

Rothstein, A. "Triumph of the Manifesto." Labour Monthly 30(1948): 73-9.

"Round Table in Commemoration of the Centenary of the Communist Manifesto: The Sociology and Economics of Class Conflict." American Economic Review 39(May 1949): 13-46.

Rovatti, Pier Aldo. "The Critique of Fetishism in Marx's 'Grundrisse'." Telos 17(1973): 56-69.

_____. "Fetishism and Economic Categories." Telos 14 (1972): 87-105.

_____. "A Phenomenological Analysis of Marxism." Telos 5(1970): 160-73.

Roy, A. "Marxist View of Liberation." Ecumenical Review 25 (1973): 202-13.

Rubel, Maximilien. "Notes on Marx's Conception of Democracy." New Politics 1 No. 2(1962): 78-90.

Rubin, Barry. "Marxism and Education - Radical Thought and Educational Theory in the 1930's." Science & Society 36 (1972): 171-201.

Ruff, Ivan. "Can There be a Sociology of Literature?" British Journal of Sociology 25(1974): 367-77.

Rugina, Anghel. "A Monetary Dialogue with Karl Marx: Its Significance for Both Capitalist and Socialist Countries." East European Quarterly 8(1974): 353-70.

Runciman, W. G. "False Consciousness." Philosophy 44 (1969): 303-13.

Runkle, Gerald. "Karl Marx and the American Civil War." Comparative Studies in Society and History 6(1964): 117-41.

──────. "Marxism and Charles Darwin." Journal of Politics 23(1961): 108-26.

Rushing, W. A. "Class, Power and Alienation." Sociometry 33(1970): 166-77.

Rutland, M. "Marx and the Communist Manifesto." Based on the "Red Prussian" by L. Schwarzschild. National Review 130(March 1948): 209-16.

──────. Review of The Socialist Tradition, by A. Gray. National Review 129(July 1947): 55-61.

Ryan, A. "A New Look at Professor Tucker's Marx." Political Studies 15(1967): 202-10.

Rytina, Joan Huber, Loomis, Charles P. "Marxist Dialectic and Pragmatism: Power as Knowledge." American Sociological Review 35(1970): 308-18. Comments, pp. 912-4; reply, pp. 915-6.

Sachs, Ignacy. "Marx and the Foundations of Socio-Economic Prevision." Social Science Information/Information sur les Sciences Sociales 7 No. 6(1968): 81-90.

Saksena, S. K. "Dialectical Materialism." Philosophy and Phenomenological Research 10(1949-50): 157-79.

Salamini, Leonardo. "Gramsci and Marxist Sociology of Knowledge: An Analysis of Hegemony-Ideology-Knowledge." Sociological Quarterly 15(1974): 359-80.

Samuel, M. "Judaism, Christianity and Marxism: Some Reflections." Midstream 18 No. 2(1972): 34-40.

Samuelson, P. A. "The Economics of Marx: An Ecumenical Reply." Journal of Economic Literature 10(1972): 50-1.

──────. "Marxian Economics as Economics." American Economic Review 57(1967): 616-23. Discussion by E. D. Domar, D. F. Gordon and H. S. Gordon, pp. 636-41.

———————. "Samuelson's Reply on Marxian Matters." Journal of Economic Literature 11(1973): 64-8.

———————. "The 'Transformation' from Marxian 'Values' to Competitive 'Prices': A Process of Rejection and Replacement." Proceedings of the National Academy of Sciences 67(1970): 423-5.

———————. "Understanding the Marxian Notion of Exploitation: A Summary of the So-Called Transformation Problem Between Marxian Values and Competitive Prices." Journal of Economic Literature 9(1971): 399-431.

———————. "Wages and Interest: A Modern Dissection of Marxian Economic Models." American Economic Review 47 (1957): 884-912.

———————. "Wages and Interest: A Modern Dissection of Marxian Economic Models: Reply." American Economic Review 50(1960): 719-21.

Sanchez, Antonio. "Vicissitudes of the Aesthetic Ideas of Marx." Monthly Review 25 No. 9(1975): 37-49.

Sanderson, J. "Demystifying the Historical Process: Karl Marx." Futures 6(June 1974): 271-6.

———————. "Programme for the Proletariat: Karl Marx." Futures 6(August 1974): 340-5.

Sanderson, John. "Marx and Engels on the State." Western Political Quarterly 16(1963): 946-55.

Santayana, G. "Some Developments of Materialism." American Scholar 18(July 1949): 271-81.

Santilli, Paul. "Marx on Species-Being and Social Essence." Studies in Soviet Thought 13(1973): 76-87.

Saran, K. "The Marxian Theory of Social Change." Inquiry 6(1963): 70-128.

Savage, D. S. "Literature and Marxism." Cambridge Journal 6(1953): 643-54.

Scanlan, James P. "A Critique of the Engels - Soviet Version of Marxian Economic Determinism." Studies in Soviet Thought 13(1973): 11-9.

Schaff, Adam. "Alienation and Social Action." Diogenes 57 (1967): 64-82.

_____. "Marx and Contemporary Humanism." Diogenes 62 (1968): 62-77.

_____. "Marxist Dialectics and the Principle of Contradiction." Translated by M. Riesic. Journal of Philosophy 57(1960): 241-50.

_____. "Marxist Theory on Revolution and Violence." Journal of the History of Ideas 34(1973): 263-70.

_____. Review of Marx's Concept of Man, by Erich Fromm, and Philosophy and Myth in Karl Marx, by Robert C. Tucker. History and Theory 2(1963): 307-18.

Scheler, M. B. "Karl Marx: False or True Prophet?" Dynamic America May 1937, pp. 14-8.

Schiebel, Joseph. "Changing the Unchangable: Historical Materialism and Six Versions of Eternal Laws of Historical Development." Studies in Soviet Thought 7(1967): 318-32.

Schlesinger, Rudolph. "The Continuity of Marx's Thought." Science & Society 29(1965): 217-24.

Schonfeld, W. R. "The Classical Marxist Conception of Liberal Democracy." Review of Politics 33(1971): 360-76.

Schoolman, Morton. "Further Reflections on Work, Alienation and Freedom in Marcuse and Marx." Canadian Journal of Political Science 6(1973): 295-302.

Schroyer, Trent. "Marx's Theory of the Crisis." Telos 14 (1972): 106-25.

Schuller, Peter M. "Karl Marx's Atheism." Science & Society 39(1975): 331-45.

Schumpeter, Joseph A. "The Communist Manifesto in Sociology and Economics." Journal of Political Economy 57(1949): 199-212.

Schur, Edwin M. "Theory, Planning and Pathology." Social Problems 6(1958-59): 221-9.

Schwartz, B. "Marx and Lenin on China." Far Eastern Survey 18(1949): 174-8.

Schwartz, H. "Marx to Khrushchev: A Four Act Drama." New York Times Magazine 12 November 1961, p. 22+.

Schwartzman, David W. "Althusser, Dialectical Materialism and the Philosophy of Science." Science & Society 39 (1975): 318-30.

Scott, Ivan. "Nineteenth Century Anarchism and Marxism." Social Science 47 No. 4(1972): 212-8.

Scott, T. "Savior of the Working Man." Forum 44(July 1910): 90-4.

Seigel, J. E. "Alienation. Marx's Conception of Man in Capitalist Society." History and Theory 12(1973): 329-42.

_____. "Marx's Early Development: Vocation, Rebellion, and Realism." Journal of Interdisciplinary History 3 (1973): 475-508.

Sellars, Roy Wood. "Existentialism, Realistic Empiricism and Materialism." Philosophy and Phenomenological Research 25(1965): 315-32.

_____. "Reflections on Dialectical Materialism." Philosophy and Phenomenological Research 5(1944-45): 157-79.

Selsam, Howard. "Ethics of the Communist Manifesto." Science & Society 12(1948): 22-32.

_____. "Friedrich Engels, Philosopher: A Discussion of the Work of Marx's Closest Collaborator." New Masses 8 October 1946, pp. 9-13.

Semenov, Yuri Ivanovich. "Theoretical Problems of 'Economic Anthropology'." Philosophy of the Social Sciences 4 (1974): 201-31.

Sen, A. "Marx, Weber, and India Today." Economic and Political Weekly 7(1972): 307-16.

Seton, F. "The 'Transformation Problem'." Review of Economic Studies 24 No. 3(1957): 149-60.

Shapiro, Gilbert; Markoff, John; and Weitman, Sasha, R. "Quantitative Studies of the French Revolution." History and Theory 12(1973): 163-91.

Sharma, T. R. "Marxian Theory, Non-Capitalist Path and the Indian Communists." Indian Political Science Review 10 (1976): 47-58.

Sharpe, M. R., et al. "Marxism and Monopoly Capitalism: A Symposium." Science & Society 30(1966): 461-96.

Shaw, Martin. "The Theory of the State and Politics: A Central Paradox of Marxism." Economy and Society 3(1974): 429-50.

Sherman, Howard J. "Marx and the Business Cycle." Science & Society 31(1967): 486-504.

_____. "Marxist Economics and Soviet Planning." Soviet Studies 18(1966): 169-88.

_____. "Marxist Models of Cyclical Growth." History of Political Economy 3(1971): 28-55.

_____. "The Marxist Theory of Value Revisited." Science & Society 34(1970): 257-92.

Shils, E. "Tradition Ecology and Institution in the History of Sociology." Daedalus 99(1970): 760-825.

Shiozawa, K. "Marx's View of Asiatic Society and His 'Asiatic Mode of Production'." Developing Economics 4 (1966): 299-315.

Shmueli, Efraim. "Can Phenomenology Accomodate Marxism?" Telos 17(1973): 169-80.

Shoul, Bernice. "Karl Marx and Say's Law." Quarterly Journal of Economics 71(1957): 611-29.

_____. "Karl Marx's Solutions to Some Theoretical Problems of Classical Economics." Science & Society 31 (1967): 448-60.

_____. "Similarities in the Work of John Stuart Mill and Karl Marx." Science & Society 29(1965): 270-95.

Shove, G. F. "Mrs. Robinson on Marxian Economics." Economic Journal 54(April 1944): 47-61.

Shtaerman, E. M. "The Society of Classical Antiquity: The Modernization of History and Historical Analogies." Soviet Sociology 10 No. 2(1971): 107-52.

Sichel, Betty A. "Karl Marx and the Rights of Man." Philosophy and Phenomenological Research 32(1972): 355-60.

Silverman, B., and Yanowitch, M. "Radical and Liberal Perspectives on the Working Class." Social Policy 4(1974): 40-9.

Simkhovitch, V. G. "Marxism vs. Socialism." Political Science Quarterly 23(1908): 193-219; 23(1908): 652-89; 24(1909): 236-68; 24(1909): 641-66; 25(1910): 393-419; 27(1912): 73-91; 27(1912): 605-30.

_____. Review of Karl Marx: His Life and Work, by John Spargo. Political Science Quarterly 26(1911): 707-11.

Simpson, Herman. "The Marxian Dialectic: A Reply." <u>New Republic</u> 28 February 1934, pp. 63-7.

Simpson, H., and Hook, S. "Understanding Karl Marx." <u>New Republic</u> 30 September 1936, pp. 232-4.

Skolimowski, Henry. "Logos and Praxis." <u>Studies in Comparative Communism</u> 3 No. 2(1970): 25-30.

_____. "Open Marxism and Its Consequences." <u>Studies in Comparative Communism</u> 4(1971): 23-8. Comments and rejoinder, pp. 29-56.

Sloan, P. A.; Thomas, L; and Levy, H. "A Discussion of Dialectical Materialism." <u>Labour Monthly</u> 15(1933): 441-52.

Slochower, H. "Freud and Marx in Contemporary Literature." <u>Sewanee Review</u> 49(1941): 316-24.

_____. "Marxist Idea of Change and Law." <u>Science & Society</u> 8(1944): 345-53.

Small, A. W. "Socialism in the Light of Social Science." <u>American Journal of Sociology</u> 17(1912): 804-19.

Small, W. A. "On the Dialectical Triad and a Necessary and Sufficient Condition for a Dialectical Process." <u>Philosophia Mathematica</u> 7(June-December 1970): 57-62.

Smith, Henry. "Marx and the Trade Cycle." <u>Economic Studies</u> 4(June 1937): 192-204.

_____. "Marx as a Pure Economist." <u>Economic History</u> 3 (February 1939): 245-58.

Smolinski, Leon. "Karl Marx and Mathematical Economics." <u>Journal of Political Economy</u> 81(1973): 1189-204.

Soares, G. A. D. "Marxism as a General Sociological Orientation." <u>British Journal of Sociology</u> 19(1968): 365-74.

Solomon, Maynard. "Marx and Bloch: Reflection on Utopia and Art." <u>Telos</u> 13(1972): 68-85.

Solovev, E. Iu. "Individual and Situation in Marx's Sociopolitical Analysis." <u>Soviet Studies in Philosophy</u> 7 (1968): 35-48.

Somerville, H. "Marx's Theory of Money." <u>Economic Journal</u> 43(1933): 334-7.

Somerville, John. "Adam Schaff and Contemporary Marxism." <u>Philosophy and Phenomenological Research</u> 34(1973): 239-74.

_____. "Marxist Ethics: Determinism; and Freedom." Philosophy and Phenomenological Research 28(1967): 17-23.

_____. "Ontology, Logic, and Dialectical Materialism." International Philosophical Quarterly 8(1968): 113-24.

_____. "The Value Problem and Marxist Social Theory." Journal of Value Inquiry 2(1968): 52-7.

Soule, G. "Psychology and Revolution." Review of Freud and Marx, by R. Osborn. New Republic 25 August 1937, pp. 66-72.

Sowell, Thomas. "Karl Marx and the Freedom of the Individual." Ethics 73 No. 2(1963): 119-25.

_____. "Marxian Value Reconsidered." Economica 30(1963): 297-308.

_____. "Marx's Capital After One Hundred Years." Canadian Journal of Economics and Political Science 33 (1967): 50-74.

_____. "Marx's 'Increasing Misery' Doctrine." American Economic Review 50(1960): 111-20.

Spargo, J. "Influence of Karl Marx on Contemporary Socialism." American Journal of Sociology 16(July 1910): 21-40.

_____. "Marx and Marxism." Saturday Review of Literature 1 June 1929, p. 1069.

"Special Issue Relating to Karl Marx Seminar, 1967." Artha Vijnana 10(September 1968): 349-588.

Spitzer, S. "Toward a Marxian Theory of Deviance." Social Problems 22(1975): 638-51.

Sprinzak, Ehud. "Marx's Historical Conception of Ideology and Science." Politics & Society 5(1975): 395-416.

Standen, A. "A Scientist Reads Das Kapital." Commonweal 10 September 1948, pp. 519-21.

Stardza, V. "Rise of the Marxian Man." South Atlantic Quarterly 51(1952): 211-21.

Stark, W. "Kierkegaard on Capitalism." (Compared to Marx). Sociological Review 42(1950): 87-114.

Stedman Jones, Gareth. "Engels and the End of Classical German Philosophy." New Left Review 79(1973): 17-36.

Steedman, I. "Marx on the Falling Rate of Profit." Australian Economic Papers 10 No. 16(1971): 61-6.

──────. "Value, Price and Profit." New Left Review 90 (1975): 71-80.

Steiner, George. "Marxism and the Literary Critic." Encounter 11(1958): 33-43.

Steinvorth, Ulrich. "Marx's Analysis of Commodity Exchange - A Reply to Carver." Inquiry 19(1976): 99-107.

Stern, Bernhard J. "Engels on the Family." Science & Society 12(1948): 42-64.

──────. "Some Aspects of Historical Materialism." Science & Society 21(1957): 10-27.

Stiernotte, Alfred. "Mysticism and Communism." Journal for the Scientific Study of Religion 6(1967): 110-2.

Stojanovic, Svetozar. "The Dialectics of Alienation and the Utopia of Dealienation." Praxis 5(1969): 387-98.

──────. "The Statist Myth of Socialism." Praxis 3(1967): 176-87.

Stolzman, James D., and Gamberg, Herbert V. "Marxist Class Analysis Versus Stratification Analysis as General Approaches to Social Inequality." Berkeley Journal of Sociology 18(1973-74): 105-25.

Strickland, D. A. "Defining 'Ideology' - A Reformulation." Res Publica 15(1974): 161-77.

Strickland, D. A., and Kontopoulos, Kyriakos. "Ideology and Praxis: Fichte to Marx." Il Politico 38(March 1973): 99-122.

Struik, D. J. "Friedrich Engels and Science." New Masses 4 December 1945, p. 10+.

──────. "Friedrich Engels in New England." New England Quarterly 22(1949): 240-3.

──────. "Marx and Mathematics." Science & Society 12 (1948): 181-96.

──────. "Marx's Economic-Philosophical Manuscripts." Science & Society 27(1963): 283-301.

Sturdya, Vlad. "The Rise of the Marxian Man." South Atlantic Quarterly 51(1952): 211-21.

Suchting, W. A. "Marx and Hanna Arendt's The Human Condition." Ethics 73 No. 1(1962): 47-55.

_____. "Marx, Popper, and 'Historicism'." Inquiry 15 (1972): 235-65.

Sukiennicki, Wiktor. "The Vision of Communism - Marx to Khruschev." Problems of Communism 9 No. 6(1960): 1-10.

Sullivan, Robert R. "Philosophy & Myth in Studies of Karl Marx." Polity 6(1974): 393-402.

Sundinski, L. "Karl Marx and Mathematical Economics." Journal of Political Economy 81(1973): 1189-204.

Sweezy, Paul M. "Marxian Socialism." Monthly Review 8 (November 1956): 227-41.

_____. "Some Problems in the Theory of Capital Accumulation." Monthly Review 26(May 1974): 38-55.

Swift, O. B. "Passing of Marxism." Bibliotheca Sacra 77 (1920): 443-59.

Swingewood, Alan. "Comte, Marx and Political Economy." Sociological Review 18(1970): 335-50.

"Symposium on the Young Marx." Science & Society 27(1963): 283-326.

Szacki, Jerzy. "Remarks on the Marxian Concept of 'False Consciousness'." Polish Sociological Bulletin 14(1966): 30-9.

Szamuely, Tibor. "The Birth of Russian Marxism." Survey 18 No. 3(1972): 56-90.

Szymanski, Al. "Malinowski, Marx and Functionalism." Insurgent Sociologist 2 No. 4(1972): 35-43.

_____. "Marx and the Laws of Competitive and Monopoly Capitalism." Social Praxis 1(1973): 299-317.

_____. "Marxism and Science." Insurgent Sociologist 3 No. 3(1973): 25-38.

_____. "Marxist Theory and International Capital Flows." Review of Radical Political Economy 6(Fall 1974): 20-40.

Tashjean, J. E. "Borkenau on Marx: An Intellectual Biography." Wiseman Review 235(Summer 1961): 149-57.

Tatsis, Nicholas C., and Zito, George V. "Marx, Durkheim, and Alienation: Toward a Heuristic Typology." Social Theory and Practice 3(1974): 223-43.

Taylor, O. H. "Schumpeter and Marx: Imperialism and Social Classes in the Schumpeterian System." Quarterly Journal of Economics 65(1951): 525-55.

Thakurdas, F. "Hegel's Philosophical Politics and its Influence on Marx." Journal of Political Studies 4 No. 1 (1971): 1-13.

Therborn, Göran. "The Theorists of Capitalism." New Left Review 87/88(1974): 125-44.

──────. "The Working Class and the Birth of Marxism." New Left Review 79(1973): 3-15.

Thomas, Paul. "Karl Marx and Max Stirner." Political Theory 3(1975): 159-79.

──────. "Marx and Science." Political Studies 24 No. 1 (1976): 1-23.

Thomas, Wendell. "What Shall We Do With Karl Marx?" Journal of Adult Education 13 No. 1(1941): 23-8.

Thompson, C. L. "Labor's Problem: Real Wages." Current History 18(1950): 154-62.

Thormer, Daniel. "Marx on India and the Asiatic Mode of Production." Contributions to Indian Sociology 9(December 1966): 33-66.

Thweatt, W. O. "A Growth Equation Analysis of the Ricardian and Marxian Theories of Growth." Indian Economic Review 4 No. 1(1958): 1-5.

Tillich, Paul. "How Much Truth is There in Karl Marx?" Christian Century 8 September 1948, pp. 906-8.

Timofeev, Timur. "Marx and Working Class Development." Social Science Information/Information sur les Sciences Sociales 7 No. 5(1968): 37-50.

Tökés, R. L. "Ethical Problems of Communist Political Development or Back to the Baby Marx." Newsletter on Comparative Studies of Communism 6 No. 4(1973): 19-26.

Topolski, Jerzy. "Levi-Strauss and Marx on History." History and Theory 12(1973): 192-207.

Trevor-Roper, Hugh R. "Marxism and the Study of History; Marxist Theory of Historical Materialism." Problems of Communism 5 No. 5(1956): 36-42.

_____. "Stalin Would Have Liquidated Marx." New York Times Magazine 30 January 1949, p. 9+.

Tribe, Keith. "Remarks on the Theoretical Significance of Marx's 'Grundrisse'." Economy and Society 3(1974): 180-210.

Trigger, Bruce G. "Engels on the Part Played by Labour in the Transition from Ape to Man: An Anticipation of Contemporary Anthropological Theory." Canadian Review of Sociology and Anthropology 4 No. 3(1967): 165-76.

Tristam, R. "Ontology and Theory; A Comment on Marx's Analysis of Some of the Problems." Sociological Review 23(1975): 759-77.

Truitt, Willis H. "Ideology, Expression and Mediation in Marx, Raphael and Lukacs." Philosophical Forum (Boston) 3(1972): 468-93.

Tsuru, S. "Business Cycle and Capitalism: Schumpeter vs. Marx." Annals of the Hitotsubashi Academy 2(April 1952): 134-47.

_____. "Marx's 'Tableau Economique' and 'Underconsumption' Theory." Indian Economic Review 1 No. 3(1953): 1-13.

Tucker, Charles W. "Marx and Sociology: Some Theoretical Implications." Pacific Sociological Review 12 No. 2 (1969): 87-94.

Tucker, G. S. L. "Ricardo and Marx." Economica 28 No. 111 (1961): 252-69.

Tucker, Robert C. "Culture, Political Culture, and Communist Society." Political Science Quarterly 88(1973): 173-90.

_____. "The Cunning of Reason in Hegel and Marx." Review of Politics 18(1956): 269-95.

_____. "The De-radicalization of Marxist Movements." American Political Science Review 61(1967): 343-58.

_____. "Marx and the End of History." Diogenes 64(1968): 165-74.

_____. "Marxism and Group Theory." Journal of Philosophy 59(1962): 678-9.

_____. "Symbolism of History in Hegel and Marx." Journal of Philosophy 54(1957): 144-5.

Turck, Dieter. "Action vs. Contemplation." Southwestern Journal of Philosophy 3(Fall 1972): 63-70.

Turner, Bryan S. "The Concept of Social 'Stationariness': Utilitarianism and Marxism." Science & Society 38(1974): 3-18.

Turner, Jonathan H. "Marx and Simmel Revisited: Reassessing the Foundations of Conflict Theory." Social Forces 53 (1975): 618-27.

Uchida, Yosshikiko. "Japan Today and Das Kapital." Japan Interpreter 6 No. 1(1970): 8-28.

Ulam, A. B. "The Historical Role of Marxism and the Soviet System." World Politics 8 No. 1(1955): 20-45.

Untermann, E. "Writings of Karl Marx." Arena 38(October 1907): 457-61.

Urbanek, Eduard. "Roles, Masks, and Characters: A Contribution to Marx's Idea of the Social Role." Social Research 34(1967): 529-62.

Urry, John. "Towards a Structural Theory of the Middle Class." Acta Sociologica 16 No. 3(1973): 175-87.

Vajda, Mihaly. "Marxism, Existentialism, Phenomenology: A Dialogue." Telos 6(1971): 3-29.

Van Der Kroef, M. "Class Structure and Communist Theory." American Behavioral Scientist 4(May 1961): 19-23.

Van Der Muhll, G. E. "Marxism, Ideologies and the Intellectuals." Indian Political Science Review 2 Nos. 3-4 (1968): 121-31.

Van de Veer, Donald. "Marx's View of Justice." Philosophy and Phenomenological Research 33(1973): 366-86.

Varela, Charles. "From Substance to Function: The Emergence of Sociology from Social Philosophy." Kinesis 2(Spring 1970): 93-105.

Varma, V. P. "Critique of Marxian Sociology." Calcutta Review 134(March 1955): 262-8; 135(June 1955): 32-8, 187-98, 299-308.

_____. "Gandhi and Marx." Indian Journal of Political Science 15 No. 2(1954): 115-33.

Vazquez, Antonio Sanchez. "Vicissitudes of the Aesthetic Ideas of Marx." Monthly Review 25 No. 9(1974): 37-49.

Veblen, Thorstein. "The Socialist Economics of Karl Marx." Quarterly Journal of Economics 20(1906): 575-95; 21 (1907): 299-322.

Veca, Salvatore. "Value, Labor and the Critique of Political Economy." Telos 9(Fall 1971): 48-64.

Veltmeyer, Henry. "Towards an Assessment of the Structuralist Interrogation of Marx: Claude Levi-Strauss and Louis Althusser." Science & Society 38(1974-75): 385-421.

Venetsanopoulos, V., et al. "Notes on the History of the Idea of Proletarian Dictatorship." World Marxist Review 17(July 1974): 64-75.

Voeglin, E. "The Formation of the Marxian Revolutionary Idea." Review of Politics 12(1950): 275-302.

Volin, Lazar. "Karl Marx and Russia." South Atlantic Quarterly 52(April 1953): 165-79.

Von Krosigk, Frederick. "Marx, Universalism, and Contemporary World Business." International Studies Quarterly 16 (1972): 530-48.

von Staden, Heinrich. "Nietzsche and Marx on Greek Art and Literature: Case Studies in Reception." Daedalus 105 No. 1(1976): 79-96.

von Weizsaker, C. C. "Morishima on Marx." Economic Journal 83(1973): 1245-52. Reply by M. Morishima, 84(1974): 387-91.

Vorob'ev, M. F. "Negation of the Negation in Logical and Historical Analysis." Soviet Studies in Philosophy 8(Fall 1969): 190-205.

Vygodsky, S. "Marx's Economic Theory and His Present Critics." Problems of Economics 1(November 1958): 12-7.

Wagner, Helmut R. "Marx and Weber as Seen by Carl Mayer." Social Research 42(1975): 720-8.

Wagner, Y., and Strauss, M. "The Programme of the Communist Manifesto and Its Theoretical Foundations." Political Studies 17(1969): 470-84.

Walker, Angus. "Karl Marx, The Declining Rate of Profit, and British Political Economy." Economica 38 No. 152(1971): 362-77.

Wall, B. "William Morris and Karl Marx." Dublin Review 202(January 1938): 39-47.

Wallace, Kyle. "Dialectical Materialism and the Problem of Knowledge." Journal of Critical Analysis 2(October 1972): 23-35.

Walton, Paul. "From Surplus Value to Surplus Theories: Marx, Marcuse, and MacIntyre." Social Research 37(1970): 644-55.

_____. "Ideology and the Middle Class in Marx and Weber." Sociology 5(1971): 389-94. Reply, pp. 395-7.

_____. "The Image of Man in Marx." Social Theory and Practice 1(Fall 1970): 69-84.

_____. "McLellan's Marx." British Journal of Sociology 23(1972): 358-61.

_____. "Marx and Marcuse." Human Context 3(1971): 159-75.

Walton, P.; Coulter, J.; and Gamble, A. "Image of Man in Marx." Social Theory and Practice 1(Fall 1970): 69-84.

_____. "Philosophical Anthropology in Marxism." Social Research 37(1970): 259-74.

Wang, Jo-Shui. "On the Problem of the Identity of Thinking and Being." Chinese Studies in Philosophy 4(Winter 1971): 147-77.

Ward, E. E. "Marx and Keynes General Theory." Economic Record Supplement 1939, pp. 152-67.

Ward, J. W. "Mill, Marx, and Modern Individualism." Virginia Quarterly Review 35(1959): 527-39.

Wayne, Y., and Strauss, M. "The Programme of the Communist Manifesto and Its Theoretical Foundations." Political Studies 17(1969): 470-84.

Weintraub, W. "Marx and the Russian Revolutionaries." Cambridge Journal 3(1950): 497-503.

Weisskopf, W. A. "The Dialectics of Abundance." Diogenes 57(1967): 1-15.

Weissman, Marsha. "Alternative Critiques of Capitalism: Marxism, Social Democracy and the New Left." Maxwell Review 11(Winter 1974-75): 37-57.

Werckmeister, O. K. "Marx on Ideology and Art." New Literary History 4(1973): 501-19.

Werlin, Robert J. "Marxist Political Analysis." Sociological Inquiry 42 Nos. 3-4(1972): 157-81.

Wesolowski, W. "Marx's Theory of Class Domination (an Attempt at Systematization)." Polish Round Table 1(1967): 21-53.

West, E. G. "The Political Economy of Alientation: Karl Marx and Adam Smith." Oxford Economic Papers 21 No. 1(1969): 1-23.

Wetter, Gustav A. "The Ambivalence of the Marxist Concept of Ideology." Studies in Soviet Thought 9 No. 3(1969): 177-83.

"When Dogma Bites Dogma, or the Difficult Marriage of Marx and Freud." Times Literary Supplement 8 January 1971, pp. 25-7.

White, D. F. "Marx Evaluates Labor." Commonweal 7 July 1939, pp. 276+.

White, Hayden V. "The Tasks of Intellectual History." Monist 53(1969): 606-30.

Wiatr, Jerzy J. "Sociology - Marxism - Reality." Social Research 34(1967): 416-34.

Willer, David. "Marx and Weber: A Theory of Historical Change." Kansas Journal of Sociology 4 No. 2(1968): 65-9.

William, M. "Is Class Conflict Necessary? The Social Interpretation of History." American Federationist 29(1922): 922-5.

Williams, John R. "The Marxist Concept of the State's Origins." International Review of History and Political Science 4 No. 2(1967): 47-56.

Williams, Raymond. "Base and Superstructure in Marxist Cultural Theory." New Left Review 82(1973): 3-16.

Williams, W. A. "On the Restoration of Brooks Adams." (Compared to Marx.) Science & Society 20(1956): 247-53.

Williamson, Colwyn. "Ideology and the Problem of Knowledge." Inquiry 10 No. 2(1967): 121-38.

Willoughby, Charles A. A. "Karl Marx: Apostle of Communism, Feared and Hated Russia." Ukrainian Quarterly 19 No. 2 (1962): 133-40.

Wilson, Edmund. "Emotional Pattern in Marx." New Republic 19 February 1940, pp. 239-42.

―――――. "Herr Vogt." New Republic 15 November 1939, pp. 106-8.

―――――. "Karl Marx: Poet of Commodities." New Republic 8 January 1940, pp. 46-7.

―――――. "Karl Marx: Prometheus and Lucifer." New Republic 6 July 1938, pp. 244-7.

―――――. "Marx and Engels: Grinding the Lens." New Republic 7 September 1938, pp. 125-7.

―――――. "Marx Decides to Change the World." New Republic 20 July 1938, pp. 301-4.

―――――. "Marx-Engels Partnership." New Republic 17 August 1938, pp. 40-3.

―――――. "Marxist History." New Republic 12 October 1932, pp. 226-8.

―――――. "Marxist Humanism." New Republic 3 May 1939, pp. 371-2.

―――――. "Some Letters After 1848: Engels to Marx, Flaubert to Maxime du Camp." New Republic 8 February 1939, pp. 21-3.

―――――. "Young Man From Manchester." New Republic 3 August 1938, pp. 352-6.

Wilson, Murray. "Was Marx Right?" Australian Quarterly 44 No. 4(1972): 44-59.

Winternitz, J. "Values and Prices: A Solution of the So-called Transformation Problem." Economic Journal 58(1948): 276-80.

Wittfogel, Karl A. "Marxism, Anarchism, and the New Left." Modern Age 14 No. 2(1970): 114-28.

―――――. "The Marxist View of Russian Society and Revolution." World Politics 12(1960): 487-508.

―――――. "Results and Problems of the Study of Oriental Despotism." Journal of Asian Studies 28(1969): 357-65.

―――――. "The Ruling Bureaucracy of Oriental Despotism: A Phenomena that Paralyzed Marx." Review of Politics 15 (1953): 350-9.

Wolfe, Alan. "New Directions in the Marxist Theory of Politics." Politics & Society 4 No. 2(1974): 131-60.

Wolfe, Bertram D. "Das Kapital One Hundred Years Later." Antioch Review 26(1966-67): 421-42.

──────. "Lenin Has Trouble With Engels." Russian Review 15(1956): 196-209.

──────. "Marx on the Truman Doctrine." 20th Century 149 (1951): 313-8.

──────. "Marxism Today." Antioch Review 18(1958): 471-87.

──────. "Marxism - Yesterday and Today. The Prophet and His Prophecies." Problems of Communism 7 No. 6(1958): 24-31.

──────. "Nationalism and Internationalism in Marx and Engels." American Slavic and East European Review 17 (1958): 403-17.

Wolff, Kurt H. "Bracketing Marx." Praxis 5(1969): 84-5.

Wolfson, Murray. "The Day Karl Marx Grew Up." History of Political Economy 3(1971): 335-52.

Wolfstetter, E. "Surplus Labour, Synchronised Labour Costs and Marx's Labour Theory of Value." Economic Journal 83 (1973): 787-809.

Wolpe, Harold. "An Examination of Some Approaches to the Problem of the Development of Revolutionary Consciousness." Telos 4(1969): 113-44.

Wood, Allen W. "The Marxian Critique of Justice." Philosophy & Public Affairs 1(1972): 244-82.

──────. "Marx's Critical Anthropology: Three Recent Interpretations." Review of Metaphysics 26(1972): 118-39.

Wood, H. G. "Marx and Science." Hibbert Journal 54(1956): 226-34.

──────. "Marxism and Religion." Contemporary Review 177 (1950): 288-91.

Woodall, Jean. "Marx Seen From Within." Government and Opposition 8(1973): 523+.

Wright, David McCord. "The Economics of a Classless Society." American Economics Review 39(1949): 27-36.

Wrong, D. H. Review of *Marxism: An Historical and Critical Study*, by G. Lichtheim. *Commentary* 32(December 1961): 542-6.

Yaffe, David S. "The Marxian Theory of Crisis, Capital and the State." *Economy and Society* 2(1973): 186-232.

Ya nan, Wang. "The Marxist Population Theory and China's Population Problem." *Chinese Economic Studies* 2(Spring-Summer 1969): 3-91.

Yanowitch, Murray. "Alienation and the Young Marx in Soviet Thought." *Slavic Review* 26(1967): 29-53.

Yin, Ch'ing - Yao. "From Marx and Lenin to Mao Tse-Tung." *Issues and Studies* 9 No. 2(1972): 11-8.

Young, Gary. "A Note on Marx's Terminology." *Science & Society* 40(1976): 72-8.

Young, J. D. "Karl Marx: Moralist, Reformist, Utopian." *New Politics* 10 No. 1(1972): 44-9.

Young, M. "Marx's Grave." *New Republic* 1 May 1935, pp. 342.

Zavadskii, K. M.; Georgievskii, A. B.; and Mozelov, A. P. "Friedrich Engels and Darwinism." *Soviet Studies in Philosophy* 10(Summer 1971): 63-80.

Zikmund, William G. "Karl Marx and Georg Simmel: A Dialogue on Socialism and Other Things." *Journal of Thought* 9 (1974): 51-5.

Ziukovic, Ljubomir. "The Structure of Marxist Sociology." *Social Research* 34(1967): 477-506.

Zivotic, Miladin. "The Dialectics of Nature and the Authenticity of Dialectics." *Praxis* 3(1967): 253-63.

_____. "The End of Ideals or of Ideology." *Praxis* 5 (1969): 409-29.

Zwick, Peter. "The Marxist Roots of National Communism." *Canadian Review of Studies in Nationalism* 3 No. 2(1976): 127-44.

DOCTORAL DISSERTATIONS ON MARX AND ENGELS

Anastasia, Diane Doherty. "Orthodox and Hegelian Marxism: A Historical and Critical Study of the Trends in Contemporary Marxism." Boston University, 1975.

Anderson, Gerald Ray. "Social Development and the Problem of Self-Determination (With Special Emphasis on the Philosophies of Hegel and Marx)." Northwestern University, 1973.

Arthur, John Hugh. "Systemic Explanation and Marxian Methodology." Vanderbilt University, 1973.

Bender, Frederic Lawrence. "The Origin and Development of Marx's Philosophical Anthropology." Northwestern University, 1968-69.

Berger, Martin Edgar. "War, Armies, and Revolution: Friedrich Engels Military Thought." University of Pittsburg, 1969.

Bevan, Ruth Anita. "The Political Philosophies of Edmund Burke and Karl Marx: An Analysis of Their Relevance to Contemporary Politics." New York University, 1968-69.

Biddulph, Howard Lowell. "Karl Marx's Early Thought in Soviet Philosophy." Indiana University, 1966.

Bisztray, George. "The Concept of Realism in Marxist Literary Criticism." University of Minnesota, 1972.

Blake, William Northrup. "Education in Marx's Concept of Labor." University of Alberta, Canada, 1967.

Blaney, Robert William. "Karl Marx's Critique of Religion." Boston University, 1965-66.

Bloom, Solomon F. "The World of Nations: A Study of the National Implications in the Work of Karl Marx." Columbia University, 1941.

Bober, Mandell Morton. "Karl Marx's Interpretation of History." Harvard University, 1925.

Borchert, Donald Marvin. "A Discussion Relating to Humanization: The Means-Ends Program of Karl Marx Analyzed On the Basis of His Major Works; The Means-Ends Program of Karl Marx Criticized from the Standpoint of Arthur Koestler's Life and Thought; The Post-Communism of Arthur Koestler Viewed from a Christian Theological Perspective." Princeton Theological Seminary, 1965-66.

Boutilier, Mary A. "Critique of Hegel's Philosophy of Right, by Karl Marx: An Analysis and Evaluation." Georgetown University, 1974.

Bowen, Elinor Rubens. "An Explanation of Conventional and Unconventional Political Behavior: Marx, Lebon, and the Survey Research Center in the Cleveland Ghetto." Case Western Reserve University, 1969.

Brown, Gladstone, L. "A Christian Criticism of the Philosophy of Karl Marx, with Special Reference to the Problem of Anthropology, Philosophically and Theologically Understood." Drew University, 1957-58.

Calhoun, Donald W. "The Reception of Marxian Sociological Theory by American Academic Sociologists." University of Chicago, 1951.

Cassidy, Frank P. "Revolutionary Politics and Normal Politics: Rousseau, Marx, and Lenin." Stanford University, 1973.

Chandler, Ludway. "Paradigms of Development in World Perspective: The Applicability of Modified Marxist Models to Developing Areas." University of Oregon, 1970.

Chang, Sherman Hsiao-Ming. "The Marxian Theory of State." University of Pennsylvania, 1930.

Chao, Paul Kwang-Yi. "Analysis of Marxist Doctrine on the Family with Testing of its Validity in Soviet Russia and Communist China." New York University, 1962-63.

Cherno, Melvin. "Ludwig Feuerbach and the Intellectual Basis of Nineteenth Century Radicalism." Stanford University, 1955.

Chung, Ho Eun. "Alienation in the Writings of Hegel, Marx, and the Existentialists." University of Pittsburg, 1962.

Clecak, Pete Emmett. "Marxism and American Literary Criticism." Stanford University, 1965.

Clickner, Edwin Kirwan. "The Influence of Classicism on Marxian Economic Thought." American University, 1962-63.

Conly, Craig Alan. "Marx's Critique of Hegel: Foundations for a Theory of Change in a Technological Society." University of Colorado, 1971.

Conway, James F. "The Marxist Critique of Religion: A New Look." Graduate Theological Union, 1972.

Cope, James R. "Religion and the Dialectical Materialism of Karl Marx." Ohio State University, 1937.

Cox, David F. "Karl Marx's Philosophy of Value." Adelphi University, 1953.

Crowder, N. David. "A Marxist's Critique of Duncan's Stratification Research." Duke University, 1971.

D'Agostino, Anthony W. "Marxism and the Russian Anarchists." University of California, Los Angeles, 1971.

De Matteis, Phillip Breed. "Individuality and the Social Organism: The Controversy between Max Stirner and Karl Marx." Southern Illinois University, 1972.

Demetz, Peter. "Marx, Engels, and the Poets." Yale University, 1956.

De Nys, Martin J. "The Hegelian Source of Marx's Concept of Man." Loyola University, Chicago, 1973.

Drysdale, Elizabeth Susan Hoecker. "The Theory of Alienation in the 1844 Manuscripts of Karl Marx." Louisiana State University, 1968-69.

Ebenreck, Clyde William. "The Relationship between Atheism and the Philosophy of Man in the Philosophy of Karl Marx." Catholic University of America, 1971-72.

Eisenstein, Zillah Ruth. "Species Life in Marx and Durkheim: Its Import as an Ideology for Women in Contemporary Society." University of Massachusetts, 1972.

Erikson, Elliot. "Karl Marx and the Communist Manifesto." Stanford University, 1954.

Erlich, Bruce Sewell. "The Idea of Politics in George Buchner: An Essay on the Problem of Knowledge in the Transition from Hegel to Marx." University of Washington, 1972.

Ewing, Curtiss Kinney. "Freud and Engels: A Comparison of Sex Rules." University of New Mexico, 1974.

Fackre, Gabriel Joseph. "A Comparison and Critique of the Interpretations of Dehumanization in the Thought of Soren Kierkegaard and Karl Marx." University of Chicago, 1962.

Ferguson, Francis Percy. "Analysis, Interpretation, and Institutional Change: Marx and the Institutionalists, Commons and Veblen." University of Wisconsin, 1971.

Fried, Marlene Gerber. "Marx's Historical Materialism and the Problem of Explanation in History." Brown University, 1971-72.

Friesen, Abraham. "The Marxist Interpretation of the Reformation." Stanford University, 1967.

Fulton, Robert B. "The Problem of Religious Assumptions in the Systems of Adam Smith and Karl Marx." Yale University, 1943.

Gandy, Daniel Ross. "Karl Marx's Philosophy of History: A New Interpretation." University of Texas, 1967.

Garlick, Geraldine S. "Communist Interpretations of the Causes of War." State University of Iowa, 1955.

Geary, Andrew C. "Marxist-Hegelian Dialectics." The Universite Laval (Canada), 1949.

Gezork, Herbert. "Philosophic and Ethical Conceptions of Marxian Socialism." Southern Baptist Theological Seminary, 1930.

Gibson, Hilden Russell. "A Pragmatic Evaluation of the Political and Social Doctrines of Karl Marx." Stanford University, 1940.

Glass, James Marshall. "Plato, Rousseau, and Marx: A Study of the Theory of Non-Alienated Being and the Transformation of Consciousness." University of California, Berkely, 1970.

Gottheil, Fred M. "The Economic Predictions of Karl Marx: An Examination of Marxian Economic Theory." Duke University, 1959-60.

Hansen, James Edwin. "The Dialectic of Praxis in Karl Marx's Das Kapital." State University of New York at Buffalo, 1970-71.

Hansen, Olaf. "The Problem of Alienation and Reconciliation: A Comparative Study of Marx and Kierkegaard in the Light of Hegel's Formulation of the Problem." Princeton Theological Seminary, 1956.

Halbrook, Stephen Porter. "The Marx-Bakunin Controversy: Intellectual Origins, 1844-1870." Florida State University, 1972.

Hampsch, George Harold. "Some Aspects of the Marxist Notion of Classless Society." University of Notre Dame, 1963.

Handman, Max Sylvius. "The Beginnings of the Social Philosophy of Karl Marx." University of Chicago, 1917.

Harris, Leonard. "Racism and the Materialist Anthropology of Karl Marx." Cornell University, 1974.

Heffner, David James. "Marx on the Relations Between Nature and Man." Saint Louis University, 1973.

Herreshaff, David Sprague. "Americanizing of Marx." University of Southern California, 1959-60.

Hildebrand, George Herbert, Jr. "The Theory of Markets and the Problem of Economic Crises, from Quesnay to Marx: A Study in the History of Economic Thought." Cornell University, 1942.

Hirai, Atsuko. "Christian-Marxist Dialogue: An Inquiry About Brotherly and Human Co-Existence." St. Louis University, 1974.

Hordern, William E. "Christian and Marxian View of History." Union Theological Seminary, New York, 1951.

Howard, Richard Charles. "From Philosophy to Political Economy: Karl Marx and the Theory-Praxis Problem." University of Texas, 1970.

Husami, Ziyad Ibrahim. "The Marxian Theory of Alienation." Princeton University, 1974.

Isham, George Frederick. "Messianism, Humanism, and Atheism: Issues in Marxist-Christian Dialogue." Columbia University, 1971-72.

Jacobson, Nolan. "The Religious Naturalism Implicit in the Works of Karl Marx." University of Chicago, 1949.

John, Puthenpeedikail Matthew. "On Alienation in Praxis: The Encounter of Alienation in Early Marx with the Problematic of Praxis." Drew University, 1973.

Kain, Phillip Joseph. "Schiller, Hegel, Marx, and the Aesthetic Ideal of Ancient Greece." University of California, San Diego, 1974.

Kang, Chi-Won. "Alienation in Hegel and Marx: The Unknown Aspects of Hegel's Metaphysical Theme of Alienation and a Reassessment of Marx's Alienation Theme." University of Toronto, 1969.

Kaschins, Edward Anthony. "Karl Marx's Theory of Economic Crisis." University of Iowa, 1973.

Kavanaugh, John Francis. "Whole and Part in Hegel, Marx, and Marcuse." Washington University, 1973.

Kim, Choon Sup. "Dialectical Method." Columbia University, 1952.

Lam, Elizabeth P. "The Place of Marx in Christian Thought." University of Chicago, 1939.

Levine, David Phillip. "Accumulation and Technical Change in Marxian Economics." Yale University, 1973.

Levinson, Belle Doree. "Marx and Malreaux: A Study in Literature and Ideas." University of Wisconsin, 1973.

Livergood, Norman David. "The Principles of Activity in Marx's Dissertation and Its Influence on His Thought." Yale University, 1962.

Lowe, Donald Ming-Dah. "The Idea of China in Marx, Lenin, and Mao: A Study in Marxist Ideological Persistence and Transformation." University of California, Berkely, 1962-63.

Lyman, George Peter. "Marx's Use of Phenomenology in the Criticism of Politics and as a Solution to the Problem of Ideology." Stanford University, 1973.

McCarthy, George Edward. "The Social Anthropology of Hegel and Marx." Boston College, 1971-72.

McCarthy, Timothy Leo. "Marx's Concept of the Revolutionary Proletariat." Brandeis University, 1973.

McCoy, Charles. "Ludwig Feuerbach and the Formation of the Marxian Revolutionary Idea." Universite Laval (Canada), 1953.

McDonald, Henry M. "Marx, Engels, and the National Question." Harvard University, 1939.

McKown, Delos Banning. "The Classical Marxist Critique of Religion: Marx, Engels, Lenin, Kautsky." Florida State University, 1971-72.

Mage, Shane Henry. "The Law of Falling Tendency of the Rate of Profit: Its Place in the Marxian Theoretical System and Relevance to the United States Economy." Columbia University, 1963.

Massaro, Vincent Gerard. "Divergent Views on Marx's Increasing Misery Doctrine." University of Notre Dame, 1963.

Megill, Kenneth Alden. "The Community as a Democratic Principle in Marx's Philosophy." Yale University, 1966.

Melville, George L. "Marxism, Communism and the Theory of Economic Development (Parts I-III)." Indiana University, 1956.

Meyers, David Benton. "Marx's Dialectical Critique." University of Texas, 1972.

Mitra, Ranadhir. "Literary Criticism as Science: Problems and Possibilities in Structuralist and Marxist Endeavors." University of California, San Diego, 1972.

Murphy, William Paul. "Karl Marx's Critique of Hegel's Philosophy of State. (1843) with an Examination of the Problem Posed by the Tension between State and Society and Its Consequences for Philosophy and Politics." University of Notre Dame, 1975.

Neuman, Robert Paul. "Socialism, the Family and Sexuality: The Marxist Tradition and German Social Democracy Before 1914." Northwestern University, 1971-72.

Nissen, Bruce Allen. "Moral Means and Ends in Social Change: Dewey and Marxism." Columbia University, 1975.

O'Connell, John Charles. "Individualistic Implications in the Sociological Theories of Thomas Hobbes, Jean Jacques Rousseau, and Karl Marx." Harvard University, 1941.

Odajynk, Walter. "Marxism and Humanism: The Question of Continuity in the Thought of Marx." Columbia University, 1969-70.

O'Hare, William Timothy. "The Significance of 'Need' in the Philosophy of Karl Marx." Marquette University, 1973.

O'Neill, John. "Marxism and Scientism: An essay in the Philosophy of Social Science." Stanford University, 1962.

Ozingo, James. "The Relevance of Marx and Lenin to the Soviet Transition to Communism." Michigan State University, 1968.

Peterson, Forrest Harold. "The Study of Power in the Philosophies of Hegel and Marx." Georgetown University, 1959-60.

Petrus, Joeseph Anthony. "Marxism, Marxists and the National Question." The University of Texas, 1965-66.

Petulla, Joseph. "Christian Political Theology: A Marxian Guide." Graduate Theological Union, 1970-71.

Pezzolo, Peter Eugene. "A Contribution to the Interpretation of Marxian Theory." Yale University, 1973.

Reith, H. "The Marxist Dialectics of Nature." Universite Laval (Canada), 1946.

Restuccia, Paul Phillip. "Marx's Concept of Alienation." Southern Illinois University, 1968.

Robert, Ellen Ruth. "Women's Roles: A Marxist-Existentialist Analysis." Western Michigan University, 1973.

Rockmore, Thomas. "Man as Activity in Fichte and Marx." Vanderbilt University, 1973.

Rodriguez, Noelie Maria. "The Archetypal Vision: A Marxist and Jungian Study of Mural Art." University of California, Los Angeles, 1974.

Romaniuk, Gertrud Ursula. "Re-Examination of Karl Marx's and Friedrich Engel's Views on Polish Independence." Loyola University, Chicago, 1970.

Rouse, David Lowry. "The Form and Content of Social Life: An Examination of Marx's Materialism." Vanderbilt University, 1974.

Samuels, Stuart Raymond. "Marx, Freud, and English Intellectuals: A Study of the Dissemination and Reconcilliation of Ideas." Stanford University, 1971.

Schifferd, Kent Drummund. "The Origins of Modern Environmental Thought: A Study of the Writings of Daniel Defoe, David Diderot, and Karl Marx." Northern Illinois University, 1974.

Schuller, Peter Michael. "Karl Marx's Ethical Theory." Boston University, 1974.

Segal, Sol. "Science and Values: A Comparative Study of the Relations Between Science and Values, Particularly Ethical Values, in the Writings of John Dewey and Friedrich Engels." New York University, 1961.

Seldman, Neil Norman. "Early Marx Interpretation in the United States During the Making of Industrial Society, 1886-1914." George Washington University, 1974.

Shishido, Miles Motoyuki. "Individual and Community in the Systems of Marx and Tillich." University of Chicago, 1968.

Shore, Maurice Joseph. "The Marxian Theory of Education." Johns-Hopkins University, 1940.

Shoul, Bernice D. "The Marxian Theory of Capitalist Breakdown." Radcliffe College, 1947.

Skelton, Oscar Douglas. "An Examination of Marxian Theory." University of Chicago, 1908.

Slaughter, John Wilson. "On Praxis: An Inquiry into Marx." Drew University, 1970.

Slomich, Sidney J. "Studies in Eschatological Politics: Reason, Fact, Value, and Law in the Historical Political Theories of Vico, Marx, Hegel, Mazzini and Kant." Harvard University, 1951.

Smulkstys, Julius Joseph. "The Marxist Concept of Democracy." Indiana University, 1968.

Somerville, John M. "Methodology in Social Science: A Critique of Marx and Engels." Columbia University, 1939.

Spencer, Richard Leroy. "Marx, Bloch, and Moltmann: Dialectical Models of History and the Question of Ends and Means." Princeton Theological Seminary, 1973.

Stell, Lance Keith. "Man, Needs, and Justice: Marx's Critique of the Division of Labor." University of Michigan, 1974.

Stern, Peter Alan. "Marx's Concept of Alienation and His Doctrine of Naturalism." New School for Social Research, 1974.

Strassmaier, James F. "Karl Grun: The Confrontation with Marx, 1844-1848." Loyola University, Chicago, 1969-70.

Sutton, Francis X. "The Radical Marxist." Harvard University, 1950.

Tarschys, Daniel. "The End of Politics: Marxist Thought on the Withering Away of The State." Princeton University, 1971-72.

Thompson, Arthington Frank. "A Comparison and a Contrast of the Marxist Theory of Party with the Christian Doctrine of the Church." McGill University, Canada, 1963.

Thompson, Paul William. "An Exposition and Analysis of Marx's Prediction of Communism." Duke University, 1970.

Traywick, Leland E. "Parallelisms in the Economic Ideas of Karl Marx and Thorstein Veblen." University of Illinois at Urbana-Champaign, 1942.

Truitt, Willis Harrison. "Social Theory and the Foundations of Aesthetic Culture: A Critique of and Contribution to the Marxian Theory of Art." Boston University, 1969.

Tucker, Robert Charles. "The Self and Revolution: A Moral Critique of Marx." Harvard University, 1957-58.

Venable, Vernon. "Human Nature: The Marxian View." Columbia University, 1946.

Vukcevich, Ivo. "Milovan Djilas and the Nyegosh Legend: Marx or Nyegosh?" New York University, 1968-69.

Wagner, Douglas H. "Marxism, Freudianism, and the Historian: A Study of the Methodological and Human Situations Current in Contemporary Historical Study." Fordham University, 1974.

Weber, Nicholas Stephen. "Marxism and the Problem of the Bourgeois Revolution." Columbia University, 1972.

Wegner, Morton Gererd. "Consumption Patterns and Class Consciousness: A Synthetical Theoretical and Empirical Analysis of the Marxian Concept of Class and the Weberian Concepts of 'Stand' and 'Status Community'." (Volumes I-VI). Temple University, 1974.

Wells, Donald A. "The Influence of Hegel on Marx and T. H. Green in the Philosophy of State." Boston University, 1946.

Whiteside, David Edward. "An Analysis of the Concept of Alienation in Karl Marx's Early Writings." University of Michigan, 1971.

Williams, Ronald Thomas. "Communication and Conflict in Karl Marx." University of Texas, 1975.

Wiltgen, Richard James. "Marxism and Population: A Reappraisal." University of Illinois at Urbana-Champaign, 1974.

Wolfson, Murry. "A Critique of Marxian Economics." University of Wisconsin, 1963-64.

Zawadsky, John Paul. "The Sources of Dialectical Materialism: Hegel, Marx, Engels, and Lenin." Harvard University, 1964-65.

Zeitlin, Irving Mordecai. "Nondogmatic Marxism: A Study in the Sociological Theory and Method of Karl Marx." Princeton University, 1963-64.

Z
855.l67
E94

DEC 15 1977